MULTICULTURAL EL

James A. Banks, ~~~~ ~~~~or

For a complete list of series titles, please visit www.tcpress.com

(continued)

Becoming an Antiracist School Leader

Dare to Be Real

Patrick A. Duffy

Foreword by James A. Banks

TEACHERS COLLEGE PRESS

TEACHERS COLLEGE | COLUMBIA UNIVERSITY
NEW YORK AND LONDON

This book is dedicated to Will and Keira.
You are inspiring me to become a real antiracist leader.

Published by Teachers College Press,® 1234 Amsterdam Avenue, New York, NY 10027

Copyright © 2023 by Teachers College, Columbia University

Front cover design by Peter Donahue. Art by Anna Musatova / iStock by Getty Images

Library of Congress Cataloging-in-Publication Data

Names: Duffy, Patrick A., author.
Title: Becoming an antiracist school leader : dare to be real / Patrick A. Duffy ;
  foreword by James A. Banks.
Description: New York, NY : Teachers College Press, 2023. | Series: Multicultural
  education series | Includes bibliographical references and index. | Summary: "This
  resource describes an adaptive framework for developing structural and curricular
  antiracist leadership with practical applications for leaders of systems, schools,
  and student groups. The text features a comprehensive study of a Midwestern high
  school, including personal narratives from a diverse group of antiracist school
  leaders."—Provided by publisher.
Identifiers: LCCN 2022054892 (print) | LCCN 2022054893 (ebook) |
  ISBN 9780807767863 (paperback) | ISBN 9780807767870 (hardcover) |
  ISBN 9780807781487 (ebook)
Subjects: LCSH: Educational leadership—Social aspects—United States. |
  Anti-racism—United States. | Racism in education—United States. | Discrimination
  in education—United States. | Culturally-relevant pedagogy—United States.
Classification: LCC LB2805 .D856 2023 (print) | LCC LB2805 (ebook) |
  DDC 371.2/011—dc23/eng/20230120
LC record available at https://lccn.loc.gov/2022054892
LC ebook record available at https://lccn.loc.gov/2022054893

ISBN 978-0-8077-6786-3 (paper)
ISBN 978-0-8077-6787-0 (hardcover)
ISBN 978-0-8077-8148-7 (ebook)

Printed on acid-free paper

Manufactured in the United States of America

Contents

Series Foreword

This book is being published at an ominous time in the United States and other nations. Democracy is fragile in nations around the world and is being challenged by right-wing and conservative movements in European nations such as France and Italy, and by the saliency of autocratic leaders such as Recep Tayyip Erdogan in Turkey, Vladimir Putin in Russia, and Viktor Orbán in Hungary (Albright, 2018). The fragility of democracy in the United States was epitomized by the refusal of past president Donald Trump and many of his supporters to accept the legitimacy of the 2020 election of President Joe Biden and by the attack on the U.S. Capitol on January 6, 2021 (*The January 6 Report*, 2023). Only 34 liberal democratic nations exist today, "which is down to the same number as in 1995" (Bokat-Lindell, 2022).

As democracy in the United States and other nations is being seriously challenged, a cultural war is taking place in the United States that includes cynical attacks on critical race theory, the teaching about race in schools (Cineas, 2020; Fortin, 2021; Schwartz, 2021; Wallace-Wells, 2012), and on the rights and identities of LGBTQ students (Saul, Mazzei, & Gabriel, 2023). Florida, where Ron DeSantis is governor, has prohibited the teaching of the first version of an AP Black history course developed by the College Board (Bouie, 2023; Hartocollis & Fawcett, 2023; Makin, 2023; Mervosh, 2022). Problems related to race, culture, and violence in the United States were manifested poignantly by the killing of Tyre Nichols, an African American, by police (the latest of many such killings as of this writing) in Memphis, Tennessee, on January 7, 2023 (Blow, 2023; Rojas & Bohra, 2023). Although the police who killed Nichols were Black, their behavior echoed and emulated the actions of White police officers who killed African Americans such as George Floyd and Breonna Taylor.

This is a propitious time for the publication of this book because of the fragility of democracy in the United States and the world, and the depth and complexity of institutionalized racism in the nation's schools, colleges, and universities. Duffy believes that public education should be an epicenter of antiracism in the nation. He details a comprehensive and field-tested plan that school administrators can use to become effective and robust antiracist leaders. Duffy describes a comprehensive, 3-year critical ethnographic study of a Midwestern high school and the complexities, challenges, and possibilities experienced by administrators, teachers, and students when they tried to become antiracists and to institutionalize antiracism in their schools.

Duffy incorporates insights and empirical findings from several theories into his framework, which consists of 10 tenets for becoming an antiracist leader. The Courageous Conversations framework, a procedure for sustained and deep dialogues and interactions developed by Glenn Singleton (2021), is incorporated into Duffy's protocol. Duffy also incorporates critical race theory (Ladson-Billings & Tate, 1995), racial identity development theories including the racial identity development theory of Janet Helms (1990), and the model of Black racial identity development theory created by William Cross (1991) into his protocol. Duffy envisions the participation of the entire school community, including administrators, parents, teachers, and students, into his intervention protocol.

The major purpose of the Multicultural Education Series is to provide preservice educators, practicing educators, graduate students, scholars, and policymakers with an interrelated and comprehensive set of books that summarizes and analyzes important research, theory, and practice related to the education of ethnic, racial, cultural, and linguistic groups in the United States and to the education of mainstream students about diversity. The dimensions of multicultural education, developed by Banks and described in the *Handbook of Research on Multicultural Education* (Banks, 2004), *The Routledge International Companion to Multicultural Education* (Banks, 2009), and the *Encyclopedia of Diversity in Education* (Banks, 2012), provide the conceptual framework for the development of the publications in the series.

The dimensions are content integration, the knowledge construction process, prejudice reduction, equity pedagogy, and an empowering institutional culture and social structure. The books in the Multicultural Education Series provide research, theoretical, and practical information about the behaviors and learning characteristics of students of color (Conchas & Vigil, 2012; Lee, 2007), language-minority students (Gándara & Hopkins, 2010; Valdés, 2001; Valdés et al., 2011), students from low-income households (Cookson, 2013; Gorski, 2018), multiracial youth (Joseph & Briscoe-Smith, 2021; Mahiri, 2017), and other minoritized population groups such as students who speak different varieties of English (Charity Hudley & Mallinson, 2011) and LGBTQ youth (Mayo, 2022).

Duffy describes why schools should and can become pivotal sites of antiracism. Other books in the Multicultural Education Series focus on *institutional and structural racism* and ways to reduce racism in schools, colleges, and universities. These books in the series reinforce and amplify the messages conveyed in this book about the need for schools to become antiracist: Ozlem Sensoy and Robin DiAngelo (2017), *Is Everyone Really Equal? An Introduction to Key Concepts in Social Justice Education* (2nd edition); Gary Howard (2016), *We Can't Teach What We Don't Know: White Teachers, Multiracial Schools* (3rd edition); Zeus Leonardo (2013), *Race Frameworks: A Multidimensional Theory of Racism and Education*; Daniel Solórzano and Lindsay Pérez Huber (2020), *Racial Microaggressions: Using Critical Race Theory in Education to Recognize and Respond to Everyday Racism*; Gloria

Ladson-Billings (2021), *Critical Race Theory in Education: A Scholar's Journey*; and Francesca López and Christine E. Sleeter (2023), *Critical Race Theory and Its Critics: Implications for Research and Teaching.*

This book contains features and case studies that school administrators, teachers, counselors, and other school participators will find informative, engaging, and helpful. Duffy's description of a high school attempting to actualize antiracism illuminates the challenges, opportunities, and possibilities of transforming a school to make it antiracist, culturally responsive, and culturally sustaining. The personal narratives from a diverse group of leaders who describe the struggles and possibilities of making their school antiracist and the author's racial autobiography contain insights that will help empower educators who want to participate in the vulnerable and risky, but essential, tasks of humanizing their schools by making them antiracist. I hope this book will inspire and encourage, and be a source of hope and support for leaders who want to take the road rarely taken of envisioning and creating antiracist schools that will empower teachers, students, and other members of the school community.

—James A. Banks

REFERENCES

Albright, M. (2018). *Fascism: A warning.* Harper/Collins.

Banks, J. A. (2004). Multicultural education: Historical development, dimensions, and practice. In J. A. Banks & C.A.M. Banks (Eds.), *Handbook of research on multicultural education* (pp. 3–29). Jossey-Bass.

Banks, J. A. (Ed.). (2009). *The Routledge international companion to multicultural education.* Routledge.

Banks, J. A. (2012). Multicultural education: Dimensions of. In J. A. Banks (Ed.), *Encyclopedia of diversity in education* (Vol. 3, pp. 1538–1547). Sage Publications.

Blow, C. M. (2023, January 27). Tyre Nichols's death is America's shame. *New York Times.* https://www.nytimes.com/2023/01/27/opinion/tyre-nichols-video.html?searchResultPosition=3

Bokat-Lindell, S. (2022, September 28). Is liberal democracy dying? *New York Times.* https://www.nytimes.com/2022/09/28/opinion/italy-meloni-democracy-authoritarianism.htm

Bouie, J. (2023, January 29). Ron DeSantis likes his culture wars for a reason. *New York Times.* https://www.nytimes.com/2023/01/24/opinion/desantis-florida-culture-w.html?searchResultPosition=1

Charity Hudley, A. H., & Mallinson, C. (2011). *Understanding language variation in U. S. schools.* Teachers College Press.

Cineas, F. (2020, September 24). Critical race theory, and Trump's war on it, explained. https://www.vox.com/2020/9/24/21451220/critical-race-theory-diversity-training-trump

Conchas, G. Q., & Vigil, J. D. (2012). *Streetsmart schoolsmart: Urban poverty and the education of adolescent boys.* Teachers College Press.

Cookson, P. W., Jr. (2013). *Class rules: Exposing inequality in American high schools.* Teachers College Press.

Cross, W. E. (1991). *Shades of Black: Diversity in African-American identity.* Temple University Press.

Fortin, J. (2021, November 8). Critical race theory: A brief history. *New York Times.* https://www.nytimes.com/article/what-is-critical-race-theory.html

Gándara, P., & Hopkins, M. (Eds.). (2010). *Forbidden language: English language learners and restrictive language policies.* Teachers College Press.

Gorski, P. C. (2018). *Reaching and teaching students in poverty: Strategies for erasing the opportunity gap* (2nd ed.). Teachers College Press.

Hartocollis, A., & Fawcett, E. (2023, February 1). The College Board strips down its A.P. curriculum for African American studies. *New York Times.* https://www.nytimes.com/2023/02/01/us/college-board-advanced-placement-african-american-studies.html?searchResultPosition=3

Helms, J. E. (Ed.) (1990). *Black and White racial identity: Theory, research, and practice.* Praeger.

Howard, G. (2016). *We can't teach what we don't know: White teachers, multiracial schools* (3rd ed.). Teachers College Press.

Howard, T. C. (2014). *Black male(d): Peril and promise in the education of African American males.* Teachers College Press.

Joseph, R. L., & Briscoe-Smith, A. (2021). *Generation mixed goes to school: Radically listening to multiracial kids.* Teachers College Press.

Ladson-Billings, G. (2021). *Critical race theory in education: A scholar's journey.* Teachers College Press.

Ladson-Billings, G., & Tate, W. F. IV. (1995). Toward a critical race theory of education. *Teachers College Record, 97*(1), 47–68.

Lee, C. D. (2007). *Culture, literacy, and learning: Taking bloom in the midst of the whirlwind.* Teachers College Press.

Leonardo, Z. (2013). *Race frameworks: A multicultural theory of racism and education.* Teachers College Press.

López, F., & Sleeter, C. E. (2023). *Critical race theory and its critics: Implications for research and teaching.* Teachers College Press.

Mahiri, J. (2017). *Deconstructing race: Multicultural education beyond the color-bind.* Teachers College Press.

Makin, K. (2023, January 27). AP African American studies: "Academic legitimacy" or "indoctrination"? *Christian Science Monitor.* https://www.csmonitor.com/Commentary/2023/0127/AP-African-American-Studies-Academic-legitimacy-or-indoctrination

Mayo, C. (2022). *LGBTQ youth and education: Policies and practices* (2nd ed.). Teachers College Press.

Mervosh, S. (2022, August 27). Back to school in DeSantis's Florida, as teachers look over their shoulders. *New York Times.* https://www.nytimes.com/2022/08/27/us/desantis-schools-dont-say-gay.html?searchResultPosition=2

Rojas, R., & Bohra, N. (2023, February 1). What we know about Tyre Nichols's lethal encounter with Memphis police. *New York Times.* https://www.nytimes.com/article/tyre-nichols-memphis-police-dead.html?searchResultPosition=1

Saul, S., Mazzei, P., & Gabriel, T. (2023, January 23). DeSantis takes on the education establishment, and builds his brand. *New York Times.* https://www.nytimes.com

/2023/01/31/us/governor-desantis-higher-education-chris-rufo.html?searchResult
Position=1

Schwartz, S. (2021, June 11). Map: Where critical race theory is under attack. *Education Week*. https://www.edweek.org/policy-politics/map-where-critical-race-theory-is-under-attack/2021/06

Sensoy, O., & DiAngelo, R. (2017). *Is everyone really equal? An introduction to key concepts in social justice education* (2nd ed.). Teachers College Press.

Singleton, G. E. (2021). *Courageous conversations about race: A field guide for achieving equity in schools and beyond* (3rd ed.). Corwin.

The January 6th Report: The Report of the Select Committee to Investigate the January 6th Attack on the United States Capitol (2023). Skyhorse Publishing.

Solórzano, D., & Huber, L. P. (2020). *Racial microaggressions: Using critical race theory in education to recognize and respond to everyday racism*. Teachers College Press.

Valdés, G. (2001). *Learning and not learning English: Latino students in American schools*. Teachers College Press.

Valdés, G., Capitelli, S., & Alvarez, L. (2011). *Latino children learning English: Steps in the journey*. Teachers College Press.

Wallace-Wells, B. (2021). How a conservative activist invented the conflict over critical race theory. *The New Yorker*. https://www.newyorker.com/news/annals-of-inquiry/how-a-conservative-activist-invented-the-conflict-over-critical-race-theory

Acknowledgments

I would like to thank the following people for their contributions and support. Without them this book would not be complete. Anthony Galloway, Astein Osei, Freida Bailey, Silvy Un Lafayette, Luis Versalles, Ezra Hudson, Daniel Shope, Ila Saxena, Maddy Wegleitner, Jill Metil, Elizabeth Huesing, Efe Mensah-Brown, Patrica Magnuson, Lee-Ann Stephens, Glenn Singleton, Gloria Ladson-Billings, Yvette Jackson, Muhammad Khalifa, James Banks, Brian Ellerbeck, Mike Olivo, Ruby Bridges, Erik Dussault, Joe Mueller, Vince Jackson, Sue Thomas, Beth Russell, Valeria Silva, Willie Jett, Suzan Samaha, Heston Lyght, Bill Blackwell, and Katie York.

Becoming an Antiracist School Leader

Introduction

"Real isn't how you are made," said the Skin Horse. "It's a thing that happens to you."

—Margery Williams (*The Velveteen Rabbit*)

DARE 2 BE REAL

My mother used to read me *The Velveteen Rabbit* when I was a little boy, and I remember it was the first book she read to me that made me cry. I'm not sure what words specifically touched me, but there was something about the notion that this stuffed rabbit could be loved so much that it could evolve into something even more real than it already was. It was an allegory that I was trying to wrap my little head and heart around at a young age. The story gave me hope about a future filled with growth, love, affinity, and belonging. My mother was an Arab American woman living in the North Woods of Minnesota trying to teach me lessons about life through children's parables. As courageous in spirit as she was tiny in stature, my mother loved God above all else—hence, she loved people, since she longed to connect with the spirit—the soul—of each person she came into contact with in our little hamlet along the North Shore of Lake Superior. Little did I know in the years following her untimely death from cancer that I would have to learn to take her lessons and apply them so consciously to the evolution of my personal and professional life as an antiracist leader.

I began this book in a season of audacious hope and completed this book in a season of heartbreak. You see, my personal and professional lives have been a mirror of each other over the past few years when for so long I worked hard to keep them separate. The early writings of this book grounded in critical race theory were inspired and written during the Obama administration. I was not naive enough to think we had gone postracial in America but, rather, shared a hope that we could make progress against the ugly permanence of systemic racism. I live and work less than 10 miles from the site of the heartbreaking George Floyd murder, but the heartbreak I feel is that which comes from the dissolving of a relationship. The relationship between citizens in this country—progressive and conservative—is quite possibly at its most partisan, and *critical race theory* is loaded language that has been weaponized to fuel the flames of division. There is a need for a bold new vision that will contemplate what an antiracist democracy will look like in the 21st century. Will we have the courage to help the children lead? Is it too late? While I lament the state of our union, I contemplate the dissolving of my 20-year marriage to the mother of my two beautiful children. Katie, my wife of 20 years and a kindergarten teacher, is one of the greatest women and teachers to come into my life. We got to a point at which perhaps our relationship needed to evolve into something else. As a hopeful romantic, Arab American and Irish Catholic, I never thought that divorce would be part of my narrative, but I had seen the statistics for so many school administrators. Those who devote their lives to "the work" often become married to the job or perhaps even to racial equity at the expense of their other relationships—indeed, this may have happened in my case. As I move into a period of coparenting with Katie and look forward to ensuring that Will and Keira, our children, know how much they are centered in our lives, my identity, worth, and belief in our relationship and family dynamics have to change. Will we have the courage to help our children lead? In this new format, will our family be redefined? After recently visiting Palestine, Israel, and my ancestral homeland of Lebanon, I saw the faithfulness and hope of so many people who still believe there is opportunity amid conflict. If one can have hope in light of those dire circumstances, I'm certain we will have the courage to help our children lead for antiracism here during these partisan times. It certainly isn't too late.

It is hard to believe that I have been working in pre-K–12 education for more than 25 years. During that time, I have had the opportunity to work in the three largest urban school districts in Minnesota and in three diverse suburban schools. Couple that with a life growing up in a rural community in northern Minnesota and you could say I have seen quite a bit. It may have been prophetic career planning that I would take some Fridays off during my senior year at Cook County High School and visit friends (mostly delivering mixtapes to girls I had met at leadership and church camps and on whom I had a crush) at other schools around the state, only to find myself critiquing the systems, structures, and lack of conscious teaching at those schools. At 18 I was living a sentient dream on the weekends as a somewhat of a cross between Ferris Bueller, Khalil Gibran, and W.E.B. Du Bois. Since those days I have devoted my life more fully to a racial-equity purpose focused on antiracist student leadership development. I have held the positions of social studies teacher; football and basketball coach; racial-equity coordinator; National Honor Society advisor; assistant principal; principal; director of leadership development; director of secondary schools; director of curriculum and instruction; adjunct professor; and director of teaching, learning, and leadership. But along the way I recognized that regardless of the position or title I hold, there are only two things that are essential in the job description: developing people and developing systems for racial equity.

I am writing this book from a place of three deeply held beliefs:

1. I believe in democracy—its unfilled promise and possibility for antiracism.
2. I believe that the most devastating factor leading to the racial predictability of achievement and fracturing of communities of color is systemic racism.
3. I believe in the power of the human spirit, particularly the collective human spirit—its capacity for truth, love, justice, and forgiveness.

With that said, I must engage a bit more deeply in why these beliefs ground this work.

The founders of our country were tragically misguided when they excluded women, Native Americans, and enslaved human beings from the "We" in the "We the People." They obviously did not consciously lay the foundations for the diversity we have today, nor did they practice anything resembling antiracism. At this moment, we have allowed our differences to fragment our civic community, creating a void that undemocratic powers are eager to fill. Indeed, we have deprived people of their freedom for reasons of racism and economic exploitation, but the promise of an antiracist democracy is what keeps me believing in our great experiment.

This book is intended to be a guide for anyone interested in becoming an antiracist leader: leaders who develop systems for racial equity—namely, principals, superintendents, school board members, teachers, students, all educators who are part of the system we call public education. You see, I am writing this book under the pretense that the purpose of public education is to not just preserve our democracy, but rather to deepen an antiracist democracy. To that end, this book is grounded in the belief that public education is the epicenter of antiracism in the United States. Indeed, for the better part of the last century, it has been. As our schools go, so does our democracy, and in a country and school system that has the potential for so much liberation, it is devastating to recognize that our school system was not created to serve all children, let alone support the development of an antiracist democracy. We have a fundamental problem in our schools. Our teachers are overwhelmed. Our schools are overmandated. Our educators and leaders are isolated and often disconnected from a mission, vision, or set of core values that speaks to their collective spirit. To go back to the roots of the earliest Afrocentric learning institutions, we must recommit to the primary work of schools being to help students develop their identity. Indeed, in the United States, in the 21st century, our schools would be irresponsible to not center the work of developing a healthy cultural and racial identity. This is the spirit work, the collaborative work, the work that will bring humanity and love back into our schools. Demystifying Afrocentric learning for our schools requires a recognition among conservatives and progressives alike that the development of the spirit is at the core of the Abramhamic faiths of Christianity, Judaism, and Islam, all of which have Pan African roots from Egypt to the Middle East. It is the "real" work.

My real work has been grounded in collaboration and reflection. These oft-repeated words in schools often sound hollow when they ignore race and culture. Indeed, race and culture are always present in collaboration, but without racially conscious and culturally proficient reflective practitioners in our leadership roles, we will continue to maintain the status quo of underperforming schools that continue to underserve our historically marginalized students of color. I have had to think deeply about how my own race and culture have impacted my career, my parenting, my marriage, and my friendships. Whether consciously or not, they have been central to the development of my relationships. Without reflection about how these identities intersect with my personal and professional lives, I will struggle to be real with myself and others. *Becoming an Antiracist Leader* is about the real work of conscious collaboration and reflection that any antiracist leader needs to engage in. The leaders at Midwest High School for 3 years participated in antiracist professional development, but as their story unfolds, you will see that a lack of racially conscious collaboration and reflection may have led to a quick demise in what was once a promising national model for courageous conversations about race. In St. Louis Park Public Schools, multiple leaders will share their reflections on how student-centered antiracist leadership tenets have helped engage, sustain, and deepen the work in that district to this day.

Becoming an Antiracist Leader asks all stakeholders in the school community to see themselves as potential leaders in our society. The potential for leadership requires us to engage in the possibility that the development of our will, skills, knowledge, and capacity for racial equity will better our school, our community, and our democracy. The problem is that when asked, most people don't see themselves as leaders. They have a narrow view of leadership defined in norms of Whiteness that suggests a dominant voice, commanding presence, and answers and directions for most problems. What has been lacking in our antiracist democracy is leaders who engage with multiple perspectives, listen with mindful inquiry, reflect with racial consciousness, learn with scholarly intent, and collaborate with a mindset of liberating our students rather than fixing their perceived deficits. What is lacking is educational love. Schools have the potential to unlock the heart of democracy, the heart of our country, and the spirit of our citizens. Indeed, energizing and enhancing the spirit of our children should be a centerpiece of our schools' mission. To do this, we must allow ourselves to love, be loved, and be real with one another with the multiple identities we bring into our daily lives as leaders. This certainly doesn't mean loving our children into low expectations but rather loving them so much that we will engage in the spirit work necessary to transform ourselves and our systems to better serve their academic and affective needs.

This book provides a framework with three phases and 10 tenets. The three phases are a progression that any individual, school, or district can use to engage in antiracist leadership development at a pace that works for themselves or for their community. The 10 tenets do not give direction but rather provide 10 questions for the self and for team reflection. Like the best teachers, the tenets provide questions throughout the book to guide critical thinking rather than answers that tell people how to think.

The framework is pulled from a set of critical ethnographic data from over 10 years of work in the field of education. It includes more than 150 stories from antiracist system leaders, students, and parents from over 40 schools around the Twin Cities metro area, most centered within 20 miles of where George Floyd was killed in 2020. It has become clear that we are juggling a lot of work in our schools but that we need to focus on how to truly engage in racial-equity transformation from within ourselves if we are ever to change the promise of teaching and learning in the United States.

It is my belief that the most devastating factor leading to the racial predictability of student achievement and the fracturing of our communities of color is systemic racism. This belief acknowledges that there are other factors but, first and foremost, it underlines what is most "devastating." *Devastating* can mean causing severe shock, distress, or grief. How could there be anything more devastating than for the one thing that we *require* our children to do between the ages of 5 and 18 years contributes to their demise? Some people—our youth—are *made* to come to school every day. Others are *paid* to come to school every day. We must find a way to engage both of these groups in life-affirming ways that develop their identities for the good of their spirit, their soul, and our democracy. To do this will require us to dare—to have the courage to do radical, but not reckless, race work. Radical work can be done with care for others; reckless work disregards the impact of transformational work on others' identity development. There is no place for recklessness in antiracist school leadership. The radical work, however, requires strategic, age-appropriate, community-appropriate, and pace-appropriate work that does not compromise the goals of antiracism and is conscious of critical race theory. The three sections of this book and the tenets outlined in those sections center and elevate student leadership development in our school systems, indeed, the highest aspiration of our work in public education.

I started this section with a number 2 in the "Dare 2 Be Real" as a reminder—not of our hometown hero Prince and his propensity for numerology in his songs, or even for 2Pac and harkening his inspirational words from *The Rose That Grew from Concrete* but, rather, of the simple fact that antiracist leadership in the 21st century, radical work, requires collaboration. When two or more are gathered in the name of antiracism, there is "real" work: evolution of the spirit, the soul, something beyond the school system that is present. To be real is to be authentic as a racial-equity ally and leader, and to do that you must engage with others and allow yourself to be vulnerable. In this vulnerability in antiracism work there is the potential for something quite real to happen that is rare in schooling—the act of love. I'm not talking about the hopeless romantic love I was trying to engage in with my cheesy mixtapes from the 1990s but, rather, the kind of love that comes when we commit to engaging and enhancing the spirit of each learner, each colleague, each day. When we create a safe and sacred space for our racial and cultural identities, we can dare to be real in our schools. The work of this book could not have been done without my years of tutelage under the amazing practitioners at Courageous Conversations (Singleton, 2022), particularly Glenn Singleton.

Starting back in 2005, I began working as a racial-equity coordinator in the suburbs of Minneapolis and learned about Singleton's model, which adhered to a systemic, 4-year progression of staff development that incorporates Singleton's "Agreements, Conditions, and Compass" of Courageous Conversations (see Figure I.1). These conditions and agreements are designed to be a protocol for participating in and facilitating interracial and intraracial dialogue about race. I describe in later chapters of this book how leaders engaged in Courageous Conversations leadership development. In the first year of the systemic transformation model, district administration and all building principals and school board members participated in intense antiracism leadership retreats or workshops. The purpose of these retreats and workshops was to bring district leadership, essential to the successful implementation of this model, to the forefront of antiracist leadership through engagement with a thorough examination of their own racial identity, critical race theory (CRT) literature, and historical and current aspects of racism. These leaders were then charged with bringing the protocol of Courageous Conversations

Figure I.1. Courageous Conversations Protocol (Agreements, Conditions, Compass)

Four Agreements:

- Stay Engaged
- Experience Discomfort
- Speak Your Truth
- Expect/Accept Non-Closure

Six Conditions:

1. Focus on Personal, Local, and Immediate
2. Isolate Race
3. Normalize Social Construction and Multiple Perspectives
4. Monitor Agreements and Conditions and Establish Parameters
5. Use a "Working Definition" for Race
6. Examine the Presence and Role of "Whiteness"

Singleton, G. (2022). *Courageous Conversations about Race, A Field Guide*. Corwin Press.

to each site in the district. The staff training needed to teach each of the protocols became the framework from which the school districts I focus on in this book have engaged most heavily in their own antiracist school leadership development.

The Courageous Conversations work in the Midwest school district that is at the center of the study of this book calls for equity leadership teams at the district and all site levels to oversee the staff development, examination of policies and procedures, advocacy for students and staff of color, and equity visioning for each school. In Year 2, principals were asked to form their equity teams by gathering staff members (teachers, counselors, etc.) who had a willingness to be antiracist leaders, skills in facilitating staff development, knowledge of culturally responsive curriculum and systems, and the capacity to learn and grow as an equity leader. These equity teams were responsible for working with existing leadership groups (i.e., curricular departments, grade-level teams, building council, student government) to institutionalize antiracist practice in all building procedures and discourse. The impact these teams had on the building made it essential for this team to be representative of the entire staff and to include as many people from different racial perspectives as possible.

Collaborative Action Research for Equity (CARE) teams were developed to build a working collaborative of teachers to model culturally and racially relevant teaching, to examine the role and presence of Whiteness in their teaching practice, to analyze the academic progression of focus students of color, and to build awareness of culturally responsive teaching throughout the building by sharing data, positive outcomes, and negative outcomes and by encouraging peer observations with all members of the staff. This staff development works in conjunction with the ongoing staff-development goals of the building equity team.

In the site of this book's study—Midwest High School—a Partnerships for Achieving Student Success (PASS) team and Students Organized for Anti-Racism (SOAR) teams were developed to bring parent and student voices, respectively, into the racial discourse. Some of those student leaders became part of my critical ethnographic study at Midwest High School that informed the Dare 2 Be Real model to sustain this work from within. This portion of the model can get complicated and requires careful planning to initiate a collective student-centered vision for antiracist transformation. Similar teams and protocols were also developed at St. Louis Park Public Schools, a district that is elevated in places in this book through multiple racial and leadership perspectives.

Overall, the Courageous Conversations model addresses multiple aspects of racial equity in the individualist paradigm and focuses on organizational change, a key component of the collectivist frame. At the time of the Midwest High School study, the Courageous Conversations model that the Pacific Educational Group (PEG) incorporated involved multiple principles of progressive equity pedagogy. A thorough examination of the broader literature shows that the PEG model incorporated ideas from many relevant scholars into their principles of equity/antiracist pedagogy, their protocol, and their leadership development model. These principles indicate strong crossover of the Courageous Conversations model and its integration of multiple strands of racial-equity pedagogy that emerged within antiracist paradigms discussed in Chapter 2.

I will not prescribe a 10-part program that promises to teach school leaders how to be antiracist or how to eliminate systemic racism from their schools. At the deepest human levels, we do need guideposts for this sort of work, but I have always been wary of peddlers with packages and programs that will supposedly fix the ills of public education. We need insight into ourselves and into our schools that will help energize and enhance our spirit while holding space for critical analysis of the problems at hand—a critical analysis that embraces critical race theory. This book attempts to offer insight through reflective questions into how to address the systems necessary for holding space for the spirit of antiracism and critical race analysis.

To be real reaches far beyond our thoughts or feelings. In schools, it points to a larger way of knowing—of receiving and reflecting educational love through our collective experiences—that goes deeper than the mind alone can take us. The heart and soul of antiracism are integrated through the imagination, emotion, intuition, and support of each other's spirit.

BECOMING ANTIRACIST SCHOOL LEADERS

The practice of identity development in schools devoid of applied leadership opportunities is noble but uncentered. By focusing our work in public education on the development of antiracist school leadership, we are centering the heart, soul, mind, and body in the pursuit of a new way of being—a way of antiracist democracy. The three phases of antiracist leadership development are shown in Figure I.2.

This framework has been grounded in the protocol for Courageous Conversations about race. The conditions for Courageous Conversations are an umbrella for the work, as it is necessary to have a protocol for engaging in antiracism if we are to have a foundation of racial literacy. There are many protocols for engaging in racial-equity work; this just happens to be the one I have become the most familiar over the course of my career and the one I believe provides the most encompassing framework for discussions that center race specifically. Each of the three phases requires some specific work.

Phase I (Know Thyself): This phase asks leaders to engage in self-reflection and to examine disaggregated student data. The data could be qualitative or quantitative in nature but are essential for centering student voice at the core of transformation. In the framework, student voice is not called upon as a token service during this phase but rather as a key component of partnership to be nurtured in the process of knowing thyself. As leaders engage students in the work, they are at once elevating their purposeful collaboration and the educational system. Staff should develop racial-equity purpose statements (REPs)

Figure I.2. Three Phases of Systemic Antiracist Leadership Development

Dare 2 Be Real - Three Phases

Personal, Local, Immediate— Keep a Spotlight on Race	Gather Multiple Perspectives— Establish Parameters	Establish a Racial-Equity Transformation Plan
PHASE I: LOOKING INWARD KNOW THYSELF	**PHASE II: LOOKING AROUND** DISTINGUISH KNOWLEDGE FROM FOOLISHNESS	**PHASE III: LOOKING OUTWARD** BUILD FOR ETERNITY
• Self-reflect on teaching • Examine disaggregated student data • Hear and reflect on student voice and community input • Be driven by well-developed REP statements • Clarify intersection of various programs • Engage in Courageous Conversation	• Research and visit regional exemplars • Engage scholars of culturally relevant pedagogy, antiracist leadership, and racial identity development • Establish criteria for adopting new materials; unpack standards • Pilot curriculum • Engage in Courageous Conversation	• Develop school belief statements and student-centered goals • Adopt new curriculum with fidelity or engage in curriculum writing • Establish collaborative team and PD plans • Develop 3-, 5-, and 8-year benchmarks • Engage in Courageous Conversation

to bring clarity to the work in which they intend to engage. These REPs become the "rep" they want to have with their students and school community when it comes to antiracist work and also serve as a mini–vision statement for each team that personalizes the work beyond that of the greater school community or district. During Phase I, student-centered antiracism should be examined at the intersections with other significant programs in the school system (i.e., International Baccalaureate, Advanced Placement, professional learning communities, technology enrichment). It is often assumed in schools that some of the other programs being implemented in the school are inherently antiracist, but rarely is that the case. Most programs are in fact colorblind in their approach—a noble vestige of the late 20th century. Although En Vogue suggested to us in the early 1990s that being colorblind would "free our mind," indeed these programs rarely if ever interrupt the status quo for our BIPOC (Black/Indigenous/people of color) students, nor have they provided any liberation of thinking for our White students to examine the presence and role of Whiteness in their lives. Without these factors we continue to churn out the same graduates who perpetuate the status quo in our society.

Phase II (Distinguish Knowledge From Foolishness): During this phase, leaders are asked to not just be real with themselves but to start looking around at the scholars in the field who can light their way. There are far too many people leading in the name of antiracism who are not grounded in scholarly literature, action research, or even honoring the wisdom of those who came before them. Where is the reverence for the scholarship of scholars such as Asa Hilliard (1992), Derrick Bell (1992), James Banks (1992), Gloria Ladson-Billings (1995), Geneva Gay (1995), and bell hooks (2018)? As this phase pushes leaders to progress down a path of educational love and antiracist democratic practice it requires that not just the heart and soul be activated but now the mind. Collectively, are we taking time in schools to be practitioners and scholars of critical race theory or is this just a partisan phrase we now run from? So many people of color, many women of color, have paved the way for us to see how we can transform our schools for our most marginalized children, but we often move to technical action (quick fixes, curriculum purchases, or structural changes) in our schools before engaging the heart, soul, and mind collectively in the work. In a postpandemic world, we should be much more comfortable with the notion of visiting regional, national, and international exemplars through Zoom calls and collectivist virtual communities. This sort of action research coupled with critical thinking and critical ethnographic study can help leaders understand not just the current reality of their community but also the racialized context in which they are operating—a racialized context that may be invisible without the guiding light of scholarship and illumination from other schools that may be engaged in racially conscious work.

Phase III (Build for Eternity). In Phase III, individuals becoming antiracist leaders must recognize that the most fragile work they are leading in a system is that which is dependent upon them. How do we build something that outlast us? Indeed, our systems and students will surely outlast most of our leaders, with the average tenure of an urban superintendent being a little over 2 years. We must even go beyond engaging multiple perspectives and help others become part of the work by recognizing their place in the transformative nature of antiracism.

WHY "STUDENT LEADERSHIP DEVELOPMENT" BELONGS IN EDUCATIONAL LEADERSHIP STUDIES

We know that educators are more likely to stay in the profession if they feel connected to the mission, vision, and core values of an organization. Do we feel connected on a spiritual level to the mission, vision, and core values of our democracy? Can we center our children at the core of our work and reenergize the workforce that in 2022 showed that 55 percent were thinking of leaving the profession? Racial-equity work over the past decade has often manifested itself in changing adult mindsets, but even those who go into teacher leadership roles and administration did not get into the work because they are passionate about adult dysfunction. Rather, most wanted to make a difference in a child's life, and that is the connection to their core purpose. Engaging our children as scholars of culturally relevant pedagogy is a core value of this book. Gloria Ladson-Billings (2021a) defines culturally relevant pedagogy as

Table I.1. Tenents for Systemic Antiracist Student Leadership Development

Tenets for Antiracist Student Leadership Development	Key Question for Reflection
Staff/Adult Collaboration	How are adult leaders positioned to collaborate with a focus on racial equity?
Student Integration	How are our students integrated, involved, and engaged?
Systemic Implementation	How embedded is leadership development in our program and school system?
Support From the Top	How well am I able to garner support from those with positional and cultural authority?
Shared Experiences	How well are we building a collective learning identity?
Safe & Sacred Space	How do students perceive the culture for being real about their race, identity, and culture?
Common Language/Protocol	How have we heightened the protocol for racial discourse and developed language for racial literacy?
Focus: Identity Development	How are we developing our individual and collective racial and cultural identity?
Active Antiracist Leadership	How do we develop students' will, skill, knowledge, and capacity as anti-racist leaders?
Family/Parent Involvement	How do we partner and communicate with families as we develop our student leaders?

having three core components: (1) a pedagogy wherein students can achieve academic success—something that is often lost in schooling due to the oppression of low expectations for our students of color; (2) cultural competence, which she defines as working toward fluency in one's own racial and cultural identity while also pursuing fluency in the identity of at least another that is different from one's own; and (3) sociopolitical or critical consciousness by which educators are expected to partner with students to apply learning at its highest potential—leadership development that can disrupt the status quo and bring equity to social and political systems. Indeed, teaching at the highest level is leadership development, this is seeing each child for their talents and developing them to their fullest. If we are to address systemic racism in our schools and society, we must be willing to isolate race in that leadership development and develop racially conscious student leaders.

Many of the school districts wanting to address inequities in our country—including Midwest School District, which is highlighted later in this book—have focused their efforts on addressing adult mindsets as the result of their leadership development efforts. Mindset work is extremely important, but this work has largely been unsuccessful and unsustainable. It does not bring joy, nor is it grounded in the purpose of most educational leaders' journeys. We are primarily here to raise children. If we prepare ourselves to teach children antiracism—not a history of oppression—but truly the action, values, choices, strategy, and liberation associated with antiracism, it centers our creative energy and strategic plans on our highest purpose.

Historically, student leadership has directly or indirectly been at the root of educational and societal reform for antiracism. I had the great honor of driving Ruby Bridges (1999) to and from the airport and between Minneapolis and St. Paul a few years ago when she came to speak to some of our students engaged in the Dare 2 Be Real student leadership summit in the region. She spoke eloquently about many parts of her childhood journey of desegregating schools but left us all with one blazing message: Racism is an adult problem. We need to address it. What became clear from my conversation with this pioneer of racial integration, however, was the notion that antiracism be a student-centered solution. As adults we have failed to address the sins of racism in society, but if we truly believe that no child is born a racist, we must also believe that children are taught racism. Therefore, they can also be taught antiracism. As adults, we can do our best to model this, but would it not be best to include those who have been engaged in racism for the shortest amount of time to be engaged with us at the highest level? Children's innocence, idealism, creativity, collaborative potential, and developmental views on schools and society are essential in breaking a partisan stronghold on the discussion of race in our society. This is not to suggest that we indoctrinate children with certain thinking about race and racism but, rather, that we open the door to let them let us in on how they are thinking about race—how could this do anything but help us to better understand what is sacred, precious— real—to them and the spirit work necessary to save our schools and develop an antiracist democracy.

PURPOSE AND ORGANIZATION

This book is intended to be a guide for antiracist school leaders and is organized as such. However, don't expect a linear process or a how-to guide that will serve as "antiracism for dummies." Do not expect this book to provide an all-encompassing overview of racism in our nation's schools. The negative consequences of systemic racism for Black and Indigenous children, children of color, and their families in the United States are well documented and require us to look at a systemic response to our history of underservice. The book is organized so that it can be used by any school leader who is dedicated to the spirt of antiracist work and the deep systemic work necessary for sustainable change. It is organized in a way that manifests the three phases of becoming an antiracist leader in narrative form.

Part I of the book is about knowing oneself. The three chapters will high-light why knowing oneself is important in becoming an antiracist leader.

1. Your personal history, particularly the racial and cultural perspective with which you enter the work, is essential to becoming an antiracist leader. Chapter 1 will model this process through excerpts from my own racial autobiography, *Looking Inward*, a grounding aspect of becoming an antiracist leader and one that must consistently be present. This part of the book includes two chapters that are about knowing oneself on a deep level. First I describe my own reflective practice and grounding work. For any school leader who wants to engage in antiracism, the practice of writing a racial autobiography is an essential self-reflection. It requires the leader to be a reflective practitioner, but it also brings familiar personal patterns having to do with race to the forefront of how themes, decisions, and relationships in the school setting may impact leadership practice. I share this because it shows the steps in how I have learned to become an antiracist school leader and because I recommend that any leader using this book to guide their practice engage regularly in reflection on the "chapters" of their racial autobiography. This should also include time for a leader to share their story.
2. Chapter 2 provides an opportunity for leaders to engage in a collective history—the context in which history, culture, and education influence the way one becomes an antiracist school leader. This chapter briefly examines the state of antiracism in schools, historically and presently. Later, in Chapters 4 and 5, pieces of critical race theory and racial-identity development are explored for additional context.
3. Chapter 3 provides the first of 10 tenets that will help antiracist leaders engage, sustain, and deepen student-centered school leadership. The first three are connected to the theme of Know Thyself, as they are deeply reliant on one's connections to the human spirit and to others. The three practical tenets are related to safe and sacred space, staff collaboration, and student integration. As in Chapters 6 and 8, voices from St. Louis Park Public Schools and practical examples from across Minnesota will be used to illustrate how these tenets can be used to become an antiracist school leader.

Part II of the book relates to the theme Distinguish Knowledge From Foolishness—the art of becoming a discerning and scholarly antiracist leader. Three chapters help explore this stage of school leadership.

1. Chapter 4 is about engaging in the scholarship of critical race theory. Through the lens of critical race theory, we will take a close look at a school that tried to become antiracist through 3 intensive years of

antiracist leadership development programming. Anyone wanting to become an antiracist school leader should not shy away from critical race theory but should lean into the tenets and understand how to apply them to a critique of any system they serve. Chapter 4 serves as an example of this.

2. Building on the lessons of Part I, antiracist school leaders should be able to analyze their actions through the lens of their own racial-identity development. Chapter 5 follows the leaders of Midwest High School through a racially disaggregated study using the models of Helms (1991), Cross (1991), and Renn (2004) to examine how the leaders navigated antiracist leadership development programming. To become an antiracist school leader, one learns important lessons about the trends among White leaders to enter into paralysis and the leaders of color to enter into periods of isolation.

3. During the phase Distinguish Knowledge From Foolishness, there are four practical, student-centered, antiracist tenets necessary to sustain school leadership. Chapter 6 highlights the tenets that will provide sustainability, stability, and longevity to work that can often be interrupted if there is not scholarly pursuit, self-critique, and collaborative reflection on the system. The tenets laid out in this chapter are systemic implementation, support from the top, common language and protocol, and identity development. Part III, Building for Eternity, asks the reader to look forward using the 10 tents for antiracist student leadership development. Becoming an antiracist leader requires that we think beyond ourselves and think about systemic antiracism as a response to systemic racism.

Part III relates to the phase Build for Eternity. It is important to look forward beyond oneself to engage in deepened antiracist school leadership. There are two chapters that will illustrate this phase.

1. Chapter 7 shares the critical ethnographic story of Midwest High School in narrative form—a story that mirrors many suburban schools that have tried and failed to engage, sustain, and deepen antiracist leadership over time. I tell this story because it illustrates a common story in America—of well-intentioned antiracist leaders who built great pockets and moments of antiracism but were unable to stay with the work over time. It may provide a glimpse into some of the tactics needed to become an antiracist school leader and cautionary tales on what might keep one from leading for "eternity."

2. Chapter 8 provides examples of tenets that will deepen the work of antiracism—namely, shared experiences, active antiracism, and family and community engagement. These tenets keep school leaders in a collaborative, reflective, and action-oriented space.

In no way does this book suggest that the three phases or the 10 tenets for antiracist student leadership development will eradicate systemic racism in our schools. Indeed, the only premise they suggest are a necessary systemic antiracist approach to addressing racism in our schools. It is time for us to find ways to dismantle the vestiges of segregation, learn from our nation's legacy of racial and social injustice in education, and advance virtues of an antiracist democracy. Alexis de Tocqueville, the French philosopher who wrote *Democracy in America* (1838) after visiting the United States in 1831, saw that American democracy would fail if generation after generation of citizens did not develop what he called "habits of the heart" (Palmer, 2011). With these words, de Tocqueville referred to deeply ingrained patterns of receiving, interpreting, and responding to experiences that involve our intellects, emotions, identities, and, some might say, contextually, a racial-equity purpose—habits that form the inward and invisible infrastructure of an antiracist democracy.

In the chapters to come, I will explore my personal antiracist story as well as the story of antiracism in our schools. This exploration of antiracist leadership can be a reminder to see both the light and the darkness that can be found in our fight for independence—a fight that must evolve into a 21st-century call for *interdependence*, reminding us that our democracy, that "We the People," is not about me but about us. We must remind ourselves of the lessons of *sankofa*—an African word from the Akan tribe in Ghana (from the Internet); that is, to fetch what has come before us, the wisdom that will move us forward if we are to lead for antiracism in such a tumultuous time. It is why I draw on my Middle Eastern and North African ancestors to support the ancient Kemetic (ancient Egyptian) wisdom of Know Thyself, Distinguish Knowledge From Foolishness, and Build for Eternity. It is why I lead with a racial autobiography that is as much about self as it is about the relationships that have formed my racial being. This practice helps develop a real soul connection to the work we are doing rather than to continue to engage in shallow technical solutions. It is why I will follow with a brief story about the context of antiracism in schooling. In *The Velveteen Rabbit*, after the rabbit becomes Real and is living with the garden rabbits, he still comes back to visit the boy whose love gave him real life. The story teaches us to never forget the people who make you who you are even if you're living in two different worlds. Some things had to come to a fiery end in that story for the rabbit to become Real, and there are reminders that "being Real doesn't happen often to people who break easily, or have sharp edges, or who have to be carefully kept. Generally, by the time you are Real, most of your hair has been loved off, and your eyes drop out and you get loose in the joints and very shabby. But these things don't matter at all, because once you are Real you can't be ugly, except to people who don't understand." Realness in antiracism has no time nor place for fragility. However, there is a need for vulnerability and sensitivity. Discernment between vulnerability and fragility can help a leader sustain the will necessary to engage in active antiracism. Loving, spirit-filled antiracist school leaders lean into the racial context of those who profess to lead us through our work and, in that same light, know that they must at least have a cursory contextual understanding of our own place within a history of antiracism in schooling if we are to become leaders who love, care for, burn down, build up, and help with the evolution of the communities we serve. We must dare to be real if we are to become antiracist leaders.

Part I

KNOW THYSELF

This above all . . . to thine own self be true.

—*William Shakespeare,* Hamlet

CHAPTER 1

My Racial Autobiography

I was born and raised in the small town of Grand Marais, Minnesota. Grand Marais is the gateway to the Boundary Waters Canoe Area. It's the largest town in Cook County and a haven for city dwellers who long for a quaint, artistic atmosphere along Lake Superior when they take the ritualistic trip "up North," as so many Minnesotans do each summer. Many locals believe Grand Marais to be quite cosmopolitan for its size and rural location, but almost all agree that it is, as my father put it quite often, "one of the most beautiful small towns in the United States." My time in Grand Marais was one that I often took for granted. I longed to leave behind the beauty of my Lake Superior bedroom view for the energy and pace of the Twin Cities or another urban experience that I only knew from the images on cable television and in movies from the local video store. However, from a young age, I learned the importance of understanding where one comes from, the importance of safe space, and, even more importantly, the importance of the people who shaped who I was and who I was to become.

Grand Marais was not unlike most small towns in America; it was dependent upon two or three chief economic staples—in this case, tourism, education, and logging—and almost entirely comprised of White people. In fact, the entire county would have been almost entirely White except for the large population of American Indians who lived on or near the Grand Portage Indian Reservation about 35 miles north of Grand Marais (including my closest friend in high school, Bill Blackwell); a handful of students of color at Sawtooth Elementary School and Cook County High School who were adopted into White families; and the Lyght family, an African American clan who settled in Lutsen in the early 20th century. In 1972, John Lyght would become the first Black sheriff in Minnesota. He quickly won the respect and trust of the county's mostly White, Scandinavian-heritage population. In 1974, the year I was born, he was elected with 97.4 percent of the vote and would hold that office for over 20 years. His biracial nephew, Heston Lyght, would become one of my best friends during my adolescence.

I was taught early about the importance of my ethnic identity. My mother, an Arab-American of 100 percent Lebanese descent, would tell me stories about her experiences growing up in Duluth, often being mistaken for Jewish, where she learned from her parents the unwritten code of voluntary assimilation and, from her own experiences, the impact of oppression on those with little or no voice. I learned much about culture and ethnic pride from my father. He was Irish Catholic, born and raised in the college town of Northfield; he instinctively practiced culturally responsive teaching with me by letting me know I couldn't fail academically because of the great accomplishments and developments of "my people" from the Middle East. For example, he instilled in me the notion that I "must succeed" in math because my ancestors introduced the Arabic numbers I was learning. He knew instinctively that I was drawn toward the humanities and social sciences, but he wanted to instill in me the belief that ancestral knowledge would carry me through an area of learning that I may not have a passion for. Peppered with a healthy dose of Irish pride, he realized that subtle aspects of my Arab American ancestry would lead some to consider me somewhat of an "Other" in the homogenous North Woods of Cook County. My mother stood out in the North Woods of Minnesota as an Arab woman. Big, thick, black hair and light brown skin on a tiny little frame of a body made others notice her, but her personality, which drew people in to hear her wisdom regardless of their background, kept their attention. An afternoon didn't go by when she didn't hold court at the Blue Water Cafe with a pot of coffee, a grilled cheese with mustard, and a healthy dose of spiritual anecdotes to share and stories to excavate from the local Norwegians, Swedes, and Germans.

I was not often conscious of my race and ethnicity, but there were various encounters throughout childhood that led me to see that I was ethnically and racially different from my peers. My middle name, Abalan, was one that was not only unique, but also a source of ridicule with many of my friends once they heard it. In elementary school and middle school, I often hid my middle name from others so they wouldn't laugh at me. I was surprised that my peers did not have Lebanese sfihas, tabouleh, Syrian bread, and hashweh with their turkey, cranberries, and pumpkin pie on Thanksgiving. Once, when I was out playing at a friend's house in my neighborhood, an older neighbor found out I was Arab American and he pulled a knife, putting it to my neck, saying he was going to kill "Ahab the Arab." I was terrified, but accepted it as part of growing up in the area I did. In middle school, one of my social studies teachers announced to the class that I must be related to Saddam Hussein, leading the class to laugh at my heritage. By this time, I had grown more secure with my ethnic identity and I had a temper that flared in the face of bigotry. I directed an expletive at the teacher and walked out of the room. When I shared this story with my father, I remember him asking me to wait in the hallway while he went to give this teacher a piece of his mind. My White father stood up for me that day, but he also subtly taught me a lesson about antiracism that I had to unlearn over time—that anger behind closed doors was how men, particularly White men, engaged in antiracist work.

Despite all of the aggressions and microaggressions toward my Arab identity, none of this made me as upset and uncomfortable as when a classmate said in a group of our peers at a very young age that my mom "can't be White." His argument: "White people can't have black hair," as my mom did, so therefore, she must be "Black." Not only was I dumbfounded by his ignorance, but for the first time, I felt a fear that others might not consider me White. This comment took place while I was in 2nd grade and I had not yet addressed my internal struggle to understand my identity development between my European White ancestry and my Brown, Arab ancestry. I did not discuss this incident with my parents. I wasn't sure how. Despite all of the conversations with my parents about ethnicity and culture, I had never had a personal conversation about race. From about 2nd grade on, I had developed a consciousness that I must not be White, I must be an "Other." I even made a point to mark "Other" on every standardized test I took through elementary, middle, and high school. Up until 2nd grade and for a long period afterward, racism was something from history that was often associated with a southern accent and often accompanied with stories about the many accomplishments of the Civil Rights movement. In my mind, it was certainly not something that I ever would have considered to be a part of my personal identity development. I was unaware of the impact that the normalization of Whiteness—colorblindness, race neutrality, and unearned and unconscious privilege—would have and how it would continue to impact my life.

Throughout my formative years, there were a number of incidents and relationships that impacted the way in which I constructed meaning about race in my own life. At 4 years old in Montessori preschool, I remember vividly my encounter with Justin Smith. The teachers had prepared the class for a new student who would be joining our class by asking us all to station ourselves in a single-file line where we would take turns shaking the new student's hand. When Justin arrived, I, like most of the students in my almost all-White class, were fascinated to see a Black student. Until the point, I had only seen fictional Black people on TV—the Huxtables, Fat Albert and Cosby Kids, the casts from Good Times and The Jeffersons—all characters from television who created an archetype in my mind that was not real. I approached to welcome him and upon shaking his hand, a practice of which I certainly was not accustomed as a 5-year-old, I noticed how we were different. I was excited that someone else was different like me, the large, Arab American kid in the class; turned and said something to one of my friends about my observations; and was quickly whisked away into a corner by one of the teachers. At the time, she told me that I was being racist and that she never wanted me to say anything ever again about how this boy was different. I was told to sit in the corner while others played with and continued to greet the new student. Before I even entered kindergarten, I learned a lesson that took me years to unlearn—I should not see difference, in particular, with people who were racially different from me, and that under no circumstance should I ever talk about it at school. It wasn't until my 20s that I reflected upon this story with my parents. They were not aware of the incident, which left me wondering about the role that parent and teacher communication—or lack thereof—plays in the formation of racial identity. Certainly, courageous conversation about this incident did not play a role in my early formation. How could it have framed my thinking and potential to interrupt further harm like this incident for not only me, in particular, but for our new Black student, who had to endure the incident and its unintended consequences?

Although I was told early to stop noticing differences, I was looking for myself in the media wherever I could. I saw little representation of Arab Americans; however, between ages 5 and 18, I often found myself identifying with people of color or some representation of them. When we watched the movie *Gandhi* on TV, Ben Kingsley, the actor who portrayed Gandhi, reminded me so much of my grandfather that I was convinced that either I was East Indian or Gandhi was Lebanese. It's not lost on me that the actor is part White, playing an East Indian man. My favorite television shows, movies, sports teams, and music featured people of color. When my brother, 10 years my senior, attended Georgetown, I was drawn not just to the basketball team, but to its Blackness. I was not trying to culturally appropriate the ways in which Georgetown players like Alonzo Mourning, Dikembe Mutombo, and Alan Iverson acted, but rather, I saw a representation of something in them and in their racially conscious coach, John Thompson, that spoke to my soul as a Brown Arab American in a small White town in the Midwest. To these prepubescent eyes, all African Americans with Muslim names were brethren to Jews and Christian Arabs, like myself. We were all related—I just didn't understand how. As mentioned earlier, my two best friends growing up were Heston and Bill, the only two students in the class who were noticeably students of color. It was not uncommon for us to hear jokes from our peers that connected us through stereotypes. On one occasion I overheard, as the three of us entered a room, that our peers weren't sure if we were going to mug them, hijack them, or scalp them. Heston and Bill lived 65 miles apart, one living in Lutsen and the other on the Grand Portage Indian Reservation, with my home about equidistant from the other two. In middle school and high school, both of them, particularly Bill, would spend numerous nights at my house because the ride home after a football game or basketball practice would get them home too late. They were like brothers to me and I learned to appreciate our differences as much as our friendship. Bill shared with me information about American Indian culture and life on the reservation. Heston and I both longed to learn more about the urban experience. We talked about the difficulties he faced being a person of mixed race in Cook County, and he often seemed to struggle with his own sense of identity. In high school, Heston moved to Minneapolis to live with one of his sisters. There, he had some athletic success, but also succumbed to new habits that would forever alter his life. Heston passed away in South Minneapolis blocks away from where George Floyd died just weeks after that tragic incident. I can only wonder how racism impacted his heart, mind, and soul throughout his life, which was cut tragically short.

As someone who passed as White and grew up as a "townie," I didn't feel the responsibility of representing an Arab American community the way that my Brown and Indigenous friends did. I think often about my diverse peer group and how we shared so much time together growing up, and cannot help but think about how our individual races impacted our various experiences and the perceptions that others had of us. I have to think though about a couple of things that were not part of my consciousness at the time of growing up with them. I believe I was unconsciously drawn into deep affinity with Bill and Heston because we were all multiracial. With a parent who was White and another parent of color, we had an unspoken kinship that brought us together despite ethnic and cultural differences. Despite this similarity, it is clear to me that I have had a much more privileged life than Bill or Heston because I pass as White in many settings. They clearly present as people of color. My relationship with them has greatly influenced many of the decisions I have made to intentionally teach about racial-identity development and privilege to my students and to intentionally reach out to students of color who are experiencing countless aggressions like the ones I witnessed growing up in a small town. It has also gotten me to reflect on the complexity of color, consciousness, and culture in racial-identity development.

Among the aggressions that had a lasting impact on me was an incident when I was walking down the sidewalk near Highway 61 in Grand Marais in the early 1990s. A couple of recent high school graduates rolled down the window and yelled out a racial epithet at my friends and me. I was so angry that I wanted to go after them. I soon was calmed down by my friends who realized that a confrontation would most likely not end well. My friends, of color had enough personal experience with this to provide me with insight into my impulsivity. However, later that night, someone spray painted "KKK" on the outer brick wall of our high school. This shocking act of intolerance in our community stayed on that wall for years as school and city authorities wrung their hands over what to do. Although they were oftentimes more subtle, I watched as continued microaggressions built upon this inaction and were implicit in a continued marginalization of people of color that went unnamed for much of my life. It was so much a part of our culture that a teacher felt comfortable ridiculing my Arab American heritage in front of the class while discussing the Gulf War in his class.

When I decided to go to college at the University of Minnesota, one of the draws was the diversity of the student population and the fact that it was in an urban setting. My brother had gone to school there a decade before me and during orientation, upon his recommendation and my father's, I approached an employee in the honors program in the College of Liberal Arts about applying for a minority scholarship. She responded with a smirk and a giggle and asked me why I would want to apply for that. I told her that my brother had received the scholarship when he attended and that I was interested in applying, as an Arab American student. She laughed and told me that Arabs were not considered to be "minorities. "At the time, I accepted this answer at face value because I had often passed as "just another White guy" and I also did not consider myself a "minority"—just someone who, at least in my small town, was a bit "ethnically unique."

The exchange in the honors office remained dormant in my memory for a few months but was rekindled during some conversations with an East Indian girlfriend. I had been invited to her house for a traditional Indian meal and was surprised to find out during conversations with her family that her parents saw me as "just White." To them, my Arab ancestry did not change the perception they had of me as a White American male. It was confusing to me at times, however, because on other occasions they elevated my status as a Lebanese Arab American. Either way, I knew I was often drawn in college to dating and engaging in close relationships with women of color, particularly multiracial women, much for the same reason I had found affinity with Bill and Heston. There was kinship in a shared experience. I reflected upon their perceptions and engaged in numerous conversations with them and with other friends about the curious subjectivity of race in the United States. At the time, the intersectionality of race, ethnicity, class, and religion was not particularly clear to me.

As an undergraduate student, one of my advisors, David Roediger, taught explicitly about the social construction of Whiteness in his U.S. History class. My studies here affirmed my thinking about the presence of a racial narrative shaping our common history and of individual and collective racial and ethnic identity in our past and present. Roediger and Dionicio Valdes, my other advisor, encouraged me to take graduate classes that would allow me to explore the impact of race and privilege and how it had impacted labor and social movements, political interactions, and foreign policy. As a junior, I audited a graduate-level class on Whiteness that was both intimidating and exhilarating. As a student leader in housing and residential life, I was exposed to antiracism teaching through a training using *The Color of Fear* (1994) and a simulation of the Underground Railroad that brought the history of antiracism alive through a powerful intellectual, emotional, and physical experience. In my teaching career, both of these opportunities became curricular staples of my own classes and training for student leaders.

I became fascinated by the social construction of race and developed an intellectual curiosity to find out more. I did some research on the topic and found that there had been a movement in Congress in the 1980s to debunk the notion that has been raised by at least one scholar: that Jesus may have been Black. The census in 1970 and 1980 suggested that people of African descent (including North Africans and Middle Easterners) were considered African American (or Black) by the U.S. government. By 1990, the census indicated that people of Middle Eastern descent had moved into a category with European Americans, who were labeled "White (Caucasian)." This shift demonstrates how the race was socially reconstructed to meet the political needs of a few powerful government officials. As I dove deeper into this phenomenon, I was surprised to find how often the social construction of race had shifted to maintain a racial hierarchy or caste in our nation. In the 1840s, I would have been considered Black because of my Irish ancestry (Ignatiev, 1995), and numerous other groups of people have had the lines of race and ethnicity blurred to impact citizenship, voting rights, housing, and internment (Zinn, 1980). It came as no surprise to me, in a post–9/11 world, that my race may once again be changed by the government to address the political climate that will most certainly want to keep track of the number of Arab Americans in the United States. To this end, I often check "Other" and welcome the opportunity to write in any explanations about the curious dichotomy between the complexity and arbitrariness of race in the United States.

Early in my professional career, I came across the book *Why Are All the Black Kids Sitting Together in the Cafeteria?* by Beverly Tatum (1997). I sat on the floor between the bookshelves at the secondhand bookstore for 2 hours, enthralled by the themes in the book and how they resonated with my own personal experiences. Over the next few years as a social studies teacher and coach, I made a point to share not only the stories of the likes of Abraham Lincoln and Thomas Jefferson but also the narratives and wisdom of pioneers with less ink in the textbook like Frederick Douglass (1857), Harriet Jacobs (1861), Chief Joseph (1911), and Dolores Huerta (1984). In doing so, I made a point to ask my students to engage in critical thinking and writing about the political, social, and economic state of our union by incorporating these multiple narratives. I heard a calling to engage in this work and felt blessed by the serendipity that led to my placement as a social studies teacher and racial-equity leader.

My professional journey, albeit a nonlinear journey, has been littered with a range of experiences that have helped me become an antiracist leader. I worked as a teacher in Hopkins Public Schools as racial-equity coordinator where I was asked, upon taking the job, why I was interested in equity. When I replied that I wanted to honor my Arab American ancestors and that I had always been drawn to issues of social justice because of my background, I was told that I must navigate my leadership journey as a White man. This came from an influential mentor whom I trusted deeply in this work. Without much question, I bought into the Black/White binary of race and at the time was perceived by many to be a very racially conscious White male. In denouncing a part of my racial identity, I was put on a pedestal by many in the racial-equity community and was soon recruited to a neighboring high-performing school district that was seen by many in the Twin Cities as the bastion of White privilege. Indeed, my time in Edina as an assistant principal was spent navigating Whiteness, but it was very much done as someone who was hired to do the work as a "racially conscious White male." After excelling in the role as a "White male," I was recruited into both Minneapolis as a principal and St. Paul as a director of leadership development. In Minneapolis we closed our racial opportunity gap by more than 20 percentage points in 2 years between Black and White students but, more importantly, created a culture of antiracist leadership development for students, parents, and staff. I then replicated that work in over 70 schools in St. Paul with superintendent Valeria Silva. I thrived in both diverse settings, feeling like I could be myself and live my purpose as an antiracist leader.

When I went to St. Paul, I thought we were doing some of the most progressive and student-centered racial-equity work in the United States. Our superintendent was being invited to the White House to consult with President Obama, our cabinet was engaged consistently in Courageous Conversations about race, our principals were being coached about systems for advancing racial equity, and systems were being dismantled. However, like in many school districts around the country, a combination of union leaders, school board, and community members rallied to remove Superintendent Silva. Her work with "critical race theory" was seen as too radical. In reality, her work to integrate classrooms and ensure that students of color served in special education got inclusion in general education brought too high a level of unproductive disequilibrium, and not enough leaders had the will, skill, knowledge, and capacity to sustain this sort of system change. I did not feel that this was a safe environment anymore and left to work in the Anoka-Hennepin school district. While there, I was taken aback by how different politically the conversation about race was. Just 15 miles removed from St. Paul, I was being asked to not lead conversations about race but rather to ensure that no one was talking about Whiteness in middle school classrooms. As kind as many of the people in the community were, I soon realized I needed to leave this district as well. I started work in St. Louis Park Public Schools as the director of teaching, learning, and leadership and have never been happier. I am expected to bring my full racial identity into the workplace and analyze complex problems through a critical race lens. All of our teachers have racial-equity instructional coaches, and I have been able to find a mentor and a team that is racially conscious and sees me. I've been able to serve, for a number of years now, as the antiracist leader in the workplace that I want to be.

A few years ago, I went to visit the classroom of the mother of my two children, who is a kindergarten teacher in their school district. She invited me in to be a guest reader in the classroom, where I was to read *Morris the Moose Goes to School*. When I entered the classroom, the students were all gathered on the floor and Katie, my wife at the time, asked them to guess who the guest speaker was, while I sat on the piano bench nearby. One White girl blurted out, "the bus driver?" Another young Black male said, "a piano player?" She went on to tell them that I was related to her children and her. One East Indian student said, "Is he your father?" Another asked if I was her grandfather—that was not the best moment of the day! Katie then went on to tell them I was Will and Keira's father and her husband. There was a moment of silence and then another White girl toward the back of the class raised her hand and asked, "Why did you marry a Black man?" Without missing a beat, Katie answered by saying, "Because I loved him." Now, this exchange to me was profound for a number of reasons. For one of the first times in a school setting, I was not asked to explain to others, not even to these kindergarten students, about my race. Indeed, I am not Black! In fact, I noticed that one Black child in the class cocked her head to the side and looked at me with a smile on her face and shook her head at the comment. However, Katie acknowledged our racial difference and honored, without explanation, the noticing that the student had about our racial difference. Katie, who is clearly White, had married a multiracial Arab American man who can sometimes pass as White, but for the first time I could remember, neither she nor the students nor anyone else tried to tell me what I was or wasn't. I felt seen. In many ways, this demonstrated just how culturally relevant a teacher Katie was. She understood the developmental needs of her children and was astute enough to not put her partner on the spot to defend, explain, or define his race. She knew she could follow up on discussions about race, color, colorism, ethnicity, melanin, and relationships through her social studies and literacy lessons or even in her morning meetings in the coming days. This was a turning point for me. I felt that I wasn't just seen as a person of color at work but was seen for who I was at home, too—something that I didn't always get throughout my life. It was one moment that gave me the confidence to stand in my full identity at home and at work.

I have noticed my capacity to keep the spotlight on race in my life to wax and wane with time. It has been tiring to be in spaces where there are few role models talking about what it is like to have a Brown mother whose parents wanted her to be White and a White father who talked of ethnicity and not of race. It is tiring to waver between two worlds, one where I am White and another where I am off-white, light brown, Arab American, Lebanese, or multiracial. In these worlds, I feel the gaze of others wishing I would just pick one and see myself the way they see me. However, the only people who tell me what they see without asking are children. Their answers are mixed . . . kind of like me. They seem to see me without prejudice and recognize the complexity, ambiguity, and social construction of my race. I'm appreciative for my experience with them and hopeful because of it. Sometimes I felt that I had the worst kind of privilege, the kind where I could choose my race, but then came to realize that my racial ambiguity was something to reflect on, not feel guilty about. Indeed, there were periods of time when I would enter a space and hope that others would just choose my race for me. That had been a familiar pattern started at the University of Minnesota, where I now teach, and had erroneously modeled for me that institutions and those who work in them can and maybe should tell you who you are. Three times in my lifetime my identity has changed in the eyes of the government. Now, I look back on how clearly I chose my own multiracial affinity in my years in Grand Marais and how alive in my whole being I felt. I just didn't see any representation of Arab Americans in the media or in the community outside of my mother. This feeling of isolation has followed me well into my adult years, when I can now embrace Arab American affinity space and am learning Arabic for the first time with peers who have experienced life in Minnesota in ways that are similar to and different from me. I can proudly say that I have overcome the fear and fatigue that have come from my identity journey, largely due to this affinity space but also because of the encounters I have had with colleagues who have helped me become an antiracist leader and realize my purpose in developing other people and systems for racial equity.

My work as an Arab American antiracist is ever-present in my leadership, scholarship, and research. I acknowledge the choice that I am making to be a racial-equity leader. I know that whether I am conscious of it or not, the depth of my impact on society can be profound, if only by the sheer number of lives that are touched by my work in schools. My choice to engage in this book is an acknowledgment that I must draw upon the power, responsibility, privilege, and navigation of Whiteness to frame my efforts toward equity for all by working to stand side by side with my other colleagues of color to ensure that the brilliance and gifts of all children—particularly Black, Brown, Arab, and Indigenous children—have space to learn and grow.

CHAPTER 2

Historical and Antiracist School Leadership Perspectives

I sometimes visualize the ongoing cycle of racism as a moving walkway at the airport. Active racist behavior is equivalent to walking fast on the conveyor belt. The person engaged in active racist behavior has identified with the ideology of White supremacy and is moving with it. Passive racist behavior is equivalent to standing still on the walkway. No overt effort is being made, but the conveyor belt moves the bystanders along to the same destination as those who are actively walking. Some of the bystanders may feel the motion of the conveyor belt, see the active racists ahead of them, and choose to turn around, unwilling to go to the same destination as the White supremacists. But unless they are walking actively in the opposite direction at a speed faster than the conveyor belt—unless they are actively antiracist—they will find themselves carried along with the others.

—Beverly Daniel Tatum

This chapter includes a brief examination of the recent research on, and models of, antiracism programs used currently in U.S. high schools, particularly those that were used at Midwest High School and St. Louis Park Public Schools—two schools highlighted throughout this book. This section provides a brief historical overview and background for systemic antiracism in U.S. schooling, a very short overview of antiracism in the United States, an overview of the tenets and origins of critical race theory in schools, and some discussion of racial-identity development theory and how it pertains to leadership studies.

A VERY BRIEF HISTORY OF ANTIRACISM IN THE UNITED STATES

With the arrival of the first African slaves in Jamestown in 1619, the complex racial development of the colonies, already present with the close proximity of Whites to Native Americans, became further entrenched. In the centuries that followed, the oppression of people of color throughout the country through White dominance was carried forward in the institution of slavery, westward expansion and imperialism, and radical forms of nativism and racism, which would create a nation of peoples made up of separate and unequal groups (Aptheker, 1992; Zinn, 1980).

Within this historical context, oppositional and critical movements concerning American racism and the educational system that perpetuated it were initiated by a substantial body of African American thought in the late 19th and early 20th centuries, as seen in the work of W.E.B. Du Bois (1903), Ida B. Wells (1892), Charles H. Wesley (1939), and others. These scholars worked to counteract stereotypes and challenge predominant assumptions about race and schooling, and they shared ideas that encouraged educators to be change agents for a better, more just society. By the 1960s, the Civil Rights Movement included many Whites and people of color on the front lines of antiracist change who looked at aspects of educational inequity that included the relevance of curricula, bias in standardized tests, and the relationship and behavior of White teachers toward students of color (Kailin, 1996). This last piece was of particular relevance to this study due to the nature of White racism and the White domination of all school leadership and teaching. It is the lack of substantive antiracist leadership by Whites that has often been associated by people of color with incremental or no organizational change for racial equity—this is the at the core of the work around critical race theory in education (Crenshaw et al., 1995; Delgado & Stefancic, 2001).

United States history, however, is not without its stories of Black, Brown, and even White triumph over racism. Notably, Whites such as John Brown, Lewis and Arthur Tappan, and Harriet Beecher Stowe provide models for many Whites who otherwise may have been exposed only to the modeling of White racists throughout history. Some historians point out that not only were people of color involved in antiracism, but many Whites were also quite aware of the moral issues at play in the United States and fought for immediate change (Aptheker, 1992). If one evaluates the actions of our founding fathers—in particular, Thomas Jefferson—not only for owning slaves but for expressing overtly racist beliefs, a common assertion would be that he was merely a "product of his time" and was expressing ideas that were prevalent in the time in which he lived. What often gets less discussion is the fact that other prominent White leaders such as Thomas Paine, who is well known for his pamphlet "Common Sense," which inspired the Declaration of Independence, was a founder of an antislavery society and wrote articles about promoting antislavery in the American colonies. Surely, Thomas Jefferson was aware of Paine and his views, yet his owning, beating, and raping of Black slaves are justified as a norm of that time. Very few students today ever learn of Paine's antiracism or that of others who were actively addressing racism—instead getting a message that racism throughout history can merely be absolved when enough time passes. Much like his counterparts of color, such as Frederick Douglass, Harriet Tubman, and Tecumseh, William Lloyd Garrison provides a role model for Whites that want to actively pursue immediate racial equity. The unique context of race relations in the United States—a context of forced and voluntary assimilation of people of color with a White culture that from its first colonization on the continent felt entitled to power and privilege as ordained by God (Winthrop, 1630)—has given antiracist actions and ideology more potential for conflict and change than anywhere else in the world.

In fact, the impact of antiracism in the United States has been far-reaching. American antiracism has become a global phenomenon (Loewen, 1996):

> Antiracism is one of America's great gifts to the world. Its relevance extends far beyond race relations. Antiracism led to a "new birth of freedom" after the Civil War, and not only for African Americans. Twice, once in each century, the movement for Black rights triggered the movement for women's rights. Twice it reinvigorated our democratic spirit, which had been atrophying. Throughout the world, from South Africa to Northern Ireland, movements of oppressed people continue to use tactics and words borrowed from our abolitionist and civil rights movements. The clandestine early meetings of anti-Communists in East Germany were marked by singing "We Shall Overcome." Iranians used nonviolent methods borrowed from Thoreau and Martin Luther King, Jr., to overthrow their hated shah. On Ho Chi Minh's desk in Hanoi on the day he died lay a biography of John Brown. Among the heroes whose ideas inspired the students in Tiananmen Square and whose words spilled from their lips was Abraham Lincoln. Yet we in America, whose antiracist idealists are admired around the globe, seem to have lost these men and women as heroes. [Our schools] . . . need to present them in such a way that we might again value our own idealism. (pp. 192–193)

Although Loewen may lament the lack of focus on antiracist idealism in our schools, there has in fact been a renaissance of antiracism in education in the recent past. Developments in antiracist education were quite prevalent during the Civil Rights era, but recent literature suggests that racial discord in the early 1990s and political pressures from the Clinton and Bush presidential administrations (despite the possibility of dissimilar ideology or motives) led to a resurgence of antiracism in the field of education that took off about a decade into the 2000s.

In the middle of the 2010s, what is now known as the Black Lives Matter movement began to organize. It started out as a grassroots organization whose mission was to build local power and to intervene when violence was inflicted on Black communities by the state and by vigilantes. Enraged by the death of Trayvon Martin and the subsequent acquittal of his killer, George Zimmerman, activism became more intense as protesters set out together on the Black Lives Matter Freedom Ride to Ferguson in search of justice for Mike Brown, another Black man killed by police. This sparked an "all lives matter" movement to counter the Black Lives Matter movement, perceived by some to be anti-White, and perhaps exacerbated issues of colorism and racial hierarchy that would impact the plight of Blacks in the United States.

Now, "Black lives matter" is painted in bright yellow letters on the road to the White House. Celebrities and chief executives are embracing it. Even

Sen. Mitt Romney, a Republican former presidential candidate, posted the phrase on Twitter (Del Real et al., 2020).

As consensus grows about the existence of systemic racism in American policing and other facets of American life, longtime organizers of the Black Lives Matter movement are trying to extend its momentum beyond the popularization of a phrase. Activists sense a once-in-a-generation opportunity to demand policy changes that once seemed far-fetched, including sharp cuts to police budgets in favor of social programs and greater accountability for officers who kill residents (Del Real et al., 2020). In the coming decade, it is quite possible we will see the murder of George Floyd in my hometown of Minneapolis as a turning point that makes antiracism part of a more mainstream progressive agenda.

A VERY BRIEF HISTORY OF ANTIRACISM IN PUBLIC EDUCATION

Theories that promote antiracist pedagogy are not new. A century ago Du Bois noted (1903) that there must be "immediate" and challenging action to eradicate the "problem of the color line." However, the view of institutional racism and its impact on educational settings made a radical shift in 1968 with the release of the Kerner Commission report (Report of the National Advisory Committee on Civil Disorders, 1968), which claimed that the reason for much of the racial discord in the United States was not because of a problem with the racially oppressed groups but rather stemmed from White individual and institutional racism. Young (1970) supported a number of the commission's findings:

> Most Americans get awfully uptight about the charge of racism, since most people are not conscious of what racism really is. Racism is not a desire to wake up every morning and lynch a Black man from a tall tree. It is not engaging in vulgar epithets. These kinds of people are just fools. It is the day-to-day indignities, the subtle humiliations that are so devastating. Racism is the assumption of superiority of one group over another, with all the gross arrogance that goes along with it. Racism is a part of us. The Kerner Commission has said that if you have been an observer you have been racist; if you have stood by idly, you are racist. (p. 730, as cited in Katz, 2003, p. 20)

A result of the new political awareness of race from the Civil Rights Movement was the impetus for diversity training that manifested in the 1970s with the advent of multicultural education. "Multicultural education" refers to an approach that began in earnest in the early 1980s (Banks, 1992; Nieto, 1995; Sleeter, 1990) that concentrates on celebrating difference and diversity and avoiding racism. Staff development in this area is seen as an antecedent to antiracism and equity programs because of its focus on understanding how culture and power act on every aspect of human behavior, especially in education (Gay, 1995). Wiedeman's analysis (2002) also suggested that this approach may have led to increased racial understanding, but it did not call for an examination of the role of institutional racism or for activism against racist actions, policies, or beliefs. Rather, a development of "White guilt" and liberal ideology provided for a lack of action on the part of Whites and people of color to change a system that was still not serving students of color. Many school leaders presented sensitivity training that challenged teachers not to see color in their approach to the classroom. The "colorblind" approach of many multicultural programs (McIntyre, 1997; Nieto, 1995) has supported a liberal gradualist ideology that is often seen as weak and ineffective to many antiracist scholars and educators (Sleeter & Delgado Bernal, 2003). Because multicultural staff development does not go deep into the power relationships in terms of racism, some antiracist scholars (Almanzan, 2006; Nieto, 1995) have seen this as a limitation of multicultural programs and do not currently associate them with antiracist staff development. In turn, some multicultural education advocates have lamented the limited scope of antiracism and its confrontational focus as a source of alienation for many White educators (Wiedeman, 2002).

As cited in Kailin (1996, p. 43), not even all who saw inequities and injustices in the educational system have shared an understanding about causality or the possibility for organizational change. When one scholar (Hacker, 1992), for example, documented the ravages of racism and debunked racist myths regarding issues such as crime and welfare, this liberal perspective was criticized for "offer[ing] no hope for change" (Roediger, 1994). Roediger critiqued Hacker's perspective as offering no vision of any counter-strategy to abolish racism (pp. 121–126). While multiculturalism and liberal gradualist ideology presented educators with tools for more awareness about the presence and impact of race, they provided few action steps for deinstitutionalizing racism. Recently, advocates for racial equity have seen the need to transcend political ideology that may impact views of people of color; instead, working to address staff-development programs that have actually focused on antiracism in secondary schools has been a relatively recent phenomenon. In the mid-1990s, a wave of programs moved beyond multiculturalism into a more radical paradigm of activist training programs. Antiracist education emerged in the mid-1980s out of concerns over the limitations of multicultural education programs. Many antiracist advocates have argued that the "watered-down, apolitical version of diversity training (seen in multicultural professional development) avoided the examination of systemic racism in relation to educational inequality" (Weideman & Stein, 2003, p. 203). Antiracism and critical race theory place racism at the center of debate over equity and focus on "the racist underpinnings and operation of White-dominated institutions . . . rather than ethnic minority cultures and lifestyles" (Troyna, 1987).

Thirty years after the Kerner Commission put White racism at the center of the discussion of inequity in the United States, the Clinton administration's Initiative on Race mirrored the findings of the commission by determining that the "absence of both knowledge and understanding about the role race played in our collective history continues to make it difficult to find solutions that will improve race relations" (Katz, 2003, p. 18). This report and the advent of the Bush administration's No Child Left Behind (NCLB, 2001) legislation, which called for disaggregated data by race and socioeconomic class, created a renewed emphasis on placing race on the political agenda and on assessing the ways in which educational institutions are serving all students, not just Whites. Despite strong opposition to NCLB by many educators, many antiracist scholars have begun to call this legislation one of the most important developments for those who are fighting to close achievement gaps (Haycock & Chenoweth, 2005).

The 2007 Supreme Court decision in the case of *Parents v. Seattle*, although not going so far as to overturn *Brown v. Board of Education*, asserted that the federal government's stance on addressing racial inequity is not a "compelling state interest." This "colorblind" approach to diversity is one that abruptly contradicts many recent race-related developments in education. All of this research suggests a permanence of racism in the United States that must be addressed with action that goes beyond multicultural awareness and calls for antiracist initiatives from the top levels of organizational power, for even presidential support for serving our students of color has not yet succeeded in eliminating our nation's racial achievement gaps.

The election of Barack Obama created another level of complexity in the realm of antiracism as scholars and media pundits debate the existence of a postracial society in light of a person of color having been elevated to the highest office in the land, thanks, in part, to a national effort by interracial voters. The triumph of Barack Obama in November 2008 can be seen as a significant individual accomplishment, but there is little evidence that this has created systemic change. In truth, the proposition that the victory of one person of color signifies a victory over racism for an entire group of people is somewhat ludicrous. As one antiracist scholar points out, "Surely, if Hillary Clinton [had] captured the nomination of her party and gone on to win in November, no one with even a scintilla of common sense would have argued that a result such as this signaled the obvious demise of sexism in the United States" (Wise, 2009, p. 27.) There have always been individually successful persons of color, as there have always been White antiracists. However, we have not seen a pattern of systemic change to alleviate racism in our recent past any more than we have seen it throughout history. It is in this context that the aforementioned antiracism resurgence in education has developed over the past two decades and has developed another layer of complexity to the notion of racial equity.

As school leaders strive to promote standards-based learning and "21st Century Learning," antiracism often contrasts sharply with the current school of thought regarding educational reform. The approach supported by the Efficacy Institute for more than 25 years emphasizes the use of accurate student achievement data and three elements of school reform: building consensus on clear targets for academic proficiency; building beliefs among all school stakeholders that standards can be achieved; and building continuous feedback through assessment work (Howard, 2016). The movement to focus on challenging institutional inequities, particularly institutional racism, has been advocated by a number of scholars and practitioners as we closed the first decade of the 21st century (Alexander, 2010; Noguera, 2008; Singleton & Linton, 2006. Pollock, 2008). Pollock suggests a synthesis of these two approaches for addressing our racially predictable achievement gaps:

> Antiracist educators must constantly negotiate between two antiracist impulses in deciding their everyday behaviors toward students. Moment to moment, they must choose between the antiracist impulse to treat all people as human beings rather than as "race" group members, and the antiracist impulse to recognize people's real experiences as race group members in order to assist them and treat them equitably. (2008. p. 2)

Within the historical context of racial oppression in the United States, antiracist reform in schools seems to call for strong leaders' racial self-awareness. Self-reflective leadership, individual and collective racial consciousness, and the presence of cross-racial dialogue are themes often implicated as essential factors for antiracist change (Singleton, 2022; Wise, 2009). As administration and staff in schools work toward systemic antiracism, awareness of the racial identity of each participant in the reform becomes a prerequisite for even beginning racial discourse, let alone for any advancement toward organizational change for racial equity.

PERSPECTIVES: RACIAL IDENTITY

This section focuses on the most commonly cited factor contributing to educator perceptions about race and racism. The literature suggests that without the ability to reflect on your own racial identity and to understand the racial-identity development of others, one cannot be an effective leader of antiracism (Singleton, 2022; Tatum, 1997). Within the context of this study, racial identity will be an important factor in analyzing school leaders' perceptions of antiracism and in the creation of meaning from multiple cross-racial perspectives on antiracism.

Some of the seminal work in the area of racial identity and education came during the period between the late 1970s and late 1990s (Helms, 1990; Katz, 2003; Tatum, 1997). Its relevance to education and staff development is that many programs started to address the personal nature of race and how it affects professional practice and the values associated with educating all students. In her study of antiracist pedagogy, Kailin (1994) argued that the inclusion of structured time for critical reflection on racial identity was a key for the success of antiracist staff development. More recently, Singleton (2022) asserted that the exploration of racial identity is one of the most important conditions for beginning Courageous Conversations About Race.

To provide more background on racial identity for this study, the following topics will be examined: (1) racial-identity development for White people,

(2) racial-identity development and privilege, and (3) leadership and Whiteness. Ensuing sections will discuss the commonly used models and research on (4) racial-identity development for people of color, (5) racial identity development and marginalization, (6) identity and leadership for people of color, (7) characteristics and implications of racial identity development for biracial people, (8) marginalization of biracial people, and (9) leadership and biracial people. The sections on privilege and marginalization are included to emphasize what the literature suggests are key factors to consider when analyzing Whites, people of color, and biracial people. It should be noted that there is a relative wealth of information on White educational leadership, but much less focused discussion on leaders of color—itself an example of privilege and marginalization in the scholarship.

IDENTITY DEVELOPMENT AND WHITE PEOPLE

Although many of the frameworks in the area of racial identity include important elements of the anti-racist model that is examined in this study, the most important purpose for reviewing the literature around these existing theories and frameworks is to understand points of reference and the perspectives on race of school leaders. Because the vast majority of school leaders in the United States are White, their racial-identity development is a key factor in differentiating between their experiences and their perceptions.

Two themes emerged from the review of the literature on White identity, or "Whiteness." The first of these is a group of characteristics consistently associated with Whiteness that suggests a subversive denial of both White privilege and the existence of racism, particularly institutional racism. The second theme is White-racial-identity development and models constructed to help analyze this development. The models are analyzed through their capacity for developing antiracist leaders and antiracist organizations.

Some scholars have argued that White people fail to see their Whiteness and perceive it as both neutral and normative (Powell, 1996). The denial of Whiteness leads Whites to "experience (them)selves as non-racialized individuals" (Scheurich, 1993). Katz and Ivey (1977, p. 11) observed: "Ask a White person what he or she is racially and you might get the answer 'Italian,' 'English,' 'Catholic,' or 'Jewish.' White people do not see themselves as White." One radical scholar sets himself apart from most White educators when he asserts that even in his all-White, German American neighborhood race was never absent (Roediger, 1999). He suggested that just as we have defined race as a color, we must also define White as a color that has had a great impact on the development of racism in American society and schools.

Many Whites' unconsciousness of their own race develops an identity that absolves them from any culpability for institutional racism. One might suggest that this is the ultimate White privilege, one that helps explain the perpetuation of the status quo regarding racism. The following section focuses on research on racial identity for Whites and the relationship between racial equity and privilege.

White People and Privilege

The literature suggests that Whites often see racism as nothing more than a manifestation of personal prejudice—overt acts of specific individuals removed from historical, political, or systemic contexts (Giroux, 1997; Kluegel & Smith, 1986; Lawrence & Tatum, 1997; Scheurich, 1993). Hollywood versions of racism, as enacted by individuals engaging in overt and intentional actions, can perpetuate this notion for most Whites through some of the recent popular films that address racism (Haggis, 2004; J. Singleton, 1991)—for example, *Crash* and *Boyz n the Hood* support the idea of racism as something individual, overt, not necessarily from the past, but most often intentional. A focus on individuals denies that structural barriers for the mobility of people of color exist (Jones & Carter, 1996; Scheurich, 1993). This relationship between our denial of the significance of race and our failure to acknowledge the existence of institutional racism is fueled and maintained by the privilege Whites experience. Peggy McIntosh (1989) defines White privilege as "an invisible knapsack of unearned assets which I can count on cashing in each day, but about which I was 'meant' to remain oblivious"(p. 18). She uses the metaphor of a "weightless knapsack of special provisions, assurances, tools, maps, guides, codebooks, passports, visas, clothes, emergency gear, and blank checks" to describe the advantage White people have in America "solely as a result of the skin color of which we adamantly deny the significance" (McIntosh, 1989).

Janet Helms (1984) linked White privilege specifically to racism, asserting that White people are born as the beneficiaries of racism. Educated to be colorblind in terms of their own identity, Whites are encouraged to deny the significance of race for others and presented with an individualistic ideology that ignores systemic racism, all the while enjoying the privilege of ignoring the whole cycle (Helms, 1984; Lawrence & Bunche, 1996). According to Helms (1990), White-identity development includes a foundational stage in which White privilege is damaging to the development of positive racial identities for White people due to the obliviousness of those in privilege to understanding their role in systemic racism.

A number of educators, psychologists, sociologists, and practitioners have developed models or typologies that suggest that privilege has a huge impact on White identity (Carney & Kahn, 1984; Ganter, 1977; Helms, 1984, 1990; Terry, 1970). Though the stages or phases in these models are named differently, they describe virtually the same processes through a "continuum of statuses" according to which White people confront increasingly difficult issues regarding their Whiteness (McIntyre, 1997). The literature suggests that the most widely accepted, reviewed, and adapted of these models is Helms's six-stage process for developing a positive White racial identity (Carter &

Goodwin, 1996; Jones & Carter, 1996; Lawrence & Bunche, 1996). Some of the most prominent contemporary antiracism frameworks have incorporated the work of Helms and McIntosh as central to their work (Derman-Sparks & Brunson Phillips, 1997; Howard, 2016; Singleton & Linton, 2006).

Helms developed her original model by informally interviewing "a few White friends and colleagues to determine how they viewed the development of their racial consciousness" (1984, p. 155). Upon analyzing the interviews, she found the coping strategies of the interviewees "rather reminiscent of the manner in which members of a visiting culture might adjust to a host culture" (1984, p. 155). As a result, she adapted culture shock theories to "explain the attitudinal evolutionary process" (1984, p. 155).

Helms's original model (1984) included five stages of White people's "racial consciousness": contact, disintegration, reintegration, pseudoindependence, and autonomy. Helms (1990) later included a sixth stage between pseudoindependence and autonomy called immersion/emersion to reflect "the contention that it is possible for Whites to seek out accurate information about their historical, political, and cultural contributions to the world, and that the process of self-examination within this context is an important component of the process of developing a positive White identity" (p. 70).

If one is a White person in the United States, it is possible to exist without ever having to acknowledge that reality. It is likely that only when Whites come into contact with people of color that Whiteness could potentially become an issue. Helms conceptualizes a two-phase process of identity development that includes Phase 1, the abandonment of racism, and Phase 2, defining a positive White identity (Helms, 1990). The first three stages of White-identity development fall under Phase 1. The first stage, contact, begins upon the first encounter that a White person has with a person of color. A person in the contact stage may or may not engage in individual racism while automatically benefitting from institutional and cultural racism "without necessarily being aware that he or she is doing so" (Helms, 1990, p. 55). One's longevity in the contact stage depends on the quality and quantity of interracial experiences, particularly with respect to racial issues. The second stage of Phase 1 is disintegration, characterized by conflicted and conscious acknowledgment of one's Whiteness.

As a White person's beliefs about race become more conscious, he or she enters the reintegration stage. In this stage, a person consciously acknowledges his or her Whiteness and grapples with feelings of guilt or denial that may be transformed into anger directed toward people of color. White people in this stage may be frustrated by the notion of being a part of a racial group rather than just individuals. Many White people never move past the reintegration stage, while others find themselves in a pseudoindependent stage. Here, an individual gains an intellectual understanding of racism as a system of advantage but does not quite now what do about it.

Stage 5 (Helms, 1990), immersion/emersion, is marked by a recognized need to find more positive self-definition. Whites need to seek new ways of thinking about Whiteness so they are able to move beyond their self-identity in the role of victimizer. It would make sense that White individuals presented with examples of other White antiracists might be able to navigate to and through this stage with more ease. The last stage in Helm's model, autonomy, represents the ability for White people to have flexible analyses and response to racial material, data, or experiences. The autonomy stage is marked by an increased effectiveness in multiracial settings.

While the 1970s produced numerous White-racial-identity models, most of the literature produced on the topic since the development of Helms's model (1984) has been based on her model. The literature suggests that Helms's model has been adopted by both education and psychology as the basis for understanding White-racial-identity development. According to Jones and Carter (1996), the model "has received empirical scrutiny," and the empirical evidence suggests "a strong relationship between the various racial identity ego statuses and prejudice" (p. 10).

IDENTITY DEVELOPMENT FOR PEOPLE OF COLOR

Although racial-identity development for people of color has many similarities to that of racial-identity development for Whites, the research on Black and Brown racial identity addresses the unique position that people of color have in the United States. There have been numerous scholars who have developed theories on racial-identity development for people of color (Cross, 1978, 1995; Helms, 1992, 1993, 1994; Tatum, 1997). Most models follow one of two strands when addressing racial identity: (a) stage models that show either cyclical or linear psychological progression of identity or (b) models that identify common identity traits in a particular group of color. This section focuses on two models that address cyclical psychological progression, two models that identify common traits within groups, and scholars who incorporate ideas between the two strands.

Cross (1978, 1995) developed a model primarily for Black Americans to understand their own experience in the United States but later did studies on a variety of groups of color in the United States. His second model is very similar to the progression of White identity seen in the Helms (1991, 1992, 1994) models. According to Cross's model, referred to most often as nigrescence theory (Cross, 1995), or "the psychology of becoming Black" (Tatum, 1997, p. 55), there are five stages of racial-identity development for Black people. The first two are often most relevant in adolescents and the last three are most common in, but not exclusive to, adults. Cross (1995, p. 42) demonstrated the dynamic progression that develops in each of these stages:

- *Preencounter.* The personal and social significance of one's racial group membership has not been realized, but unconsciously, the child is learning that Whites are more valued in society.

- *Encounter.* Something happens that forces the young person to see the personal impact of racism, and he or she grapples with what it means to be a member of a group targeted by racism.
- *Immersion.* The period, often in adolescence or early adulthood, when a person of color is energized by learning more about his or her cultural history and by spending time mostly with peers of the same race. This is also an attempt to redefine oneself based on an affirmation of one's racial group identity.
- *Internalization.* The stage characterized by a sense of security about one's racial identity; usually this is the time one is willing to establish meaningful relationships across group boundaries, including with Whites who are respectful of a person of color's new self-definition.
- *Internalization-commitment.* The stage when the individual has found ways to translate his or her personal sense of racial identity into ongoing action that expresses a commitment to the concerns of his or her racial group.

Nigrescence theory (Cross, 1978) is indicative of much of the literature on racial-identity development for people of color. Cross refers to this model as a framework for understanding identity for people of color but exclusively refers to Black people when addressing specific examples. By interchanging Black experiences of identity with those of people of color, the work implies that it includes all people of color but does not specifically address the development of those who identify as something other than Black. More recently, Cross has worked to critique his own work by suggesting that his research, as well as research on Black racial identity, would benefit from longitudinal studies, the examination of the existence of overarching racial-identity constructs, and an acknowledgment of multiple nationalistic indentures (Worrell et al., 2001). However, this model does provide some important elements to use to address the challenge of marginalization and the impact on leadership for people of color. It is important to note that in all of the cognitive models of racial-identity development, the process is ongoing, often occurring in cycles. After someone "reaches" a stage, he or she will return to a former stage as a result of encounters with racism. Such encounters perpetuate the marginalization of people of color and have a profound impact on their identity. Updates of the Cross model have addressed the discovery of a multiculturalist racial identity (Worrell et al., 2001). In the original model (e.g., Hall et al., 1972), the "internalized" individual was described as focusing on things other than himself and his own ethnic group. The revised model (Cross, 1991) modified this stance to say that internalized individuals give "high salience to Blackness," and this salience can leave "little room for other considerations," as in the case of Black Nationalists (p. 210). The multiculturalist racial identity falls somewhere between these two notions and was not hypothesized until the 21st century. Some questions Cross considers are whether an identity that is based on accepting other oppressed minorities should be considered a steppingstone to an inclusive identity or an end point. In addition, he wonders if a viable subscale can be created to measure this identity, and if not, whether it can be described using profiles regarding assimilation, anti-White sentiment, or multicultural inclusivity.

IDENTITY DEVELOPMENT FOR MULTIRACIAL PEOPLE

A growing field of study on biracial (or multiracial) people has stimulated debate about how to assess racial-identity development for this group. In recent scholarship the complexity associated with this has come through many multiracial peoples' self-identification process. The development of self-identification has been illustrated through the changes in the naming process for multiracial people (Renn, 2004):

1. Monoracial Identity: Students in this group identified with one of their monoracial heritage groups either some or all of the time. (p. 95)
2. Multiple Monoracial Identities: Students in this group held two or more monoracial identities at various stages of their lives. These students often experienced shifts in their monoracial identity due to encounters with racism. (p. 124)
3. Multiracial Identity: Students in this group did not conform to the monoracial categories that exist in the United States. They expressed a new construction of identity such as hapa, biracial, multiracial, mixed, etc. (p. 156)
4. Extra-Racial Identity: Students in this group chose not to identify themselves by any racial classification and do not accept the construction of racial identities. According to Renn, this pattern is not that common. (p. 194)
5. Situational Identity: Students in this group identify with two or more of the four patterns described above. This can be a conscious or an unconscious shift based on the situation. For them, identity is fluid and contextual. (p. 220)

As illustrated in frameworks for multiracial identity (Poston, 1990; Renn, 2004), the process of racial-identity development for multiracial children depends on a number of factors, including the racial combination, the involvement of both parents in the child's socialization, and the acceptance of their parents' union by extended family members. These frameworks also suggest that physical traits and a person's environment have a profound impact on multiracial identity. A young person's appearance—whether visibly identifiable as a person of color, apparently White, or racially ambiguous—plays a major role in identity development. In addition, living arrangements—whether a person lives in a community of color, a predominantly White community, or one that is racially mixed—will impact the way the person sees him- or herself and others who are racially different.

THEORETICAL BASE: CRITICAL RACE THEORY

Sometimes explicit and often implied, critical race theory (CRT) is at the core of most antiracism models and the backdrop for any understanding of racial-identity development. Critical race theory provides a bridge between the literature of racial identity and the literature on antiracist reform in public education through the commonality of their theoretical underpinnings. In fact, the research on organizational change for racial equity overwhelmingly demonstrates a reliance on the tenets of CRT.

Critical race theory originated in the mid-1970s as a critique of the effectiveness of civil rights strategies used by legal scholars. Unlike many other traditional civil rights or social-justice-oriented movements that focus on the dangers of conservatism and the status quo related to race and racism, CRT questions the very foundations of liberal thinking by not embracing incremental change and step-by-step progress (Delgado & Stefancic, 2001). Critical race theorists argue that racism is permanent and deeply embedded in our laws, institutions, cultures, and psyche (Tate, 1997). Although CRT finds its origins in the work of Derrick Bell, Richard Delgado, Kimberlé Crenshaw, and Alan Freeman—legal scholars who challenged traditional views of race— some scholars have linked CRT's origins to numerous European philosophers such as Antonio Gramsci and Jacques Derrida, to ethnic studies, to Marxism, to critical feminism, and to cultural nationalism such as the radical tradition in the United States exemplified by Frederick Douglass, W.E.B. Du Bois, Cesar Chavez, and the Black Power and Chicano movements of the 1960s and 1970s (Delgado & Stefancic, 2001; Solórzano & Bernal, 2001; Yosso et al., 2004).

Lynn and Adams (2002) reported that some legal scholars (Parker & Lynn, 2002; Tate, 1997) found that CRT has roots in African American literature that are just as strong as those based in legal scholarship. Storytellers from communities of color and many other writers, poets, and artists who were courageous enough to be critical of the racial past of the United States are part of these multifaceted roots. In this way, CRT is unique in how it builds upon the intellectual and historical perspectives from marginalized communities that have existed for centuries yet have rarely been given voice in traditionally White scholarship. CRT has become a tool for scholars in the past decade, particularly those interested in fighting for racial equity in education and society. This section includes brief discussions of (a) how CRT has been manifested in factors related to racial equity, and (b) how CRT has historically manifested itself in public education, specifically in leadership and reform.

CRT Manifested in Racial-Equity Movements

In their case study on a U.S. high school, DeCuir and Dixson (2004) outlined what they believe to be the five basic tenets of critical race theory and used examples of these in a study of student perceptions of racism in a Midwestern private high school. This section draws heavily on the five tenets that they described because they are most universally accepted in the literature. Numerous scholars (Delgado & Stefancic, 2001; Lynn & Adams, 2002; Smith-Maddox & Solórzano, 2002) have used many of the same tenets to illustrate the basic aspects of CRT. In this subsection, these five tenets are briefly discussed in the context of racial equity, specifically in relation to what much of the scholarship (Diamond, 2006; Katz, 2003; Ladson-Billings, 1999; Singleton, 2022) identifies as two of the main points for achieving racial equity on an individual level and an institutional level: antiracism and the understanding of one's racial identity.

Racial equity, as defined earlier in the context of education, is the raising of achievement for all students while narrowing the gap between the highest- and lowest-achieving students and eliminating the racial predictability and disproportional nature according to which students are in the highest and lowest achievement groups. CRT attempts to address the troublesome nature of the racial predictability of racially marginalized groups being among those who are the lowest-achieving. The five basic tenets demonstrate how CRT has manifested itself in the fight for racial equity. Although not always formally recognized, the tenets are commonly seen throughout race-related educational literature. The five tenets are:

1. *Counter-storytelling.* The notion that each perception of reality can be seen from a counter-racial perspective is key to CRT. Counter-storytelling proposes that all people searching for racial equity should use the CRT lens to validate multiple perspectives and search for data that might help identify factors contributing to inequity. Additionally, it is argued that counter-storytelling helps antiracist leaders analyze experiences of students of color and critically reflect on alternate views of reality, rather than just allowing them to be a part of an "Othering" process that does not normalize different racial experiences (DeCuir & Dixson, 2004). By highlighting marginalized accounts of people of color, "CRT hopes to demystify the notion of a racially neutral society and tell another story of highly racialized social order: a story where social institutions and practices serve the interest of White individuals" (López, 2003, p. 85). All of these notions are key factors in bringing about racial equity.

2. *The Permanence of Racism.* Bell (1992) argued that racism is a permanent component of American life. Delgado and Stefancic (2001)

stated that racism is an ordinary, "normal science": the usual way society does business (p. 7). According to some CRT scholarship on court cases (Bell, 1980) and school practice (DeCuir & Dixson, 2004; Lawrence, 1995), this tenet requires one to recognize the dominant role that racism played and continues to play in American society. This scholarship also asserts that structures and institutions may promote conscious and unconscious, intentional and unintentional racism and provide for White privilege. Because of the ordinary nature of racism, individuals often fail to see how it functions and shapes individual, cultural, and institutional ways of thinking.

3. *Whiteness as Property.* Ladson-Billings and Tate (1995) suggest that tracking, Advanced Placement, honors classes, and gifted/challenge programs are ways that schools, in essence, have been resegregated. The formal admission and registration processes are often navigated more fluidly by and guaranteed more readily to White students and/or their familial advocates. In the seminal studies on the property value of Whiteness (Lipsitz, 2006), scholars concluded that the history of racism in the United States has provided Whiteness with more value for transfer than that of people of color. For example, the history of racism in our country has contributed to a disproportionate number of White leaders compared to leaders of color. A part of the integration movement, commonly regarded as a positive achievement for Blacks in the South, that has often been ignored is the impact that it had on principals, teachers, and students of color. As segregated schools closed it was rare for staff and students of color to be put in leadership roles. Two generations later some organizations are advancing the value of leaders of color.

4. *Interest Convergence.* This tenet is concerned with the motivation behind antiracist work. It suggests that civil rights and antiracist gains by people of color often come only when they converge with the self-interests of Whites (Bell, 1992). For example, although students of color who attend a suburban high school as part of its new desegregation program have access to a rigorous educational experience, the school itself has benefited from not having to pay legal fees to fight the NAACP over desegregation policy and has received positive publicity from the numerous state championship basketball teams that include a majority of students of color from outside the district lines. CRT examines critically whether desegregation policy makes as substantive a difference in the lives of people of color as it does for the organization. Interest convergence ensures that racism stays intact and that equity advances at the pace that White people determine is reasonable and judicious (Bell, 1992).

5. *Critique of Liberalism.* According to DeCuir and Dixson (2004), CRT scholars "are critical of the basic notions that have been embraced by liberal legal ideology: the notion of colorblindness, the

neutrality of the law, and incremental change" (p. 29). All of these ideas may seem quite positive to White liberals, but these ideas do not address structural inequities that have resulted from a history of racism in the United States—for example, the idea that the law is colorblind and that policies are neutral does not take into account the effect of White privilege nor acknowledge that race, let alone racism, even exists. Also, the argument against incremental change, a key component of CRT, is identified as crucial in the development of antiracist institutions. DeCuir and Dixson argue that under the "notion of incremental change, gains for marginalized groups must come at a slow pace that is palatable for those in power" (p. 29), and equality rather than equity is sought. The ideal of equality presupposes that all people have the same opportunities or experiences, regardless of race. A concern for equity recognizes the uneven playing field and attempts to address the marginalization of those who are most directly and adversely affected by racism. In seeking equity rather than equality, the policies, practices, and structures that promote inequity are addressed and eliminated.

Since No Child Left Behind (NCLB; 2001) legislation created a legal, if not yet moral, call for equity in schools, public educators have become quite interested in how to address the racial predictability of achievement. CRT scholars are not motivated by the "interest convergence" of funding that accompanies compliance with political legislation; they became entrenched in a discussion of racial equity in education in the decade preceding such laws. As one school district's equity strategy framework reads, "We will consciously and deliberately act to eliminate the gap between our mission of high levels of achievement for all students, and the policies, practices, and structures in our school system that may perpetuate inequities based on race" (Midwest High School). There are numerous frameworks for addressing racial inequity (Derman-Sparks & Brunson Phillips, 1997; Singleton, 2022), and proponents of equity in public education have benefited from the manifestation of CRT thinking in public education.

CRT Manifested in Public Education

The impact of this CRT scholarship has recently been seen at the core of race-related education research. As one scholar notes, it is implicit in many of the core aspects of education:

> What can critical race theory, a movement that has its roots in legal scholarship, contribute to research in education? Plenty, as it turns out. Much of the national dialogue on race relations takes place in the context of education—in continuing desegregation and affirmative action battles, in debates about bilingual education programs, and in the controversy surrounding race and ethnicity

studies departments at colleges and universities. More centrally, the use of critical race theory offers a way to understand how ostensibly race neutral structures in education—knowledge, truth, merit, objectivity, and "good education"—are in fact ways of forming and policing the racial boundaries of White supremacy and racism. (Roithmayr, 1999, p. 4)

According to CRT scholars (Delgado & Stefancic, 2001; Lynn & Adams, 2002), critical race theorist William Tate (1993, 1994) introduced CRT to the educational community by using CRT as a tool to expose the racist under-pinnings of math tests in the United States. Ladson-Billings and Tate (1995) addressed the development of CRT's link with education and they documented propositions connecting "race and property as a central construct" toward understanding the "property functions of Whiteness" in relation to school-ing (pp. 58–59). Lynn and Adams (2002) argued that Ladson-Billings and Tate's critical race analysis "moved beyond the boundaries of the educational research literature to include arguments and new perspectives from law and social sciences and demonstrated the centrality of race-focused analysis to educational inequality in U.S. schools and schooling" (p. 88). Ladson-Billings (2021b) later focused on the emergence of critical race theory in education by examining curriculum, instruction, assessment, and other school policy issues through a critical race perspective in numerous articles, including the incendiary title, "Just What Is Critical Race Theory, and What's It Doing in a *Nice* Field Like Education?"

In early 21st century, two education journals devoted entire issues to de-velopments in CRT in the field of education. *Qualitative Inquiry* (2002) in-cluded an issue edited by Lynn, Yosso, Solórzano, and Parker focusing on the relationship between qualitative research and race theorizing in qualitative educational research through the use of storytelling that counters the master narratives in education. Later that year, *Equity and Excellence in Education* (2002) took a step beyond examining CRT as just a theory and method cre-ation in education. In this issue, edited by Lynn and Adams, CRT was docu-mented as a means for practitioners to bring about social justice through the school experiences of all children and empowering staff of color.

The very recent linkage between public education and CRT in the United States has been growing more prominent in educational literature. The research on institutional practices and policies has dominated much of the CRT educa-tional literature, but it has also contributed to two areas in public education that are significant in their relation to change for racial equity: leadership and reform movements. As the next two sections demonstrate, CRT-related liter-ature suggests that these two areas are essential for racial equity in education.

CRT Manifested in Educational Leadership

Tenets of CRT are often implied in the educational leadership literature as important aspects of cultural proficiency (Lindsey, Robins, & Terrell, 2009), promoting positive interracial relations (Henze et al., 2002), and political inclusion (López, 2003). Although very little scholarship explicitly addresses CRT and leadership, the tenets of "Whiteness and property" and "counter-storytelling" are present in literature that addresses culturally competent public educational leadership (Delgado & Stefancic, 2001). Despite the fact that CRT has been found to most often be in the margins of educational leadership literature (Bernier & Rocco, 2003), there are a few notable exceptions that explicitly address CRT.

More often than not, school leaders face the prospect of institutional change in response to a growing population of color. Evans (2007) found in her critical qualitative examination of the words and actions of school leaders that school leaders' ability to make sense of racial issues influenced their willingness to change structures in their schools that might perpetuate racism. The "sensemaking" of school administrators about changing racial demographics in their suburban schools and the resulting issues, such as labeling and racial stereotyping, "helps people make sense of race in an efficient manner but also justifies one group's legitimacy and dominance over other groups" (Evans, 2007). White leaders often made sense of race in ways that were based on their own unconscious experiences. The implications of this are immediately significant for school leaders who are affected by racial integration in their districts. Just as culturally responsive instruction calls for teachers to help students understand how their own experience contributes to their "sensemaking" of the curriculum (Gay, 2005), leaders must be given direction concerning how to better understand their own racial identities and how those shape their leadership and views on race.

In his CRT review of leadership in the political arenas of education, López (2003) argues that people of color have been silenced by the belief of most White educational leaders that "colorblindness" leads to "racially neutral" schools and policies. This belief has huge implications about the roles of power and marginalization in leadership. López suggests that racial avoidance in the politics of education has made it uncommon and difficult for even well-intentioned leaders to engage in provocative discussions on race and racism and how they affect power, conflict, government, and educational policy. If leaders are unwilling to have discussions about race, it becomes nearly impossible for organizations to recruit, retain, or support staff of color. This conundrum makes it crucial for educational leaders who want to create diversity and inclusion in their organization to engage in dialogue and professional development that invites racial counter-storytelling and an exploration of racial identity (López, 2003; Singleton, 2022).

Numerous scholars have pointed out the importance of support from district and site leadership as a key to positive perceptions of antiracist staff development. Lawrence (2005) and Singleton agree that even the perception of support from principals and superintendents has a profound impact on antiracist staff development. In fact, staff of color have much greater feelings of safety and support when they are given direct guidance and mentorship from people in positions of power (Elliot & Nieto, 1996; G. Singleton, 2012). Notable scholars and practitioners (Kailin, 1996; Ladson-Billings, 2021a; Landsman, 2001; Lawrence & Bunche, 1996; G. Singleton, 2012) took it a step further and argued that antiracist staff development is not received or perceived well unless White leaders and staff of color in a building work together to achieve their goals. The ability to recognize Whiteness as property and find value in counter-storytelling seems to be the key to effective antiracism leadership. Any systemic antiracist reform must take multiple racial perspectives into account and work to normalize social constructions of race that have been developed through racial-identity development (Singleton, 2022).

CRT Manifested in Educational Reform

The discussion of the permanence of racism that has been the hallmark of CRT since its inception has been among the most prominent presences of CRT in educational reform literature. As with educational leadership, there are a number of studies that address the difficulty of educational reform for equity, but few that explicitly address this issue through a CRT lens. This section documents a sampling of the explicit examples of CRT in educational reform literature.

In the introductory chapter to *Race Is . . . Race Isn't: Critical Race Theory and Qualitative Studies in Education* (Parker, Deyhle, & Villenas, 1999), Ladson Billings (1999) described the ways that racism is maintained and practiced in schools on a daily basis. She argued that what many administrators believe to be real about race is nothing more than a social construction that lacks the counter-story of people of color. She called for radical transformations and bold solutions to problems of racism in society. She asserted that CRT provides the lens for this radical transformation by working to provide tools for antiracist reform.

Using CRT in a study of secondary schools in the United Kingdom, Gillborn (2005) addressed the intentionality of racism in numerous organizational policies that had been identified as institutionally racist. He stated that although racial inequity may not be a deliberate goal of the educational policies or procedures, neither is it accidental because of a structural pattern of domination—"acts of White supremacy that routinely privilege the White interests that go unremarked by the political mainstream" (p. 485). He concluded that antiracism must act counter to the mainstream to address goals of racial equity. As these samples of the literature suggest, very little educational reform includes CRT without also addressing antiracism.

Antiracism literature has made a much greater use of CRT in recent years. In the creation of a staff-development course they teach, Smith-Maddox and Solórzano (2002) suggested that CRT provide teachers with the space to, as one scholar put it, "address the ideological blinders they may have developed as a result of their own cultural and educational experiences" (Wiedeman, 2002). Singleton and Linton (2006) also claim that CRT is the foundation for all antiracist reform. They argued that unless people within an organization are able to act on their understanding of the tenets of CRT, organizations will change little more than the words they use to eliminate racism.

Numerous studies (DeCuir & Dixson, 2004; Duncan, 2002; Ladson-Billings & Tate, 1995; Solórzano & Yosso, 2002) have used CRT to discuss the marginalization and lack of service to students of color. However, few U.S. studies have included CRT in their analysis of staff. Those that have done so (Howard, 2016; Kailin, 1996; Ladson-Billings, 2000; S. M. Lawrence & Tatum, 1997; Sleeter, 1990) have focused solely on teachers, often ignoring the experience of support staff and administrators as part of their creation of knowledge. Although the research here is limited, the work that has been done with students and teachers has provided the basis of a framework for using CRT in educational research.

Critical race theorists imply that when addressing any race-related reform movement, the motivation and impact of these changes must be examined. A review of CRT literature found that often, without addressing them specifically, the tenets of critiquing liberalism and the concept of interest convergence were major factors in assessing perceptions of organizational change for racial equity (Bell, 1992; Duncan, 2002; Singleton, 2022). The tenet that recognizes the permanence of racism sets antiracism apart from many other multicultural or diversity-related reform movements in education.

Models for antiracist staff development that address systemic racial inequities draw from the concepts addressed in critical race theory and racial-identity development. Antiracist staff-development models can be placed in two paradigms. The first describes the developmental paradigm of antiracist staff programming that focuses on the personal and professional development of individual educators as they move along a continuum of antiracism. The second discusses the structural paradigm of staff development, which addresses the systemic, collaborative effort involved in bringing about organizational change for racial equity, often using a colorblind or nuanced antiracist approach. A third and uncommon paradigm crosses paradigms for developing antiracist school leaders and systems with the potential of emancipating school systems from racism. This model develops out of the need for both structural and developmental needs that came from the study of Midwest High School. In addition, the notion of cross-paradigm work for antiracist leadership development influences the Dare 2 Be Real framework shown in tenets throughout this book.

Whatever the outcome of the study outlined in the chapters ahead and the subsequent framework for antiracist student leadership development, the implications of substantive change for racial equity are vast for our underserved students. Much of the program evaluation and scholarship encountered in the literature follows the thinking of the Supreme Court through its colorblind evaluation of programs that affect historically oppressed groups of students and staff. With a few notable exceptions (e.g., Landsman, 2001; S. M. Lawrence, 2005; Roediger, 2002; Scheurich, 2002), White scholars often ignore the impact of their own Whiteness on their work. Antiracist studies must take into account the problems of gradualism and the denial of racism as a normal occurrence as impediments to recognizing complacency in modern education. This research is important because to remain silent regarding racial oppression in education is to give consent for continuing another generation of racism and inequity.

CHAPTER 3

Engaging in Antiracist Leadership

In this chapter, three of the 10 tenets of Dare 2 Be Real will be explored through the lens of leaders from the St. Louis Park School District in Minnesota, with some practical applications for the district-, school-, and student-leadership levels. Seven voices from the field will provide a tapestry of the diversity of antiracist school leadership that is required to engage, sustain, and deepen antiracism in a school system. Each tenet is introduced with a key question for self- and organizational reflection. These questions are designed to help leaders audit the readiness of their system for student-centered antiracist school leadership. The Dare 2 Be Real tenets are set up to help any student, teacher, parent, or administrator center their antiracist efforts on the true purpose of education—the development of our students as active antiracist leaders in our democracy.

SAFE AND SACRED SPACE

How Safe and Sacred Is the Space for Being Real About Race and Culture?

We need to ask teachers to think deeply about what it means to demonstrate care in their classrooms. Teachers may think of caring as unconditional praise or as quickly incorporating cultural components into the curriculum . . . or even lowering standards (Duncan-Andrade, 2008; Nieto, 2008). What is needed to have a safe and sacred space for learning is for students to feel like they can fully be real about their cultural and racial identities. In other words, can they be their full selves while having their spirit enhanced and energized? Teachers must understand individual students in their sociopolitical context (Gay, 2012; Ladson-Billings, 2021b) and devise specific pedagogical and curricular strategies to help the students navigate those contexts safely. As many scholars have suggested, this safety and sacredness begin with helping students feel a sense of care, hope, and belonging (Chenoweth, 2017; Duncan-Andrade, 2008; Nieto, 2008; Singleton, 2012). The following section asks us to consider what it means to have a *safe space* by determining both the structural limits needed for a space to be safe for students' identity development and also how we create a sense of hope and security among our students when they share their racialized experiences. In addition, the notion of a

Table 3.1. Tenets for Systemic Antiracist Student Leadership Development

Tenets for Antiracist Student Leadership Development	Key Questions for Reflection
Staff/Adult Collaboration	How are adult leaders positioned to collaborate with a focus on equity?
Student Integration	How are our students integrated, involved, and engaged?
Systemic Implementation	How embedded is leadership development in our program and school system?
Support From the Top	How well am I able to garner support from those with positional and cultural authority?
Shared Experiences	How well are we building a collective learning identity?
Safe and Sacred Space	How do students perceive the culture for being real about race, identity, and culture?
Common Language/Protocol	How have we heightened the protocol for racial discourse and developed language for racial literacy?
Focus: Identity Development	How are we developing our individual and collective racial and cultural identities?
Active Antiracist Leadership	How do we develop students' will, skill, knowledge, and capacity as antiracist leaders?
Family/Parent Involvement	How do we partner and communicate with families as we develop our student leaders?

sacred space will be discussed in terms of aspects of a space for healing and leading and the necessity for energizing and enhancing the spirit.

Safe Antiracist Space

Several scholars have contended that effective school leaders with an awareness of the broad social and cultural realities of the children they serve and the children's school and home experiences will actively critique marginalizing behaviors and attitudes in their own teaching and leadership style and practices as well as those of others in their school community (Brooks & Arnold, 2013; Dantley & Tillman, 2009). Also, democratic principles such as active listening, mindful inquiry, and the antiracist structures of providing clear roles and group norms in the classroom could be practiced and professed by any aspiring antiracist educator.

As a school administrator, I have seen many teacher-leaders with social-justice awareness and passion be quick to move into a "White savior" mode rather than one that liberates students of color. This savior mentality, nested deeply in the context of our racist school systems and White guilt and pity, draws from liberal ideology about the stereotypical plight of Black and Brown communities. I have often cut through this by simply asking questions rooted in identity rather than trauma. The best way to create a safe space for students is not to ask them to bare their soul to you as an educator. This sort of mentality creates a one-way relationship dynamic that actually hurts safety in many ways. It is important to give students opportunities to share who they are and what their racialized experiences are but not ask students to do so in a vacuum. One tool that I have found helpful in doing this is "step-ins."

Step-ins is an activity that provides a safe environment for students (or staff for that matter) to get real about race, identity, racism, or whatever becomes the topic that the facilitator or group thinks is necessary to discuss. As a social studies teacher, I often used step-ins as a pre-assessment activity for my students before we started a unit. Students are asked to get into a circle and then are given a statement that is somewhat ambiguous about a topic. The key to the statement is that it must be something that could elicit a spectrum of responses. Students then are asked to step into the circle if they agree and stay sitting if they disagree. Either way, they are making a kinesthetic decision to step in or keep their seat. The facilitator then asks students to share why they stepped in or why they didn't—being careful to let students know both that they are not in a debate and that everyone can speak their truth, and that each person's voice is valuable, so throughout the activity each will be called on at least once. It is important to note to the participants that in this space there will be no clowning, no put-downs, and no pressure to step in. Students should speak their truth and not speak for others. Step-ins is much more effective than a large-group discussion in that there is structure and movement that enable all students to speak and move throughout the activity, and multiple questions can be asked.

In my role as the director of curriculum and instruction, I was helping facilitate a consulting team of approximately 30 math teachers through their fourth math program review. It was determined that at this point in the process it would be good to bring in student voices. That morning at 8:00, I went to the high school's main office and I gave the names of five students to the lead secretary, asking her if she would send these students to the room where we would be conducting the review at 9:00 that morning. These five students were students I had noticed in classrooms visited when on learning walks with the principal over the past year who showed passion for racial equity and school improvement. I knew this because I always engaged students in questions that would critique their curriculum and instruction through these lenses when I did class walkthroughs. I then went to the nontraditional academy classroom, a class for students who were far behind in their progress toward graduation, and approached a teacher who had been getting accolades from our district racial-equity coaches. The reputation he had was that his expectations for students were high and that his students worked hard in his class. I asked him if he would be willing to send five of his students to work with me at 9:00 that morning to talk about their experiences in math. He looked at me and did exactly what I would have done when I was a social studies teacher. He told me no. I accepted the answer and left his room. About two minutes later he found me in the hallway and said, "Where do you need them?"

I believe that I had built a level of trust with this teacher and with these five students through my presence in the school and the racially conscious learning walks. Now came the time to leverage that. The 10 students arrived outside the door at 8:59 that morning. I smiled at them and told them to be themselves. I then walked them into the room and made a circle in the middle of the room for us to sit. I asked all of the teachers in the room to not speak while the students were in the room. Their only job was to listen. I began by asking the students, "What aspect of your identity is most important to you?" I modeled by talking about being Arab American and Irish Catholic, how my color is what people see and how that is important to them but that my ancestors are what is most important to me. We went around and the students shared, unprompted, that their race, their culture, or their religion was the most important thing they bring into their classroom. I then asked if they believed that part of themselves is honored or dishonored in school and then specifically about that honoring in math classrooms. I asked when they felt good at math and when they felt bad at math. I concluded by asking them what questions they hoped the teachers would ask themselves after the students left. I thanked the students and they went back to class. The teachers overwhelmingly said they had never seen a conversation like this in their classrooms before, and they were blown away by how much they could learn about math when they just created a space for students to first be real about race and culture.

Sacred Antiracist Space

The anecdote above underscores the importance of creating opportunities for students to share who they are with their peers and with their teachers if they are to be leaders. Let me be clear: The students who walked into that math program review that day demonstrated antiracist leadership. They helped transform the trajectory of the math review and had a profound impact not only on the way the math teachers across the district looked at how they approached their classrooms but on how they approached their classrooms the very next day. I was able to get the responses from them because they trusted me as an antiracist leader and had seen me developing antiracist adult leaders throughout the school on a consistent basis over the previous two years.

The space in this math program review room was not just a safe space on this day but also brought with it a sense of the sacred. When I say sacred, I am not speaking specifically to anything religious, lest the public-school educators who are reading this become nervous, but rather something that enhances and energizes the spirit while leading and healing. There were tears among the students and the teachers that day, but they were not manufactured. We did not create discomfort in the room, but there was a social contract because of the level of trust and authenticity that allowed for one's full humanity to be on display. I opened the contract by bringing my ancestors into the space and the students completed it by talking freely about their racial, ethnic, and religious identities. By asking the teachers to stop and listen, there was also a different power dynamic in the room that energized the spirit of the students and, much to the surprise of many of the teachers, energized and enhanced theirs as well. You see, watching the students engaged in active antiracism energized the teachers' spirit and left them with a feeling that stuck with them well into the following weeks.

Like step-ins, another activity I have used often to create a sacred space for students or staff is concentric circles. A concentric circle activity starts by asking the group to count off by twos, and then the 1s sit facing out while the 2s sit in a circle facing the 1s, knee to knee. The facilitator then asks participants to respond to a question. Each partner takes a turn answering the question. The facilitator, in an effort to be equitable with voice, may need to be dictatorial about time, giving each person 1 minute to respond to the question without interruptions. One of the circles moves one seat to the right after each set of questions, setting up a sort of "antiracist speed dating" scenario that at once provides safety for students who are afraid of being "stuck" with the same partner for the duration of class period. Asking questions about identity can bring a depth of discussion like the questions in the math review did, but the sharing of racial autobiographical pieces can invoke the most spiritual responses from student participants. If the facilitator shares a story about someone who had an impact on his or her life in a certain way and then asks the students to think about and share with their partner the name of the person they are thinking about and how they impacted the student, they are invoking the spirit of that person into the space. This act changes the dynamic of the space as well. The work of creating a sacred space does not always have to be deeply personal. It can also be a collective historical experience. Invoking the names and experiences of those who came before us is an essential part of grounding students in the curriculum and in antiracist leadership development.

Voices From the Field: Luis Versailles—Parent at St. Louis Park and Partner With Pacific Educational Group

Ancient Nile Valley wisdom instructs those of us of African descent that core to one's purpose in life is the responsibility to "build for eternity," to leave the world a better place for generations to come. I come to this writing as the grandson of two Afro-Cuban and two White Cuban grandparents. I come to this writing as the son of two Afro-Cuban parents, who immigrated to the United States from their native Havana in the early 1960s and too often encountered a Twin Cities that didn't know what it was to see their sacredness nor provide a true sense of safety for them or their children.

As is the case for many immigrant parents, my parents operated from a belief that educators and the schools in general were to be trusted, that family support means getting out of the way and letting those better educated and suited to handle schooling the children do their work. This left me and my two older siblings—my sister, Caridad, 5 years my senior, and my brother, Lázaro, Jr.—navigating a schooling process that had not deemed it a priority to educate us equitably, that instead chose a colorblind approach, one that frequently left me without windows into the historical contributions of Afro-Latinx people, or people of the African diaspora, or people of color, more generally, and therefore as a result, this opportunity was also denied to our White counterparts and schoolmates.

My earliest memories of schooling and race were therefore categorized by omnipresent feelings of "Othering" . . . of feeling "Othered" due to the color of my skin, the smell of my mother's Cuban cuisine in my clothes, the languages represented on my home language questionnaire. Coexisting with the unanswerable question, what would it feel like to truly feel like this school was for me and the other handful of kids of color who populated the Bloomington Public Schools at that point in time? was a deep desire to learn, to be academically challenged, to move with wonder and inquisitiveness in the world. Yet too often, my educators, by and large, a group of people I would generally describe as caring and kind, did not hold me to the same standard, it seemed, as my White counterparts. For those educators, it seemed to me, my presence in school and overall sense of "being okay" sufficed; I was not from a troubled or fractured home and I did not have behavioral outbursts in school or exhibit a learning disability of any kind, so my matriculation from grade to grade seemed to be sufficient. I never was taught to see myself as gifted in any way or that I had any particular academic aptitude.

I later learned that my experience had been the same, previously, for my sister, Caridad, who would go on to become the regional manager of the highest-producing region of a major coffee company, and for my older brother, Lázaro, Jr., a creative in a golf media organization whose writing has been published in many of the major golf publications of the industry. I now reflect and ask myself, what would it have been to have felt seen by my educators, and, therefore, not only safe but truly sacred, special, to have been nurtured and molded to unleash my potential?

In my experience the past 11 years with Courageous Conversations, yes, even decades later, as I partner with educators around the country seeking to unapologetically transform systems to create this sense of sacredness and safety for all students—with particular care for those who our racialized histories and systems have intentionally and systemically Otherized—while creating a much more humane, empathetic, challenging, and nourishing experience for their White counterparts who too, we believe, are owed a racially conscious and socially just schooling process, I have found that too often, all of these years later, my experience is replicated by our systems and felt by our students. While I have worked in 34 states, each with their regionalisms and particularities, there is one commonality: They exist in the backdrop of a racial history of systemic racism that too often has offered a false choice of denying one's fullness in exchange for what we have constructed "academic success" and "college and career" readiness to mean. Too often missing from those narrow definitions is a need to elevate one's own racial literacy and consciousness so that our young people of all races can truly move forward with the leadership qualities needed to humanize themselves and our society. This is a significant component of my "why" and what compels me to truly build for an eternity.

I fast-forward to 2020, in the midst of a global pandemic, now the parent of two middle school–aged children in the St. Louis Park Public Schools, a first-ring suburb to the west of Minneapolis. Through our work with this district since the early 2000s, part of the district's journey involved an organizational shift in philosophy from learning about the racial and cultural identities of the students to truly centering organizational adult-learning practices that create priority for the ongoing work of increasing the capacity of the adults in the system to deeply know the racialized lenses they bring to the environment, in hopes of building a community of learning wherein the relationship between one's racialized experience and how those experiences begin to frame one's beliefs around what it means to live the district's mission and show up on a continual basis—personally, professionally, and organizationally.

Our work teaches that whether we are conscious of them or not, these beliefs are connected to behaviors, which ultimately produce the outcomes we see in our lives. The question that St. Louis Park Public Schools posed to itself was, What would a racially conscious, adaptive, transformative process for strategic planning entail? and, What are our beliefs about the degree to which strategic planning can serve as an accelerant to racial-equity transformation?

As a testament to the work of [Dare 2 Be Real], our student leadership arm of programming; Students Organized Against Racism (SOAR); [Dr. Lee-Ann Stephens, Dr. Astein Osei]; and other powerful student leadership structures existing in the district, as a design feature of [St. Louis Park Public School District's] strategic plan, racially conscious student voice was situated to speak to the strategic priorities of the previous plan and to inspire the core planning team to envision what a more racially conscious, bold, and empowering stance could look like in the next iteration of this work. As an aspect of the work, I guided a process of reflection centered in the Courageous Conversations protocol, which created space for ongoing introspection and ultimately the beginning of articulating one's personal racial-equity purpose, or "PREP." Central to this process was my belief that the content of the strategic plan could only be delivered upon powerfully to the degree that the core planning members themselves had authentically begun/ were continuing their process of racial self-reflection and that as we cocreated the space, we were authentically living what it would take to embody the powerfully articulated vision, mission, and core values of the system. Our work then would be to continue to replicate this process of transformation at every opportunity to authentically embody and step into our PREP, personally and professionally, as racial-equity leaders for the community.

In the spirit of accepting and expecting nonclosure, much work remains for the St. Louis Park Public Schools in the quest for racial justice in education, and I must say as a parent and community member, I am proud of so much of the work that has been initiated. In addition to a deeply committed cadre of central office leaders from the cabinet and board-director levels and throughout, the district features a powerful racial-equity instructional coaching model with coaches situated at all six campuses, a districtwide, culturally relevant talent-development process that, in response to racially conscious student voices being centered through the processes of curriculum revision, has been implemented, replacing what had historically been a deeply racially segregated gifted and talented, pull-out model. Plans are in place for all middle school and high school students in the system to have been offered intentional development in antiracist leadership development prior to matriculating for the middle school and high school. Again, what I am describing is by no means perfect work, but I do assess this to be a system producing evidence of grappling with a different, more courageous set of questions as it strives to ensure that each child, young person, and adult in the system is having the experience of truly feeling sacred and safe as a result of institutionalizing the need for safe and sacred spaces, be those spaces in the classroom environment, in adult-learning contexts, or in the community at large.

I close by reflecting on the distinction between my experience in the skin I was in as a student and the experience of my two biracial, Afro-Latinx children, Lucía (age 14) and Río (age 12). I can see how they have benefitted by being developed by antiracist educators of all races through their experiences in St. Louis Park. I can see how spaces have been created to ensure their psychological, social, emotional, and racialized safety through powerful affinity programming. This reminds children that they have a story that is essential to give voice to and that, for the system to truly serve all children, it is critical for them to have the courage to speak their truths and for the adults tasked with creating schooling systems that serve them to have the courage to receive those truths and act courageously when our systemic practices create any sense of Othering or distancing from what we believe to be every child's birthright, a racially conscious and socially just schooling process that nurture's the children's potential.

And yet, even with the backdrop of our city resident and fallen brother, Mr. George Floyd, as the world seemingly beckoned for true systems change and racial justice, my children, like many around the nation, watch as adults seek to make off-limits the very kinds of scholarship that signal to young people that despite the narratives offered up by our nation, what is true is that people of all races have historically locked arms and taken up the struggle for racial justice, so that future generations might have it better than them. I am grateful that my children have been raised to think deeply about their own racialized experiences and about race and racism more generally, but it pains me to see our nation too often replicate its historical pattern of racial dominance through the attempted silencing of the voices and scholarship that cause us to collectively experience the necessary discomfort of confronting the difficult history of the construction of race and racism in American society. As I write this piece, I do so in an immediate racial context in which at least 36 states have adopted or introduced laws or policies that restrict speaking, teaching, and training about race, racial bigotry, and systemic racism. What must I do to stay engaged in this context? In what ways does this deeply racialized experience inform my beliefs, behaviors, and the outcomes I am committed to as they relate to racial justice? There are no neat answers to these questions for me, but my ancestral loyalty compels me to sojourn forth.

I close by stating what I have always believed, that as these notions of race and racism have historically been created by human beings, albeit in the least of our humanity, through education we can collectively turn the tide. But the question remains, do we have the courage to truly build for eternity and to do what is necessary? I believe our children's sacredness and safety requires us to do so . . . as our ancestor Frederick Douglass famously asserted, "It may be moral, it may be physical . . . but power concedes nothing without a demand . . . it never has, and it never will."

Safe-and-Sacred-Space Tenet Application

District-Level Application. Like a number of school districts across our country, St. Louis Park Public Schools decided in 2021 to partake in a statement of land acknowledgment before each school board meeting to honor the legacy of the Indigenous people on whose land the school district stands. In doing so, the district embraced the values of Indigenous culture and committed to a number of things.

A land acknowledgment statement is a formal statement that recognizes and respects Indigenous peoples as traditional stewards of this land and the enduring relationship that exists between Indigenous peoples and their traditional territories. St. Louis Park leaders believed they should engage in a land acknowledgment statement, not as a token act of recognition but, rather, because doing so would align closely with the district's clear strategic plan for racial equity, which called out the elevation and centering of the voices and stories of Black, Brown, and Indigenous peoples. It was also an opportunity to recognize and honor Indigenous students and families who have traditionally been invisible in our school systems—even an outwardly antiracist school system such as St. Louis Park.

The land acknowledgment is an opportunity to honor the sacredness of the space in which we teach and learn and also provide more safety to the people whose legacy is being honored. Before each school board meeting, the board chair reads the following statement: "*We are gathered on the land of the Dakota and Ojibwe peoples. I ask you to join me in acknowledging the Dakota and Ojibwe community, their elders both past and present, as well as future generations. St. Louis Park Public Schools also acknowledges that it was founded upon exclusions and erasures of many Indigenous Peoples, including those on whose land this school district is located. This acknowledgement demonstrates a commitment to dismantling the ongoing legacies of colonial mistrust and the district's desire to supporting the ongoing work of local Indigenous communities to thrive in our schools.*"

A land acknowledgment, while a step in the direction of justice, is only a first step and must be accompanied by actions that allow our Indigenous students and their families and communities to thrive in our schools. The work was done in partnership with our American Indian Parent Advisory Council and has been accompanied by the inclusion of Ojibwe language and culture classes in our schools, American Indian Student Advisory Leadership Groups, and related professional-development opportunities.

School-Level Application. Sustaining a safe and sacred space in school can be very difficult without a combination of trust and vulnerability. This often comes when staff are willing to share their lived experiences in staff meetings, collaborative teams, and professional development settings. In various schools in which I have worked, racial autobiography has been a key component of sustaining a safe and sacred space for being real about race and culture in schools. Leaders who are not willing to share "chapters" from their racial autobiography with their staff cannot expect their staff, let alone their students, to speak openly and honestly about the impact of race on their own teaching and learning experience.

I have often started my professional-development sessions or retreats for staff by asking them to consider how their parents or family talked to them about race when they were the age of the students with whom they currently serve. In addition, I ask them to consider how this is similar to or different from how they talk to their own children or the children they serve about race now. This conversation is fluid because teachers, leaders, and support staff are often evolving in their own understanding of how to talk about race with their students and also in how to reflect upon the experiences they had as a child.

It may be difficult for a staff member to share their entire life story in one collaborative team session, but they can certainly share their earliest memory of race and their most recent memory of how race has played out in their life. These bookends are just chapters in a racial autobiography. In addition, leaders may want to take time to acknowledge to their colleagues how they identify racially and what factors have contributed to this identification. This normalizes the conversation about race and also opens the door for others to talk about influencing factors, both personal and professional, that have led them to feel discomfort about their own racial identity.

I started this book with samples of my own racial autobiography because I believe in the power of sharing one's story before getting into any technical—or even adaptive—conversations about race and leadership. The power of one's story is sacred in its uniqueness and also provides the potential for spiritual connection to any who read it, hear it, or experience it.

Student-Group-Level Application. As I worked with various Dare 2 Be Real student leadership groups over the years, it became important to find strategies for engaging students in leadership development kinesthetically, emotionally, and communally. One of the strategies that allows for this is step-ins, a student favorite. Students create their own circle of chairs and are asked to engage in a discussion, not a debate, about topics that are presented in intentionally open-ended, somewhat ambiguous, and thought-provoking ways. The facilitator makes it clear that the students should speak their truth, first, with their feet by "stepping in" to the circle if they agree with a statement that was shared and if they disagree by staying in their seat. Students then are called on by the facilitator to share why they stepped in or why they stayed seated. Either way, they are making a conscious decision to contribute to the discussion, provide perspective, and develop community. The facilitator is key in this process, as they ensure that multiple perspectives are heard and time the statements to determine a pace and progression that will engage, sustain, and deepen the conversations about race and culture in the room. If the facilitator sets clear parameters up front, students will feel much more comfortable and able to be real about their perspectives on race.

STAFF COLLABORATION

How Are Adult Leaders Positioned to Collaborate With a Focus on Equity?

To begin engaging students in antiracist leadership development, staff must recognize that they cannot expect students to do any work the staff are not willing to do themselves. If the intention is to build an antiracist leadership team for students, adults must be ready to accept antiracist roles and responsibilities on their team as well. An adult collaborative team should utilize the professional strengths of its members and allow for diverse lived experiences to inform growth. That means that any attempts to bring about interracial student leadership development must include staff collaboration that captures the diversity of the community being served. In addition, staff must be willing to examine their authenticity with one another and to make a commitment to courageous conversations using protocol and practices that are going to elevate their own leadership. Staff who engage in regular racial discourse, with protocol (at least weekly), are more likely to stay out of White paralysis and less likely to experience isolation in their work for racial equity.

The isolating nature of practicing antiracism in schools has been documented in literature (McIntyre, 2008; Parmar & Steinberg, 2008), and the intensity associated with a heightened awareness of racial identity during engagement in equity work indicates how important it is that school leaders develop a culture of collaboration marked by structures that support this culture. Norms of collaboration such as agreements and conditions of Courageous Conversation (Singleton & Hays; 2008) should be established, and leaders should model the art of mindful inquiry as a way of facilitating cross-cultural and interracial dialogue. The study indicates that these models are necessary for keeping leaders engaged and collaborative, but the allocation of time is important as well. Emergent in the data was the feeling among most staff that the most impact on their own learning happened when they were engaged in retreat-type learning settings or in regular, weekly meetings that provided enough time to go deeply into a broad set of experiences and consciousness that may have previously been unexplored.

Debunking the Mythology of the Lone Hero

For decades, popular culture has depicted antiracism as the act of a heroic individual. Films like *Freedom Writers* (2004), *Dangerous Minds* (1996), *Lean on Me* (1987), and *Stand and Deliver* (1986) depict individuals working to teach students of color against all odds. In the process, audiences see the results of such folly in the form of divorce, job loss, depression, heart attacks, or physical beatings meet the heroes of these films. The message is clear: if you are willing to sacrifice your body, your relationships, or your life, you may be able to make a difference in the lives of "other people's children." Even films that are lauded for their depiction of racism in society, such as the Oscar-winning film *Crash* (2004), rarely show groups of people engaged in antiracism or examples of institutional and cultural oppression. Hollywood may believe that it is not as sexy to depict a group of adults working behind the scenes to dismantle barriers and establish functional protocols that allow all team members, regardless of personal and professional identity, to show up as their best selves. While some scholars have lamented the invisibility of antiracism in most historical narratives (Darling-Hammond, 2011; Loewen, 2005), the Dare 2 Be Real framework supports the notion that collaborative action for equity must be visible, modeled, and supported.

We only teach two things: Who we are and what we know (Hartoonian, 1997). Most of our teacher and leadership preparation programs focus their efforts on developing future educators in what they know, leaving out at least half of what we teach. Knowing oneself and being conscious of how one's identity impacts others as one collaborates across various intersections present in school and society are crucial to helping students understand this truth as well. Strategies for engaging adult teams may include the sharing of racial autobiographies, antiracist professional growth plans, and aligning student development goals with state or district mandates such as school improvement plans, ESSA requirements, or World's Best Workforce planning.

Collaboration across positional and racial diversity helps develop a team capable of supporting antiracist leadership in students. Often, schools have someone who is positionally or racially marginalized working alone with groups of students around race-related issues. Collaborative positional diversity means administrators, teachers, and support staff working together as a team to ensure that student leadership is nurtured and that organizational blind spots are addressed. Having multiple perspectives among the roles of adults is crucial for engaging students in antiracism work. Without this, a "lone hero" can easily be burned out, moved out, or moved up in an organization, leaving students without a trusted staff member to guide them along their journey.

Staff should ask what characteristics there are among the adults that would bring credibility among other staff and students. If teachers from the dominant culture and key administrators do not respect the adults leading the work, it will very easily be marginalized. If students do not see themselves reflected in the diversity of the adults leading them, they may have a harder time seeing themselves actualized as a racial-equity leader. It is highly recommended that the team work on elevating their knowledge of critical race theory, culturally relevant teaching, and racially conscious pedagogy and protocols. Bringing multiple perspectives into the development of youth is a responsible action to ensure students are engaged effectively and consistently over time. One person working alone or in affinity with another adult who is very similar in identity runs a greater risk of missing key developmental touchpoints in the growth of the student-leadership team. Two leaders working in collaboration may not be able to transform an entire system alone, but their collaboration can transform a small corner of their school for the students they serve.

Voices From the Field: Elizabeth Huesing, Efe Mensah-Brown, Jill Metil, Maddy Wegleitner, and Ila Saxena—Teacher-Leaders on the Math Design Team, St. Louis Park Public Schools

"We need a BIG change in math."
   This was the belief of the math design team of St. Louis Park Public Schools when we started our Racial Equity Transformation Plan. When we started working together, we were not sure how to position ourselves to collaborate with a focus on equity, but with guidance and time, as well as through the sharing of our racial autobiographies, we were able to develop the trust and mutual respect necessary to consistently collaborate with a focus on equity. Below are some of [the team members'] own words related to the gestation of the team. They illustrate that the work of antiracist staff collaboration is not linear, nor is it clean. To build an antiracist democracy there need to be multiple perspectives positioned for the purpose of equity—even when working on something like mathematics!
   Ila: Wait, what?? I had to go on a 20-minute walk and talk with depth of feeling about math with a complete stranger??? And a HS teacher no less? Someone who knows way more than I do about mathematics? I barely got through math classes in high school and college! (Why was I on this team anyway? Doesn't everyone know how bad I am at math?)
   From that moment to this, it was funny (in a wondrous sort of way) to think how quickly our math design team came together. We were a team that bonded despite the times when one of us was on leave for a period of time. (Perhaps the births and deaths that were experienced during our time together provided the the the glue that bound us to each other.) In the past days we've all asked why and how that happened. What I've landed on is that we almost automatically learned that we had a similar conviction that math should (and could) be different for our students. No matter that there were two elementary and three secondary "experts" among us; no matter that our own mathematics education

varied in scope, depth, and the ways it made us feel. We were uncomfortable and outraged enough with the status quo of mathematics in our district to push through any differences and seek the necessary changes for the whole school.

Liz: The idea of collaborating with teachers from across grade levels to "transform" the math experiences of St. Louis Park students was intriguing. Not even sure what transforming a math experience really meant, we turned in applications to be part of the district design team.

Efe: We began our journey in the summer, with no real idea what our new roles were, what they meant, or how we could even make such a change. We embarked on a 2-day workshop attended by two elementary school teachers, two middle school teachers, and one high school teacher, and we were tasked to come up with a 3-, 5-, and 8-year plan to transform how math was being taught. Engaging in our racial autobiographies helped us build rapport with each other.

Maddy: I think our time really began when we met over the summer in the district office, bonding over the common theme of "we need a BIG change in math" and also having no idea what our new roles were/meant. We were told to collaborate with/use the resources of the director of curriculum and instruction, assessment, SPED, technology, the superintendent, and so forth, but we weren't sure how. Eventually we decided we needed something to bring us together, so we adopted a racial-equity purpose statement. Having a common purpose statement, focused on racial-equity transformation in math, served to be instrumental during the infancy of our team until its close.

Liz: We struggled and spun in circles for quite some time about what our role was going to be. What was the direction we were going? How do we come up with a plan? At one meeting, we took a look at the secondary racial-equity purpose statement:

Our Why: All SLP [St. Louis Park Schools] students will see themselves as successful in math regardless of race or background.

Our How: As a math department we believe that we can transform every mathematics class at SLP to mirror the racial demographics of the school. We will do this by analyzing and reflecting on our own mindsets and beliefs surrounding mathematics and culture to enable all students to see themselves as mathematicians in and out of the classroom, regardless of race, gender, or background. We will promote a classroom culture that will value and encourage our students' authentic selves as well as value the skills of a mathematician: asking questions, thinking and listening critically, questioning answers, communicating effectively, objectively evaluating without bias, and describing patterns so that all students will understand how they can use math to change the world.

This statement would drive our learning and vision throughout the process. The group, in its infancy . . .

At the workshop we were introduced to the different phases of the design team process. Phase I, Knowing Thyself, Phase II, Distinguishing Knowledge From Foolishness, and Phase III, Building for Eternity. Throughout all these phases, our design team was constantly learning from each other, about ourselves, and about our role in the transformational process. Knowing that this process would not work if it was just the five of us who were on board with the idea of transforming the math experience in SLP, we gathered multiple times with the math consulting team and other district leaders. By working with other people, we were able to make it happen on a broader scale with integrity and broader implementation. Simply put, the more we had greater buy-in from a multitude of parties, the more collaborative we became.

Ila: Our district is one that uses Courageous Conversations About Race for its protocol between colleagues, among peers, and in classrooms. Because of that, the secondary mathematics team had created a [REP] statement that we tried on for size to guide the work of the math consulting team. We deemed it satisfactory enough to have it apply to all parties in our group (including early learning, special education, admin, etc.). Soon after, we began to analyze the NCTM Eight Effective Math Practices (Principals to Actions: Ensuring Mathematical Success for AIL, National Council of Teachers of Mathematics [NCTM], 2014) and add in a practice about development of math identity because we felt that it would better reflect the strategic direction of our district. These two documents have been both the guiding light and an evaluation tool for us as we dream about and put into place structural changes to math at every level of our organization. Once we landed on those two documents, I hung onto those as a lifeline. In my experience as a Brown woman, I find it easier to depersonalize a bit and dig into what the collective is putting out as the "way things should be." This is something I've done to protect myself and keep my heart intact. Having both the REP and the frameworks gave me the green light to be myself within the words found on each (not hard to do, as they are encompassing and match my beliefs). We came together so quickly because of a similar strength of conviction, the REP and frameworks, but mostly, time together. We spent time together in and out of formal meetings; texts between us are rapid and with great volume. Fortunately, what was happening on a personal front with the math design team along with the REP and frameworks was creating a snowball effect on the idea of our group collaborating to transform mathematics in a racially equitable way.

Jill: Our team has been positioned to collaborate with a focus on equity because our entire district, from our school board to our district-level staff to our building-level staff, has a clear focus on our district's mission, vision, and values, which center on equity.

When you step inside St. Louis Park Schools there's a clear understanding that our mission, vision, and core values drive the work we do on a daily basis. With a focus on equity at the forefront of the work, it makes it easy to stand in my purpose as a multiracial Latina teacher on an interracial team of teacher-leaders. When we came together as a team one of our first steps was to create a racial-equity purpose statement that connected our work to our mission, vision, and core values.

Throughout our 3 years together, we were equally outraged at the persistence of the injustice of math in schools, which provided us with the motivation and sense of urgency to trudge a path forward. We began, and continue to operate, with a high level of trust in one another. We knew that we were all committed to the same mission because . . . although everyone has gone on leave at one point or another, the perspectives of the missing were always represented. We were committed to ensuring that multiple perspectives were sought and that the vested parties were heard. Gone were the days of teaching in silos, each school separate from the others. We sought to create a system that flowed from early elementary school education through high school graduation. Without collaboration across the district, we would simply be recreating the very system we were attempting to transform.

That unifying statement—a common racial-equity purpose statement—was the critical element that bound us together. Our statement allowed us to work together, unified in a common purpose to become antiracist school leaders for transformational change in mathematics.

Staff-Collaboration Tenet Application

District-Level Application. In St. Louis Park Public Schools our Teaching and Learning Team has been positioned to collaborate with a focus on racial equity for about 4 years. Racially and culturally our Black male superintendent has crafted a team consisting of a Cambodian American refugee, an Arab American, a Black woman, a Biracial woman, and two White Americans. This team establishes trust with check-ins on a regular basis that ask us to review questions ranging from "How are the children?" to "How has interest convergence impacted the decision-making in this curriculum review process?" We share personal and professional intersections about how the work shows up for us and make space in every meeting to have fun. But, make no mistake, we are laser-focused on racial-equity transformation. We know that with high levels of antiracism come the need for high levels of trust and that trust comes from a healthy combination of fun, truth telling, and space for reflective practice. I send out the agenda items on the day of the meeting each week, inviting team members throughout the week to contribute to the agenda with their own topics. This allows the team to have some shared ownership of the agenda and allows for flexibility in which voices are heard and in facilitating sections of the meeting.

School-Level Application. In St. Louis Park Public Schools, we are using a model for antiracist collaboration called CARE (Collaborative Action Research for Equity) teams. Inspired by the work of Courageous Conversations and influenced by the Coalition of Essential Schools, this CARE team model has replaced PLCs (professional learning communities) as a potentially more intentionally student-centered antiracist form of schoolwide collaboration. In this model, educators choose a small group of focal students of color whom they elevate as partners in their journey as antiracist leaders. These students become the focus of the lesson planning, the educators' sounding board for reflection on culturally relevant practice, and data points to assess the effectiveness of teaching. This flips the model of collaboration that often has focused on the deficits of children being the focus of data discussion or intervention during team time to that of elevating the voice, work, and brilliance of students to influence teacher practice. Educators during this cycle develop a racial-equity purpose statement—that is, a purpose statement that grounds them in isolating race in their discussions and reminds them of the presence and role of Whiteness in their teaching and in student learning. By revisiting this purpose statement and engaging in the sharing of racial autobiographical reflection, educators position themselves to engage student voices, sustain conversations about race, and deepen reflective practice that challenges the status quo.

Student Group-Level Application. Collaboration across positional and racial diversity helps develop a team capable of supporting antiracist leadership in students. Often, schools have someone who is positionally or racially marginalized working alone with groups of students around race-related issues. Collaborative positional diversity means administrators, teachers, and support staff working together as a team to ensure that student leadership is nurtured and organizational blind spots are addressed. Having multiple perspectives among the roles of adults is crucial for engaging students in antiracism work. It is so common for antiracist leaders to burn out or turn over, so for the sake of continuity and safety for students there needs to be at least two multiple adult perspectives—ideally a team of adults—working with interracial student leadership groups. When a beloved, trusted leader leaves a school and there is no other adult there with an established relationship in the space, students are set up for heartbreak.

Anthony Galloway and I worked together for years to ensure that student groups in various school districts not only were implemented with fidelity but were gaining the political credibility necessary for success. We built trust with each other quickly through the sharing of our values and deepened that trust through personal time together. It became important for us to not just discuss how we were similar in our spiritual identities and passion for racial equity and student leadership development but also how different our lived experiences had been for an African American man growing up in St. Paul and an Arab American/White man growing up in a small town in the North Woods. Our interest in and respect for our differences allowed us space to build on each other's strengths and help students build on theirs.

STUDENT INTEGRATION

How Integrated, Involved, and Engaged Are Students in the Antiracist Leadership of the District?

Often, students who may flourish in a racial-equity leadership program are those who do not fit the dominant culture's definition of leader. Many times, students who ended up in my office when I was assistant principal were there because they did not have the skill or capacity to use their voice in a way that adults could hear it. Seeing students' potential for leadership is a skill that adult teams can use when deciding how to get students integrated into the system. One of the first things to look for is student interest in antiracism. Conversations in the cafeteria can help unseat some nascent racial consciousness, but what is most helpful in uncovering potential for leadership is observation in classroom settings. If teachers are embedding social-justice issues into their curriculum, they may begin to see passion bubbling up.

To get buy-in from the entire school community, it makes sense to gather staff input on which students should be encouraged to be a part of a racial-equity leadership team. In various settings I have gone to teams to gather their perspectives on who should be a part of a Dare 2 Be Real team. In some more conservative settings, I have had to refer to the group as a multicultural leadership group so as not to disarm the staff before even working with them. Over the course of a decade the outcome has been eerily similar. Staff begin by giving the names of assimilated girls of color. After reminding staff that this is an interracial group, some White girls are mentioned as potentials. Assimilated males of color often get peppered into the discussion at some point, and after careful consideration, some may even mention students of color who are typically not perceived as leaders. To shift a leadership paradigm in your school, adults must be open to advocating for some students who may not be thriving in the mainstream setting of the school. This is not only important to let the staff know that certain students were recommended for the group but also is essential for the self-esteem of the new leader. Letting a child know that multiple adults recommended you for a leadership group because they saw your potential can be a life-changing experience. In addition, it has been common for adults to find it difficult to identify White males who may show interest in antiracism. This is not often because there are no White males interested in this work but rather because adults have not been engaging in racially conscious dialogue with their White students; therefore, the adults do not have a mental model of White males who can work in this regard. Gathering staff input can produce a "canary in the mine," uncovering how discussions of antiracism are manifested—or not—in your school. With all of this in mind, three essential ingredients are necessary when looking at systematically developing student leaders for antiracism: (1) integration, (2) involvement, and (3) engagement. The following paragraphs highlight what is needed to have these pieces in place for system student leadership development.

Let us begin diving into the words of the second tenet by addressing some foregrounding and assumptions that are the basis of the Dare 2 Be Real framework. To be a truly antiracist student-leadership-development program, integration must be a goal and a reality within the program. There is certainly a place for racial affinity, whether that be ethnic study courses, Black student unions, or other programs that support the development of ethnic and racial pride. However, to engage in active antiracism, Dare 2 Be Real and the research behind it assumes that integration must be present. This means that there is an interracial group of students present in the program, classroom, class, or model that bears its name.

If a goal of antiracism is to have student integration, an organization should aim to engage an interracial group that is indicative of the racial demographics of the organization. It should be noted that the group should not be developed based on racial quotas, but rather on racial consciousness. White participants should be particularly open to alliances with other students of color. It should be ensured that there is not one dominant racial group, but in a predominantly White school like Midwest, it is essential to have White students and White advisors involved in the group to not further isolate students of color who are already historically marginalized and hypervisible within the system. A group focused on "race talk" is going to quickly be labeled as the "Black Group," so intentionally engaging students that mirror the population allows a school to redefine antiracism as an issue in which students of all backgrounds should engage. We know that until White students see this work as their own—in alliance with their peers of color—students of color will continue to be asked to fix the problem of systemic racism for White people. If all students do not see a place for themselves to be engaged and involved in antiracism, the student leadership team will predictably be marginalized as a fringe group that is not really bringing substantive change to the organization. The centering of student equity groups comes from the implementation of the sustaining structural tenets.

In addition, students need to be involved in the process of developing the program and in school improvement. Dare 2 Be Real assumes that students can be school leaders, not just student leaders. When we think of student leadership, we usually think of elected student councils and other means by which students are encouraged to provide leadership for their class or school. All too often, student councils become preoccupied with school dances or become a transparent attempt to coopt students into the service of teachers' and administrators' goals. Seldom are they a forum for students to make what they believe in happen. Currently much is being said about the value of "student voice," particularly to harness adolescents' energy, idealism, and moral outrage about social justice issues.

In a middle school where I was assistant principal, rather than just engaging student voice, we trained students to use their passion to better the school community through the facilitation of Courageous Conversations with younger students, the presentation of spoken word at all-school assemblies, and the development of antiracism lessons for younger students that would be cotaught with an interracial team of peers. Voice was not just a cute afterthought, but rather was harnessed to integrate and involve students in the school. This engaged the entire school community in the work of Dare 2 Be Real and heightened an awareness of antiracism throughout the campus.

Indeed, all of our students need to be integrated fully into an antiracist community of learners. We can speculate about what a school focused on developing antiracist school leadership would look like but, as Ladson-Billings points out regarding our most historically marginalized in our schools,

Parents, teachers, and neighbors need to help arm African American children with the knowledge, skills, and attitude needed to struggle successfully against oppression. These, more than test scores, more than high grade point averages, are the critical features of education for African Americans. If students are to be equipped to struggle against racism, they need excellent skills from the basics of reading, writing, and math, to understanding history, thinking critically, solving problems, and making decisions; they must go beyond merely filling in test sheet bubbles with Number 2 pencils. (Ladson-Billings, 2009, p. 153)

Voices From the Field: Danny Shoppe—White Male High School Student, St. Louis Park High School

In the summer of 2020, the St. Louis Park Public School District hired me, along with five other students, to research race and equity in our schools. As a White male high school student who had not been exposed to this before, being able to work with teachers and administrators gave me and the other student interns a completely unique chance to have an impact on our own education.

I'll be honest—looking back, I didn't know much about the antiracist work being done by the district before I started this internship. As a White male student, I had not been explicitly exposed to it. The goal of our youth data analyst team was to do research on something relevant to us as students, but we didn't jump straight in. Instead, we spent weeks reading a variety of different texts about race, equity, and education. We analyzed data that had previously been collected by the district and talked about what it meant to us as students. On top of that, we reflected on our own racial and ethnic identities and how they influenced our beliefs and values as researchers.

The best part about this research project was that it was centered around students, who are usually (and ironically) not consulted with as much as they should be in decisions about education. We chose the research question and decided how to approach it, and the racially conscious administrators responsible for the program gave us complete control over the presentation of our findings. Beyond that, we interviewed and surveyed other students to gain as many perspectives as possible. And it worked—after presenting our data about advanced classes to over one hundred teachers, administrators, and school board members, real changes happened. The district extended the gifted and talented (GT) programs to all students at the high school, middle school, and elementary schools, rather than offering it only to students who had high standardized test scores. The district created an antiracist talent development program at the elementary schools that provided gifted education to every student in our district multiple times a week. They also responded to our research presentation by making changes to how advanced classes work at all levels, expecting all students in the district, regardless of their status, to take Advanced Placement, IB, or concurrent college enrollment courses.

While these changes certainly aren't entirely the results of our work alone, I feel like we had a genuine impact on the decisions. I was impressed with how open adults in the district were to our ideas, many of which challenged the existing foundation of our schools. In fact, many adults said that our research had an even bigger impact on them since we were students.

The purpose of this project was to introduce our voices as students, but support from adults in the district was crucial to making it work. By providing us with knowledge, facilitating our discussions, and helping us plan and organize our research, our advisors, Dr. Silvy Lafayette and Gao Thor, helped us find the best way to express our own ideas. In order for our voices to be heard, it was important for administrators and teachers to not only give us the tools to do the research but also be open to having conversations with us about our experiences, even when it might be uncomfortable. This collaboration between students and adults is vital to ensure that everyone's voice is heard when making important decisions.

At St. Louis Park, the administration has been very intentional about giving students a say in the conversations about race and equity. The fact that they were willing to pay me and the five other interns to do this research made me feel like the district valued our perspectives as students. And the positive results of the internship, both in policy changes and the personal growth of the interns, show that this investment was worth it. Since then, the district has continued to put time and money into engaging students in leadership around antiracism and equity. They paid another five interns to conduct similar research in the summer of 2021 and continue to collect input from students in other ways, turning this into a student-centered antiracist system.

Education should center around students and their perspectives, and St. Louis Park has shown that they're committed to listening to what students have to say. Asking students for their perspectives is a powerful tool to make progress that is beneficial and lasting. Also, the experience of being in leadership positions related to antiracist work enriches students' education and sets them up to be successful and conscious leaders in and beyond their time at St. Louis Park.

Student Integration Tenet Application

District-Level Application. The St. Louis Park Public Schools incorporated a Youth Data Analyst Program in the summer of 2019 and have engaged youth in the strategic planning of their work ever since. Youth Data Analyst Interns met 2 hours a day, 3 days a week in the summers and were paid a $1,200 stipend to essentially work as members of the Assessment, Research, and Evaluation department for St. Louis Park Public Schools for a summer internship. During this time, they assessed project needs, engaged in intensive research training, and were expected to complete reading assignments prior to each meeting. The purpose of reading assignments was to provide new learning from researchers in the field. Most of the scholars that they read were people of color. Their unique lens would help the group enter into conversations about race, equity, and the opportunity gap. District leaders shared racial autobiographical information, introduced new learning, and shared aggregate district data with the student interns. Interns were expected to engage in ethnographic and quantitative research that then would be shared at a data retreat with all staff in August. The purpose of this retreat was to inform the strategic direction of the district and provide student-centered, research-based recommendations to transformative antiracist change. Changes from former exclusionary practices to restorative practices, from exclusive gifted and talented programs to antiracist talent development programming, and to communications plans that de-weaponized White parent perspectives were all attributed to the work of interns over the course of 3 years in St. Louis Park. This is an exemplary model of student integration of antiracist leadership.

School-Level Application. When I was a principal at Barton Open School in Minneapolis, I inherited a very good school. I had a goal to get into each teacher's classroom at least once a week as a principal and to provide feedback of some kind. To make the work more systemic, I started including the teachers from my equity team on learning walks once a month. On these walks we would look for evidence that our professional development on culturally relevant pedagogy was being applied in classrooms. At the end of the learning walks we would pull students from our Dare 2 Be Real student leadership group and ask them to share with us their perspectives from the classroom on the themes we had just seen throughout our walk. The students would then sit with us and corroborate or debunk the relative urgency of professional-development areas based on the themes we had observed. Then, we would strategically plan how adults and students together would bring their voice to the next professional-development session for staff. It was a partnership that had a profound impact. Within a year of this integrated student leadership practice, we closed our racialized achievement gaps between Black and White students by 26 percent and garnered the highest scores in reading, math, and science in the city of Minneapolis.

Student Group-Level Application. At South View Middle School in Edina, Barton Open School in Minneapolis, and St. Louis Park Middle School in St. Louis Park, we made a conscious effort to integrate antiracist student leadership development not only into our school day but into the fabric of our community site council. As was the case in most schools in which I have had contact, the site council was often disconnected from the day-to-day operations of the school, yet still seen as an important vestige of school/community relations. We took student representatives from our Dare 2 Be Real leadership group and asked them to not only sit in as token members of the site council but actually bring their goals as a leadership team to the council and ask for their support in meeting them. This partnership exponentially raised the practicality of the team and also elevated the level of purposeful collaboration between school and community stakeholders—centering antiracist student needs at the core of the work. By asking the students to bring their antiracist goals to the table, it at once deescalated the potential for partisan posturing that could come from an adult bringing this to the table and also kept the work of the group firm on the involvement and engagement of children.

Part II

DISTINGUISHING KNOWLEDGE FROM FOOLISHNESS

Not everything that is faced can be changed, but nothing can be changed until it is faced.

—James Baldwin

CHAPTER 4

Critical Race Theory at Midwest High School

Critical race theorists (DeCuir & Dixson, 2004; Delgado & Stefancic, 2001) suggest a cycle of oppression that accompanied antiracist reform throughout U.S. history. Recent scholarship draws upon the tenets of critical race theory (CRT) to help explain the maintenance of racially predictable achievement (Gregoryet al., 2010) and the mass incarceration of Black males (Alexander, 2010). Midwest High School showed substantial growth in racially conscious language and extravagant displays of antiracism that would have been silenced in their infancy a decade or two ago. However, the potential for a Golden Age of antiracism was lost through short-sighted programming that provided strategies for closing racially predictable opportunity gaps and that was steeped in Whiteness that blinded many of the participants to the pain that these gaps caused adults and children of color; a leadership that provided some cursory monetary resources to implement a vision for racial equity but lacked the will, skill, knowledge, and capacity to sustain the work beyond its implementation; and a plethora of individual accomplishments to celebrate that were met with disdain and often subtle subversion by members of the Midwest school community that squelched long-term reform.

The following sections review the central themes that emerged through the coding and analysis of data from participant interviews, focus groups, email and personal correspondence, meeting agendas and minutes, and personal journals throughout the "Gilded Age of Antiracism" at Midwest High School. The clustered themes are discussed in the following two chapters while grouped according to two major themes: those related to critical race theory and those related to racial-identity development. Both of these major themes are discussed with examples and analysis of the 67 subthemes that emerged from the data and help frame the landscape of antiracism at Midwest High School. The data reveal a Black/White dichotomy of racial consciousness for participants in this study as well as the complexities they navigated while working as antiracist leaders in this school system.

Among the findings of the study of antiracist leaders at Midwest High School were numerous emergent themes that showed a manifestation of the tenets of critical race theory. These subthemes are (1) interest convergence, (2) counter-storytelling, (3) Whiteness as property, (4) critique of liberalism, and (5) the permanence of racism. Present in all of these themes is a socially constructed notion of race that permeated the culture of Midwest High School. These themes presented themselves in various ways and are addressed in the following five sections. Within each of these sections, I identified three or four clustered themes that fall under each of the five tenets of CRT. These themes are discussed in the following pages. (See also the online appendix to this book at tcpress.com/antiracist-online-materials for the coding of participants and a listing of clustered themes.)

INTEREST CONVERGENCE

Some of the greatest reform movements in U.S. history came as a result of converging interests that were mutually beneficial to those in power and those in need (Loewen, 1996). Whether intentional or not, major Civil Rights legislation was not realized until deep into the Cold War period, as images of Black children being chased by dogs and hit with fire hoses were being published all over the globe as an example of the moral corruption of Capitalism and the "American Way" (Zinn, 1980). Lincoln signed the Emancipation Proclamation soon after hearing that one more Confederate victory at Antietam would most likely get England to support their side in the Civil War. Slaves were freed in the Confederate States, although slaves in the five border states were to stay in bondage as a provision of this proclamation, hence allowing Lincoln an opportunity to show moral superiority over the Confederacy to our European counterparts and maintain loyalty to the slave-holding elite from the states that did not secede from the Union (Takaki, 1993; Zinn, 1980). In the age of No Child Left Behind, Race to the Top, and standardization, interest convergence has become a way of life in public schools (Noguera, 2008; Singleton & Hays, 2008). Schools show progress across multiple demographic categories, including race, to keep their name off the list of underperforming schools. This political reality provided a lot of momentum for antiracist reform at Midwest over the past decade, but for some school districts, this sense of coercion only provided fuel for surface-level reform.

Interest convergence is the notion that racial progress for people of color happens only when those in power also gain something from the change. Numerous participants alluded, either explicitly or implicitly, to this phenomenon at Midwest High School. This theme of interest convergence arose when Whites gained power as leaders in equity work, when developers of courses and programming claimed to have the "answers" to racial disparities in achievement, when racial "tokenism" eased White leaders of their guilt and responsibility to do equity work, and when public perceptions and structural changes were honored over truth and cultural change. Data from participant interviews were captured in subthemes that are explained in the following four sections. These subthemes are (1) Whites gaining power as leaders, (2) racial tokenism, (3) course offerings and staffing decisions, and (4) programming answers.

Whites Gaining Power as Leaders

Numerous participants of color spoke of their experiences with Whites who were leading the work and gaining power in the organization. Three participants of color shared frustration with the fact that some ideas originally had come from people of color or Whites who were more racially conscious than those who were being recognized for their work. This theme was quite common from some of the participants of color. The interest convergence became clear once individuals received personal gain for work without giving credit for the idea to others, thus maintaining the power dynamics they were claiming to address. One Black teacher reported,

> We were talking about race, it was about getting some resources for our students of color, and everybody's agreeing saying this is the best idea they had ever heard and I'm sitting there about to just bust open because we had a conversation a couple of years ago about the same topic, but no one listened at that time when the Black staff were presenting it. Now, because the White teacher says it is a good deal, he gets credit for being so equitable. (TBF 14)

It was commonly found in personal correspondence with White staff that people of color were deemed dangerous, ineffective, radical, or negative at Midwest High School. It was much more common for Black staff to be linked to others in their racial group than for Whites who may have exhibited similar characteristics and skill sets. In fact, throughout the period 2004 to 2008, every African American staff member was seen and described that way by multiple White staff at Midwest. Although White nonparticipants were more likely to share unsolicited perceptions about staff of color, White participants shared stories and perceptions about people of color at Midwest High School but rarely had individual conversations with them. More than half of the participants of the study and numerous pieces of personal correspondence illustrate that White leaders who shared similar sentiments and led similar reform as their Black counterparts were considered smart, politically savvy, and courageous for their actions by their peers. This characteristic of the culture at Midwest High School mirrors the work of other scholars who have studied interracial group dynamics (Ladson-Billings, 2005a; Singleton, 2012; Wise, 2009).

While some White leaders may have not been conscious of the presence of interest convergence in their practice, other White leaders were more explicit about their search for power. One participant shared a conversation she had with a staff member involved with the equity initiative about her ambitions to do the work "just enough" to gain positional power in the organization:

> She was very overt with me and we had the conversation where she told me that her goal was to be the next principal . . . so it was something on my mind in the first year [of our equity work]. I think I got too much exposure early on in this

work in speaking my truth, so it became a career-limiting move. She thought she would say the right things and gain favor for her work even if she was [covertly] subverting reform when she got a chance. I never heard the people at the district office who seemed to know her intentions ever say anything that wouldn't back that up and give her the idea that she was a viable candidate for the next principal and that that was a realistic expectation for her to have. I'm pretty sure the behind-the-scenes conversations went differently. (AWF 20)

There were numerous political moves alluded to throughout the process. Many staff members sought to develop the perception that they were authentically engaged in antiracist leadership so they could make personal gain. Although more common among participants of color, one White teacher developed a concern that she was only being invited to things because of her role as an equity leader. She felt that although she was at the table, her presence solidified the agenda of those who invited her despite their unwillingness to value her opinion or input, particularly as administrative prioritization on equity became less focused:

> For equity, right now, the only context in which they ever give us any time is when they want to invite us to the table so they can say that they included the equity team in the process. This year, I wasn't even invited to the meeting where they discussed how they were going to do staff development this whole year. Last year [2007], they at least invited me, even though they had already made the decision for how to allocate staff-development time before I got there, and I didn't realize that until I got there and saw that the calendar was already set . . . one person gets to decide who is invited, who sets the calendar, and then puts my name on it as a collaborator so she can appear inclusive. (TWF 5)

Racial Tokenism

The sentiments shared by the White teacher in the previous section only underscore the feelings of many staff of color at Midwest High School. Racial tokenism in the school workplace is certainly not unique to Midwest. Other studies have examined the difference between civil equality (equal opportunity or access to resources) and social equality (equality of treatment in addition to access to resources) for Black educators (Kantor & Lowe, 1995; Kelly, 2009). The feelings of racial tokenism were quite profound in certain Midwest settings. A person of color suggested that her involvement in activities seemed to be a token gesture that supported the interests of her White peers rather than one of genuine partnership.

> I'm involved in every district committee because they know that I can work with Black children. Why am I the only one that is going to speak for them? If I wasn't there, I'm not sure that any of these [racial-equity] conversations would happen. They count on me to tell them what to do, but then turn around and complain

that I'm not getting the work done [at the same pace] as my White colleagues. How is that fair? How is that equitable? (TWF 9)

This Black teacher expressed a frustration that was common among participants of color. They shared a sense that they were invited to meetings to provide equitable representation but were often the ones who had to speak for students of color, allowing White educators to remain sheltered from speaking through an antiracist lens. Others felt silenced because they were the "only" person of color in the room. One participant shared:

> My wound is being the only dark piece of pepper in the salt shaker. And so, if everybody, it sounds like everybody saying we all have our own pain, or things where we are vulnerable, we have to be able to share that with the world. For most people at this school, when I walk out in front of them, I can't say anything about race, because I am already the poster boy for equity just because of the skin I'm in. If I start to mention race, the arms start to fold, the eyes avert, and the tone of the room changes. They are okay with me being in the room, as long as I don't speak about [race]. That is a hard place to be. (ABM 13)

Some staff of color even expressed a sense of fatigue, being the only ones to be called upon to be on district committees and then often being the ones that have to provide the consciousness for the group of mostly White educators.

> I got tired of having to help [White colleagues] struggle through their Whiteness. Just once, I would like to see them put me on a committee and have someone else call out the ignorance . . . I'm often the one who has to speak for the kids of my race. (TWF 3)

As the building developed more racially conscious White leaders who could do just that, they often found themselves working through political and cultural structures of Whiteness—a social construction that often relied on conscious or unconscious interest convergence for any hope of reform. Many of the perceptions gained from these structural changes were designed with stakeholder interests in mind and were supported by White people as long as they were able to articulate some sort of mutual benefit.

Course Offerings and Staffing Decisions

During the 3 years of the equity initiative, there were numerous times when curricular or sweeping course changes were suggested as a way to develop more inclusion and multiple perspectives in the classroom. The ideas often surfaced when students and parents of color lamented the lack of diverse racial perspectives in literature and curricular materials. Although these changes led to more relevant curricular opportunities that reflected the experiences of people of color, they often did not happen until there was a mutual benefit for students, teachers, and administrators. Administration was asked to report to the school board with accessible examples that demonstrated progress with the school's equity work. One White participant suggested:

> It is the right thing to do, to offer AP World History because it makes sense for all kids, but it is also the right thing to do because it helps make our department more relevant to the decision-makers that are seeing all the reasons to add staffing to math and language arts classes, but not social studies. Since we don't have a state test assessing us, we need to make sure that we at least can show them how we are addressing our equity goals. If we want to gain any ground in a community that has loved its AP Euro and AP U.S. History, we need to show them how it meets our mutual interests. (TWM 1)

The plan described above would not only provide a more diverse curriculum, but a means for recruiting more students of color to take advanced classes. The hope among some equity leaders was that this would help desegregate a class in a department that had had only three Black or Latinx students take an AP class over the course of a decade despite over 20 percent of the school being students of color for most of that time.

Although many departments, including social studies, looked at ways to develop more racially inclusive curriculum, the political nature of interest convergence helped provide urgency for new initiatives among those who did not share the same passion for this curricular content or the vision for developing a program that would provide more opportunities for students from all backgrounds. This was an important distinction throughout the time period. It also allowed many staff to individually or collectively provide a perception to outsiders that they were doing the work of imbedding racial equity. One teacher talked about the grant money that was awarded her class by a foundation that may have wanted to appear more racially enlightened:

> I was able to add this drum and dance class this year because the funding was there for equity. Last year I had 13 or 15 students of color. This year, I thought I had less, but there was, I counted, the same 12 or 13, but it was a really tight, good group of kids. How did things differ this year? Well, one the thing was, I started out having an ally in a colleague who knew about the resources. My challenge now is to create a space where there are enough African American kids that they feel empowered, where they can speak. Because they won't [feel comfortable or even want to take the class] if there's not enough of their friends there. Maybe that won't happen in my class, but if my colleagues can [create a comfortable space for Black and Brown students], too . . . (TWF 18)

Interest convergence manifested when White staff were absolved from learning culturally responsive teaching practices because they would not have to work with students of color. In some departments, teachers of color or members of the equity team had students scheduled into their classes because it was assumed that their practices were going to be better for kids of color. One person of color reflected,

> I am told to work with kids from all backgrounds, yet the Black boys keep getting sent to me and [my other Black colleague] because we are told that we can work with them so well. What would happen if I couldn't work with White students? I think we all know that I would lose my job. Why can someone openly acknowledge that some people in my department can't work with Black students and then say it is okay to just give those students to me? Why do those teachers still have a job? (TBF 14)

This lack of accountability seemed to be made possible by a schedule that pushed clusters of Black and Latinx students into the classes of a handful of teachers while others had virtually racially homogenous classes. Peers and administration did not have to confront the lack of results with certain teachers, meeting their own self-interest, albeit often unconscious, to avoid discomfort while addressing antiracism.

Programming Answers

Throughout the equity initiative at Midwest High School, there was a frequent rallying cry among many of the staff members for answers, strategies, or programs that would address the increasing consciousness of their ineffectiveness with students of color and the guilt and fear associated with this issue. These programs came in many shapes and sizes and had varied results. Some teachers incorporated parts of programs into existing curricular programs, while others developed programs that further segregated students of color out of the mainstream classroom. Avoiding discomfort was never more prevalent than in the development of programs that were expected to be the "answer." Many teachers and administrators shared the perception that many programs like AVID (Advancement Via Individual Determination) and NUA (the National Urban Alliance), which were introduced during this period, or existing programs like special education or Sophomore Academy became the places to send Black and Brown kids when staff ran out of answers for serving students of color in a core curricular classroom. One participant noted,

> AVID has taken a lot off our plates. Now we have a place to send students who need the skills to make it through school. I know I probably shouldn't think this, but it has gotten too difficult to differentiate for all of my students. We need more programming for kids who just cannot be successful without the extra support. It is a great place for our Black kids to get what they need. (TWM 8)

The thought among some participants was that certain programs allowed staff members to hide behind a "silver bullet" approach to addressing racial equity. Some staff recognized the limitations of programs for students of color but also recognized the necessity for providing programming that would address the various levels and complexity of racial predictability in the school. By Year 3, over 75 percent of Black boys were enrolled in special programming at Midwest High School, a result of increased consciousness for addressing opportunity gaps, but a problem lamented by one participant for the lack of integration that this caused in the school and the interests it may have served:

> As a system, we have done a disservice to our young Black men because their involvement in all our programming has limited their opportunities for elective classes and courses like [music and art] that typically allow for some form of self-expression. This manifests itself in some interesting ways . . . at the same time you have the district feeling good about themselves because they can report to the board that we have this percentage of Black kids in program X and this percentage of Black kids in program Y. It continues to perpetuate the problem that they were supposed to address. (SBF 22)

During a focus group another teacher animatedly suggested,

> AVID has become an easy out for our staff. It is a program where we can "stick" Black boys who are not yet "ready for AP" and most teachers no longer have to worry about them. If the student struggles, most teachers can now blame the program and take responsibility off of themselves . . . right now; over 75 percent of the Black boys in our building are in special programming. Integration has gone out the window. Differentiation in the classroom has been thrown out the window. Instead, we are trying to figure out what programming we can throw at them next. (TWM 4)

Although there is little empirical evidence to support that special programming has perpetuated the problem as the participant suggests, these initiatives may have undermined some of the efforts of the equity team to create system-wide accountability for the teaching and learning of students of color. Special programs are an essential piece for schools to consider when addressing institutional racism (Gregory et al., 2010), but not all teachers saw this as a piece of the puzzle rather than as a tier of intervention that includes culturally responsive instruction in general education settings. Some staff saw this symbiotic relationship, but these were often staff who had participated in extensive training associated with both racial equity and instructional pedagogy. In fact, many White participants suggested that integration of multiple racial perspectives into their daily work may have been a key factor in maintaining their passion and persistence for racial equity. These perspectives are shared more in depth in the next section.

COUNTER-STORYTELLING

Storytelling is a powerful means of creating meaning and challenging stereotypes or myths (Delgado & Stefanic, 2001). Counter-storytelling is a tool that CRT scholars utilize to contradict racist or racially unconscious characterizations of certain events. Counter-storytelling also aims to expose race-neutral discourse to reveal how White privilege operates in an ideological framework to reinforce and support unequal societal relations between Whites and people of color. Solórzano and Yosso (2002) define counter-storytelling as "a method of telling the stories of those people whose experiences are not often told," including people of color, women, gay people, and the poor (p. 26). Counter-stories or counter-narratives stand in opposition to narratives of dominance. Dominant or majoritarian narratives can carry multiple layers of assumptions that serve as filters in discussions of racism or other forms of oppression. In short, dominant stories privilege Whites, men, the middle and/or upper class, and heterosexuals by naming these social locations as normative points of reference and the normalized reality. Counter-storytelling can often become empowering for people of color but also can serve the interests of Whites who want to become more color-conscious but lack the perspective to normalize multiple racial perspectives. The data suggest strong use of counter-storytelling at Midwest High School. The following sections address the data that fell under counter-storytelling themes. These sections are the importance of staff of color, hearing from parents of color, student voices influencing practice, and staff dissention.

Importance of Staff of Color

One White teacher at Midwest talked about the importance of staff of color in the quest to provide multiple perspectives in the Courageous Conversations About Race:

> We have a very low number in the school district and in the school. We're disproportionately low. And that's not that unusual for a suburban school district, well, probably for any school, but it doesn't make it okay. And it also does not—I think we are disproportionately lower. I don't know. I mean if we know that it's a goal of ours, well, first of all just to know it's a goal of ours in the district to have more staff of color, and you know, the reasons behind it are many, to reflect our students and our parents, our community, to be more representative of our society in general, to I think, enrich our school community and staff with multiple perspectives on life. (TWM 21)

Other participants talked about how important it has been to have leaders who can share a different racial lens than the majority of the staff:

> You know, I think that it's huge that we have a Black principal. I really do. And I told him he can't leave until after I retire. And you know, well I guess we'll see how long he lasts. I feel bad because I do think that in many cases a lot of pressure is put on [Black administration] that probably isn't appropriate. You know, having a Black man in front of us speaks for all types of things, sometimes. I feel badly because we expect him to represent all Blacks. (AWF 24)

The perspective shared above mirrors a comment by an administrator of color who shared how he often sees himself as the "poster boy for equity" just by walking into the room. The burden to represent a perspective greater than your own is one that most White educators do not have to face. A White teacher shared a conversation he had with a biracial teacher once he had developed a bit more consciousness about the burden placed on the racial "Other" at Midwest.

> So, you know, finally, I go and sit down with [biracial teacher] and say, "I kinda get it. I know you know, and I know how much I didn't get it before." . . . to have her smile because she's been talking about [racial consciousness] for years. And I, you know, her patience and waiting for other people to come along and finally start into this journey is very impressive. I don't think I could be as graceful under that pressure. (TWM 6)

The pressure to provide a perpetually silenced perspective is a theme that resonated with many staff as they participated in the racial-equity work. A White teacher shared his perspectives, as well as possible solutions:

> Somehow, I think we need to bring in—I don't want to say inspirational speakers because I hate that phrase—but, you know what I mean? We need to be rejuvenated sometimes. We need to hear from some people [of color] outside of the system that can tell us what they see. (TWM 21)

Another perspective from a White counselor demonstrated his sense of urgency to get the staff to hear multiple perspectives but also a limited understanding of how to get staff to share the same will to learn from others.

> It is so important when we are going and hearing people of color deliver a message [that we are not used to hearing], because I think it's going to be the same handful of White teachers that are going to go and seek that out, and you know that. I mean, we're going to seek that stuff out all the time, but most teachers in this building won't. So, I think we have to force it on them. They need to hear what they don't know they need to hear. (SMF 5)

These perspectives demonstrate a desire by White staff leaders, engaged in the antiracism work, to hear the perspectives of people of color. With such small numbers of staff of color, White staff often wanted to call on consultants or experts from Black, Asian, or Latinx communities. One theme that developed was a desire to hear from parents of students of color.

Hearing From Parents of Color

As Midwest's staff became more entrenched in the work, our Partnership for Academically Successful Students (PASS) team worked to develop authentic partnerships with parents of students of color. This included racial affinity focus groups and an opportunity in 2008 to have individual parents and panels of parents speak to our staff about what their children need and what their expectations are of the staff. A number of White staff members spoke about the importance of these experiences and their desire to learn from more parents of color. White staff often looked at this experience with a critical eye and wanted to make sure that they were getting the truth from parents, not just compliments:

> I want to have more parents [of color] attend. So, we can hear from them about what it is, where's the mismatch, what is standing in the way of you getting more engaged and your child getting more involved in school and more successful. I'd like to get more of that input. When the panel of parents were here, I had the distinct impression that we were being patted on the back, kind of as a way to cajole us into listening to what the parents were about to say. (TWF 9)

Another White teacher talked about her experience working on a committee with parents of color and shared similar concerns:

> I went to the PASS team meeting . . . on the one hand I felt like, you know, certainly some parents were very vocal and very, it seemed to me, very genuine in what they were saying. But I wondered to what extent they were trying to please us, or saying things that they thought we wanted to hear. . . . You know, some of the kids and parents that were there, were the more—looked to me—to be some of the parents of the achieving kids anyway, and the parents might want us to maintain their status. (TWF 12)

This perspective expresses a concern that was common among White leaders in this work. Despite their call for perspectives from people of color, there was often an underlying distrust that what was being shared was the whole truth. In fact, some staff were concerned that the people of color at these meetings were not the "right people of color." When pushed on this perspective, many White staff members alluded to wanting to hear from staff who demonstrated more aspects of socially constructed "Blackness." Parents who shared characteristics often associated with White identity were not seen as authentically Black to those White leaders who considered themselves "woke." There was a perceived assimilation among parents of color who seemed to easily navigate Whiteness, and this caused some White staff to dismiss these perspectives as "real" perspectives that could lead to systemic change. Although relationships never got deep enough to go beyond perceptions of this assertion, the continued partnership remained something that the administration valued when deciding who to put in front of the staff for a panel. Despite the perceived identity differences and differing perspectives of parents of color, numerous White participants still valued the perspectives of any parents of color over the perspectives of their peers who were staff of color. One White female teacher suggested that these perspectives coupled with a concerted effort from the district to use data might be a winning formula:

> Our involvement with parents of color has been great, but it needs to move from just talking to the actual action where we are seeing the ideas generated from the talking—it needs to be a lot more data driven. We need to start looking at test scores and we have gotten a good start on that. (TWF 12)

Another White male suggests a similar path of action, but reiterates his perception that parents of color are experts in the field. Staff of color are not given the same credibility:

> I get the research perspective. I mean, in terms of antiracism work. I mean, I read the book. I talk to my [students] all the time. I talk to other staff all the time. To get parents' perspectives who are that close to [students of color] and, you know, who are not invited into schools as frequently as they should be, who don't get as much say about—what I don't see, who I don't talk to as often and, you know, have something I don't [a relationship and perspective on how to motivate Black and Brown children]. I would like to get their perspective, and to get their insight, and to get this totally different view of here's what we're doing at home, here's what's happening at home, here's what we know, here's what we want, here's what's important to us. I mean, I guess this is a whole different perspective than one I could ever hear from my colleagues at school or certainly from what I heard when I was in school to become a teacher. (TWM 4)

Multiple participants shared a concern that we needed to move beyond talking about the problem, to some action-oriented, data-driven equity work. Others suggested strongly that we should be cultivating more authentic partnership with parents and community members of color. However, there was nothing that drove more staff to reform their own practice than the counter-stories of students.

Student Voices Influencing Practice

Although there was very little direction from antiracist consultants and virtually no urgency from district or building administration, the space for antiracist student dialogue became a great motivating factor in developing not only the will but the skill for many White staff and staff of color to engage in active antiracism. Hearing from students motivated many educators, at their core, to develop opportunities for leadership, change instruction, and examine policies or practices that might be perpetuating racial inequities at Midwest High School.

> Being a counselor, I hear from kids and get a lot of feedback on teachers. They come in and tell me who sucks, and they come in and tell me who's really good.

And you can't always take them at face value, but you hear the same thing enough and you start to take it as truth. So, being in the building for [a few years], there's been a few situations in which I thought a teacher didn't handle it well with a student of color, I thought they could have handled a situation better. I thought the practices in the room were racist. You hear this from multiple kids; it starts to become the truth. You want to make a change immediately so more kids aren't affected the way these kids have been. (SWM 2)

A Black female staff member shared her perspective on how to change the system based on what she had been hearing from the students of color who frequent her office. She suggests that we must create space and time to talk about acts of racism and to use them as teachable moments:

What needs to change is students and teachers thinking that it's okay if something [racist] happens on the stairs to be able to talk about it in class. I understand if you're teaching math and science, but still give an announcement about it—find out if anyone wants to talk about it. If you're a math teacher, I mean, why not at the beginning of the class be like, "That incident on the steps, what's going on with that?" And talk to these students to try to figure out what that is all about if you don't understand it. If you do understand it, this is a great opportunity to educate [students] about race. (SBF 22)

Staff who had engaged students in dialogue about race shared a great passion for continuing to do so. In fact, the staff members who talked about the racial-equity work in the most positive terms were those who had worked most directly with students of color or with interracial groups of students on a regular or semiregular basis. One student argued that it is essential to have an intentional space for students of color to talk about race so they can learn how to be more proficient when they address the inevitabilities of racism that come with interracial schools. This White student actually saw a change in her teachers after engaging side-by-side with them in interracial dialogue:

Having groups like Dare 2 Be Real and having people get out there and do what they feel is right, talking about race, but not to be a rebel—it allows people to stand up for what you believe in and get people aware of what's going on from your perspective. It gets the students aware of what the racial problems are in school. People like me who weren't necessarily affected directly by it but can still be aware of it are at least having conversations with our other Black friends. Because the [White] kids are more aware, it's kind of like the teachers were kind of getting more aware of it, too. Like, "whoa, these kids' attitudes are really changing, maybe we should try to figure this out." I could see a change in them. They wanted to talk about racism more. (CWF 29)

Student and staff alike recognized the power of student voices in the development of an antiracist school. A White male teacher shared his desire to get students into the middle of the equity work while understanding the importance of creating a safe space for them to speak their truth:

> I want to say that I wish we could have something that I don't think we can, because it puts kids at risk. I said from the very first day that it would be great to hear it from the horse's mouth. I'd love to hear a Black kid go, "Mr. Nelson, you don't do shit for the Black kids." And put him on the spot . . . you don't actually have to put their names out there, but to hear from kids saying, "Look, there are teachers out there who are doing this."—That would be powerful. If we could get our staff to shut up and listen, it would be really powerful. (TWM 21)

All students interviewed wished to get into the middle of the conversation as well. They expressed great pride in wanting to share their perspectives with teachers and believed that it would be a key factor for creating racial equity at Midwest High School. One Black male lamented the lack of action by most staff members at Midwest. He suggested that courage was key:

> We need to have more people like you guys who aren't afraid. And even, not just teachers, administrators, and students, who aren't afraid to do something, I mean it's kind of embarrassing to say, but there are not a whole lot of people who are not afraid to talk about race and to do something when they see racism. I mean, some of them can't even see racism because they don't take the time to hear or believe our story, but most don't even do something when they do hear it. (CBM 27)

When it came to hearing multiple counter-stories, staff participants at Midwest were divided when expressing the need to hear a voice different from their own. There were multiple examples from participants in the study who shared the impact of hearing counter-stories from their colleagues as well.

Staff Dissension

At the heart of the racial-equity work at Midwest High School was the commitment to using protocol for Courageous Conversations about race. Staff participated in various degrees with this protocol and worked through numerous activities and professional learning communities to engage in these conversations. Nearly two-thirds of all participants mentioned some example of a conversation they had had with a colleague about race that they believed would not have taken place before they engaged in the focused learning of this racial-equity protocol. One staff member recalled a conversation he had in a fishbowl in front of the entire staff at Midwest:

> I remember going into the fishbowl saying to a colleague, "I'd want to really see what the issue is if we all look at these kids [of color], what if these were all our own [biological children] in our classroom?" I think I remember saying, "I think what we should try to do as a staff is to look at each child as if they were your

kid, how would you treat them in your classroom? Would you let them listen to the iPod in your class? Would you let them pull out the cell phone or say, put that thing away or I'm gonna take it away right now? (TWM 8)

When this staff member shared this story in a focus group, other participants nodded and responded with affirmation, remembering this fishbowl activity and the subsequent conversations. All focus-group participants remembered some fallout from the activity because people broke protocol. They thought the real power came from those who shared perspectives counter to the common perception that others had of them. One participant remembered an incident with a colleague from his department:

> When [White teacher] who had been badmouthing the work for about a year and half stood up in front of the staff, he shared a story that had a profound effect on another participant. He had been reflecting on the work we were doing and realized that he had been doing something racist. There were two Black girls that were sitting in the hallway, talking loudly, disrupting my class while they should have been in another classroom. He said, "I walked by them every day and didn't say anything because I thought that they might say I was racist. I figured it was just a cultural thing. I realize now that by not sending them to class or confronting them on their behavior and by not holding them to the same expectations that I have for my White students, that that was racist." (TWM 23)

Another White teacher reflected,

> When he told us that he realized that he had been racist by not holding the Black girls to the same standards as the White students in the hallway because of his own fears, it sold me a little bit more on this [equity] work. I knew it was the right work to be doing, but it gave me hope that even the biggest critics can change their views if we remain persistent and make the work personal. (TWF 17)

Midwest High School, like most suburban schools, is predominantly White and is steeped in a Whiteness that permeates the culture and practices of the school. Whites engaged in Courageous Conversations about race (Singleton, 2022)—like those at Midwest High School—had an opportunity to learn alternative ways of teaching and communicating that might help address the needs of all students. Many participants reflected on the very personal journey and how it requires staff to examine their own mental models related to racial capital and deficits. This theme is central to the next section related to Whiteness as property.

WHITENESS AS PROPERTY

The notion of Whiteness as property suggests that Whites are encouraged to "invest" in Whiteness like property, giving them an artificial identity that ensures resources, power, and opportunity. This investment becomes "possessive" as Whites hoard their privileges, denying communities of color like opportunities to accumulate assets and become socially mobile (Lipsitz, 2006). Discriminatory lending, opportunity-rich educations, insider networks, and intergenerational transfers of wealth maintain these racial hierarchies.

The Whiteness that Whites create and invest in can in turn come to "possess" them, unless they strive to develop antiracist identities and to disinvest in White privilege (Lipsitz, 2006). White people typically have not come to realize how we radicalize human rights, educational opportunities, and achievement in the United States. In fact, it may be much easier for White educators to imagine that we would have been active in the Civil Rights Movement in the 1960s, when our school policies and beliefs about the abilities of our Black and Brown students and colleagues are more in line with those who supported, intentionally or unintentionally, the oppression of that time (Alexander, 2010; Loewen, 2005). This intermittent, unconscious maintenance of racial hierarchies was present in the participant responses from Midwest High School. In fact, many of the participants saw emotions and reactions from their peers who worked to maintain the possessive investment of Whiteness present at Midwest. The following sections follow participant responses that demonstrate some form of Whiteness as property. These themes include staff anger toward antiracism, choosing to disengage, struggles with the definition of race, and being acknowledged as an equity leader.

Staff Anger Toward Antiracism

About 50 percent of the participants in this study shared a story about an experience they had had with a peer who was angry with the course of the antiracism work. Almost all White teachers shared examples of the difficulty they faced while trying to lead this work with their colleagues. Sometimes, this manifested itself in detours of the work by angry White staff:

> This person in my professional learning community completely shifted the focus to, "We're all fine, it's the kids who need to change their attitudes and meld themselves into the mold of the perfect student or whatever . . ." I was a little overwhelmed, like I said, and surprised and disappointed by that, so I kind of shut up at that time because that's what I do in situations like that. I need to process it before I can address it, so I didn't directly address it in the conversation. There was one other person in the group who tried to focus the conversation a little more when it became very single-focused, very laser-focused in on that issue instead of being on the issue of what we could do to address racial equity—where the conversation had started. (TWF 18)

As in the example above, other staff members were surprised by the energy put into subversion of the antiracism work at Midwest High School. Seven White teachers shared examples of strong reactions from their colleagues. For example,

> It wasn't so much that my colleagues were slightly annoyed by the fact that we're focusing on [racial equity] still. It was the level of energy they were putting into being exasperated by it. It was like a throwing up of the hands, like, "I've had enough of this stuff!"—that's what it felt like to me. (TBF 24)

Another remembered an equity-team meeting when a White male with considerable positional power became extremely angry with the continued focus on Courageous Conversations during a professional development planning session.

> And then he pounded on the table and said, "Goddamn it! I'm the principal of this school, not Glenn Singleton!" It became very clear that there was a frustration mounting because of a power shift that might be taking place at our school. Right there, it became clear to me that it was not safe to speak my truth in this setting. (TWM 23)

Numerous participants in the study shared their beliefs that the racial-equity work at Midwest High School had, indeed, created a shift in power that was felt very strongly in the first year of focused professional development at the site. This shift brought discomfort for those who seemed to have the most invested in their status before any reform movements had begun. Numerous participants shared examples highlighting how they had had conversations with people who were concerned about losing individual power and wanted to maintain solidarity through Whiteness at all costs:

> She wanted me to tell her right there that I would not do the [racial-equity] work. The third year of implementation was that we would start having a building equity team and we would have to pick who is going to be on this team. So, I'm stuck in this position where [my colleagues] are, in my opinion, not invested, number one. And number two, they're actually overtly sabotaging it. And then, going into the point where they say they won't be involved in it. They won't do the work. They had power to keep this from gaining any momentum. They wanted to find people to be on the team that would challenge it or hurt the work. I felt stuck. (TMF 7)

In this case, another White equity leader at Midwest felt silenced by a strong presence and role of Whiteness that existed, despite the challenge she was facing to engage in the protocol of Courageous Conversations:

> That is the first mistake I made, is that I should never have been a truth-teller with this group of people [district and site administration]. They were not trustworthy. And, looking back on it, that was part of the career limiting move—I should not have ever, I should not have spoken my truth. (AWF 20)

The difficulty of doing authentic racial-equity work became quite transparent for numerous staff at Midwest. Unlike all of the participants of color who felt that this work was a part of their personal and professional life, it was not a choice; White staff had a choice to disengage if the work became too difficult.

Choosing to Disengage

Numerous staff members shared their concerns about remaining involved in the racial-equity work because of the personal toll it was taking on them. Two-thirds of the participants shared that they felt fatigued at some point during their work as a racial-equity leader, and some talked about how it might be easier to remain unconscious of this work. One Black female staff member shared,

> It's very uncomfortable professionally for a lot of people and it's uncomfortable for me, especially being only one of a few Black people in the building. I feel like the pressure—the microscope is always on about, okay, well, if I say this, how am I going to impact how somebody feels? I feel like I oftentimes have to be very filtered about what I'm saying, because I think people are going to take it in the wrong context because of how they see me . . . I just can't disengage, no matter how hard it gets. (SBF 18)

This demonstrates a commitment that was quite common among participants of color. Despite discomfort, they remained engaged in the equity work. White participants also showed resilience in remaining engaged, but were often frustrated by the possessive investment in Whiteness that their colleagues demonstrated. One White male shared his frustration:

> We need to be more assertive and not afraid of conflict in pointing out practices within classrooms and within departments that are inherently racist or are not antiracist. If you're not being actively antiracist, you're maintaining the status quo, like I said, you're being racist. So, I struggle with this because I'm not a conflict person, I'm [an educator]. I'm constantly trying to diffuse conflict. But I think we need to do that. (TWM 1)

This educator pointed out something that was a common theme among White staff and staff of color at Midwest—a desire to try to diffuse conflict rather than seek truth. In fact, almost all adults interviewed shared times that they sought to diffuse conflict rather than seek understanding from others that might lead to discomfort. This truth-seeking was often seen as an *ideal* for staff, but a *reality* for student participants. Students saw many of the same inherently racist practices alluded to by staff, but sought to better understand the source of these practices in the moment. Despite this assertive take on antiracism, the viewpoints seemed to come from a place of less judgment than their adult counterparts. One White student leader from Midwest's student antiracist leadership program shared her perspectives shortly after graduation from Midwest:

I think that's the way the math department is set up [to not be very accessible to students of color]. I'm not gonna name names on this one, but there's been a math teacher, and I think you've probably heard stories about this one before—at least I hope you have. But there's this [African American] boy, and he's kind of the class clown, so I understand being a little frustrated with him. And he came in late sometimes. And this teacher would just rain down on him, and she was so angry—visibly and audibly. And then, there was another student who was a White girl, who came in 15 minutes late one day with Caribou Coffee in her hand and no pass—she had been in school earlier that day and had left campus to get coffee. She was not excused. And she came in, and this teacher saw her sit down and didn't say a word, smiled, and continued on. And that may not have to do with race, but for me, seeing her behave toward students of color who were slightly obnoxious versus White students who were slightly obnoxious was so different. And I don't think it was something that she was doing on purpose—at least I hope not, but I think you give these kids labels of being disruptive in class and all these kinds of things and it becomes true to the whole class—most kids never thought twice about the girl coming in late with her coffee. That becomes normalized like the Black boy getting yelled at for his "misbehavior." (CWF 29)

What is striking about this student observation is the way she specifies practices in a classroom and has internalized the knowledge about a deficit model (Solórzano & Yosso, 2002) that many students of color face when coming into the classroom as well as the privileges that White students have when entering a room (Jensen, 2005). Although a common reaction from student participants, adult leaders rarely gave specific examples of either of these manifestations of racial property at Midwest. Another student comment questioned the institutionalized practices at Midwest that may be perpetuating racial inequities:

I see the least racial integration in music and art, and of the academic subjects, it is math. There is something to be said there. Don't they say that math is a gateway to higher level thinking? It seems like you told us that more and more CEOs are looking for people with art and music backgrounds that can think those ways. Why is that [racist practice] happening? (CWF 30)

These sorts of questions were commonplace among student participants. Staff often were looking for answers but had a harder time speaking their truth about what Midwest seemed to value in its programming choices. As mentioned earlier, most White adult participants looked for programming answers that did not address the heart of the problem but shifted students into different settings. Adult participants involved in CARE (Collaborative Action Research for Equity) were the only ones to talk specifically of the need for antiracism work to be done in the core classrooms. One member of CARE talked about how frustrating it was to collaborate with staff on racial-equity work because of their unwillingness to engage. Another staff member also offered a glimmer of hope from a different source:

> I think being involved in CARE team opened my eyes a little bit to how difficult it is to talk to the faculty and people who view [the racial-equity work] as just that latest, new fad in education that's going to come and go. Sometimes it feels like we've come a long way, and other times I think, whoa. I think being involved with that team has helped me reflect on that. How are students modeled antiracism? Our AP classes are disproportionately underserving our students of color, and many of us feel like we are not able to do anything about it. (TWM 1)

Another staff member spoke of a similar feeling of discomfort with staff but offered a glimmer of hope:

> Sometimes I go home at night with a pain in my gut because of the conflict I have engaged in with my colleagues. Other times, it is a deep feeling of guilt because I have not had the conversation with a colleague that I should have—and they just keep hurting kids. I feel the opposite way when I work with students. They want to learn more and their energy for doing antiracist work is infectious. I want to come to school the next day and dive into it some more. (TWM 6)

In both cases, staff members showed a willingness to disengage from work with adult staff because of the discomfort it brought. A common theme throughout my data collection was the feeling that staff could turn this work on or off when they chose to do so. This discomfort often came when they needed to confront Whiteness in the organization.

Struggling With the Definition of Race

All of the participants involved in this study shared a belief that racial-equity work was something that should be a focus of work at Midwest High School; however, a common theme among White male participants was that they struggled with the working definition of race that had been laid out at Midwest. Midwest had adopted the notion that race is primarily a color—an assertion shared by the consultants working with Midwest High School and also something supported by various historical situations in the United States. The lack of consensus among staff members about the working definitions for race and racism (Katz, 2003; Singleton, 2022) caused some confusion and led some participants to question the focus of the antiracist work. Despite a considerable amount of time on the front end of the work regarding the importance of these working definitions, there were participants who saw the focus in many different ways. One White male saw things this way:

> There are few people in this world who are more qualified to talk about math instruction than I am I have a math degree, a bachelor's in mathematics, a master's

in math education. I have many credits beyond that. However, I cannot say that I am the definitive person on math education even though there are very few people who have more education on math education than I do, or mathematics. So, I would say that, although people can come to talk to us about racism, I would say that they're not the definitive answer on what racism is or how to be around it. There could be other underlying factors. (TWM 21)

Throughout my time in the field, I had various conversations with White staff at Midwest who asked why we continued to focus on race. They questioned the definitions of race, racism, and particularly the need to be antiracist rather than colorblind. The lack of consistency among staff in this regard served to maintain racially predictable outcomes. One White female teacher reflected,

> I think the definition has focused primarily on academic impact. How racist practices have brought about the achievement gap, or at least have a role in that. And so, the opposite, antiracist practices would presumably bring about a closing of, an elimination of that achievement gap. So, I think that's kind of been the broader definition—how that has been implemented has been a lot of resources made available so that people could become more aware of and more equipped to start looking at the practices that have to do with the achievement gap. (TWF 19)

This teacher, like many other participants, talked about how they had become more equipped to "start looking at the practices that have to do with the achievement gap," but after 3 years, only a few had taken those tools and put them into practice. Participants shared that there were numerous examples of racism given, but they did not seem to internalize antiracism in the same way. With nothing to replace the racist practices, it seemed more likely that the cycle would not be interrupted at Midwest High School. One student shared her observations:

> I haven't heard somebody tell me, "This is what antiracism is . . ." No that's not true, because in Dare 2 Be Real, we talked about antiracism. But I guess in a classroom setting, we've never talked about that. We talked about race—should say racism—in almost every class. Even in science, like environmental science, we talked about environmental racism. So, race comes up, but I don't think antiracism has ever been defined. I don't think it's been defined to me as a student outside of Dare 2 Be Real. (CWF 29)

Other than in isolated settings, students and staff saw few examples of antiracism to coexist with their much more strongly, socially constructed notions of race and racism as a historical problem. Across all demographics, participants were much more descriptive in their examples of racism than they were in their examples of antiracism.

Being Acknowledged as an Equity Leader

Another theme that emerged throughout the study was the notion of participants gaining power as they were acknowledged as equity leaders by those
who had positional or political power in the Midwest school system. For one
participant, being identified by a consultant was something that gave her a
feeling of perceived power among her peers.

> Gary Howard picked me out of the whole crowd and he and [the district administra-
> tor] had a personal conversation with me about what my background was. And they
> wanted . . . Gary had very specifically said to me that I seemed to be really advanced
> in my understanding of the topic, and where I was, and kind of was just interested
> in who I was and everything. The other leaders were listening, but I was also kind of
> scared about presenting myself and was not pushing too hard. (AWF 20)

Administrative participants all shared some perception of how the role of
Whiteness in other individuals and throughout the system had created a sense
of competitiveness with other White colleagues. They all shared reflections
upon moments in their work as racial-equity leaders that had created tension
in the workplace. One participant recalled how this may have even impacted
her career:

> I was pumped to be a part of the Midwest School District just because of the
> reputation it had. The fact that I got the job with no experience before and then
> getting chosen, then to come and say, "This is my passion, and this is the work
> I want to do. And the very first professional experience I'm having is happen-
> ing." . . . When I look back with 20/20 vision, I think that, then, helped set me up
> for a couple things that happened later on, which, professionally, I was asked to
> be on the DELT (District Equity Leadership Team) when some of my colleagues
> who had been there much longer, were not asked to be on the team. And, later on,
> that caused a lot of problems. I realized that that really pissed Mary off. I didn't
> know that at the time, but that was the first, probably, strike, looking back on
> it, where tension started to arise and there was an impact on me, professionally,
> and on my career goals and where I was going to go just because I was chosen to
> be on that, and she wasn't. So . . . and that history comes out a lot, later in the
> story. But anyway, professionally, just in general . . . I think that professionally,
> being a part of the equity antiracist work was a career-limiting move for me in the
> Midwest School District. (AWF 20)

Administrators, not teachers or support staff, shared some reflection on how
the perception of their equity leadership had an impact on their career. For
teacher and support staff, the acknowledgment of their work as leaders resulted in different reflections and feelings. Those who even acknowledged how
others saw them often felt positive about how their colleagues viewed them as
a resource for either their department or for students. The following example

is reflective of the positive feelings numerous participants associated with collegial affirmation of racial proficiency.

> God knows you don't get affirmation from the kids most of the time, but I think it's the affirmation that there are adults in this building who believe that what I'm doing and how I do it is a safe place for kids to be. Even with the frustration. There are a lot of people whose judgment I value—I really do appreciate it. I don't ask for it, but I get it. (TWF 3)

Celebration of progress in the equity work was something that equity leaders appreciated. Four staff and all five student participants shared stories of conversations with others that encouraged them to keep doing the work. For more than two-thirds of the participants in the study, there was also an indication that they felt conflicted with their need for celebration and their need to maintain the urgency necessary to change the system. Staff at Midwest who followed the protocol of Courageous Conversations on a regular basis shared that they felt that the burden of closing the achievement gaps rested on them. At times, it felt as though there were numerous roadblocks in their path. Participants across all demographics shared their critique of the progress at Midwest High School.

CRITIQUE OF LIBERALISM

Another theme that emerged in the study involved the tenet regarding a critique of liberalism. (See the online appendix for this book at tcpress.com/antiracist-online-materials.) Participants across all demographics provided experiences that fell under this tenet. These dominant ideological assumptions result in a deficit analysis of differences between Whites and people of color. This deficit model can perpetuate the victimization of people of color rather than supporting side-by-side, interracial work to deconstruct paradigms of power asymmetry and unearned privilege afforded to dominant groups (Gorski, 2008; Solórzano & Yosso, 2002). Within this predominant paradigm of colorblindness and meritocracy, a Latina worker's failure to be promoted would be attributed exclusively to individual deficiencies, with factors such as an "old boys club" being ignored or discounted (Gorski, 2008). Even individual acts of racism, such as from a bigoted manager, provide easy detours for those who discount deep-seated institutional racial dynamics as nothing more than a myth (Bonilla-Silva, 2006).

Numerous participants in the study shared their perceptions regarding practices of liberalism at Midwest High School through answers that fell under four main themes: colorblindness, slow progress, structural slowdowns, and the notion of reflection over action. Those themes are discussed in the following sections.

Colorblindness

Liberalism's cautious, colorblind, approach, which in essence invalidates multiple racial experiences (DeCuir & Dixson, 2004), is opposed by critical race theorists in favor of the more aggressive approach of racial consciousness. Race neutrality and the myth of equal opportunity ignore the reality of deeply embedded racial stratification in the United States and the impact it has on quality of life. Participants demonstrated either their own colorblindness or their perceptions of the presence of colorblindness at Midwest.

Demonstrating their own colorblindness, 10 of 30 antiracist leaders did not specifically talk about race in their answers unless probed by the interviewer. Conversely, two-thirds of the participants talked openly about race and about how their consciousness had been raised during the course of their leadership training and committee work at Midwest High School.

Numerous participants, teachers in particular, talked and shared a point of view that argued that staff at Midwest were not often treating students fairly. Some teachers shared that they had often been taught not to notice race. Their immersion in the racial-equity work had taught them the folly of this practice. They had always noticed race, but had not felt permission to talk about what they were noticing and how it was impacting their results with students.

Fourteen participants shared their concerns about how colorblindness was impacting student discipline. A couple of participants articulated how a colorblind approach to student discipline was actually creating more inequities. One teacher commented on the inequity in the context of staff conversations between teachers who are finding very different results from students of color in their classrooms:

> I think a lot of the time, we just focus on, Oh, that kid, man, what a, why's that kid such a jerk? But that kid is doing exactly what they are supposed to be doing in another [classroom] setting. What I'm getting at is that there is some asynchronous quality to the way in which kids are treated in our building, but we don't often talk about it. (TWM 1)

This colorblind approach to student issues was something lamented by most participants of color. Many of them shared concerns about how students were treated by staff at Midwest High School and the accompanying silence among colleagues when faced with subtle and overt racist comments. A number of participants shared that since the school started doing racial-equity work, that they had had their eyes opened to so many more racial inequities in the system. Despite this feeling of enlightenment, all but two White participants acknowledged that they still don't always "see" things through a racially conscious lens unless they are intentional about doing so.

Slow Progress

Many participants were concerned about the pace of change at Midwest High School. Across all demographics, participants shared their perspectives regarding the lack of substantive change in the system that would have benefited students of color. Often, this concern was attributed to a lack of attention to achievement data within the system.

> I certainly see people's awareness level up, and I think it's cool to be in a place where people are talking about it. I don't see the achievement gap closing that much. I don't have the numbers, but I bet if you looked at Black achievement 3 or 4 years ago here it would be pretty similar to today. I don't even know if that is true or not . . . that might be a problem. (TWM 7)

There were also numerous participants who shared concerns about the issues that kept staff from making progress toward racial equity. A few participants shared their concerns about the drama that accompanied many equity-team meetings. Participants alluded to the judgments and arguments among staff that took focus away from what was best for students. One participant shared his perspective:

> One of the things that I think characterized a lot of the equity-team meetings was anger and denial and frustration, rather than move to action, there seems to be lots of conversation about how we judge what people are doing and how we judge where people were, and it felt like we were trying to find ways to not get at the work, but to be able to, you know . . . it all felt like an unconscious avoidance strategy. In retrospect, I look back at some of those meetings and think "What were we talking about?" We had agendas and we had conversations, but did those conversations somehow create a feeling and sense of greater comfort and connection for students of color and the Black students and Black faculty at our school? (SWM 15)

A few student leaders also shared a concern about the lack of coherence with their racial-equity work and the impact it had on their results. Three of five student participants shared how their passion for the work was squelched by a perceived lack of follow-through and a lack of courage by staff leaders. One student shared,

> When I was a sophomore, students from START came into my homeroom and talked about racism with us. It was kinda cool that they talked about it because I had never experienced something like that before. After having some deeper conversations about it in my history class, I was really pumped to be a part of that leadership group my junior year. I liked the meetings, but by winter, I was like, "Oh, we're spinning our wheels a little bit." It seemed like the staff didn't want us to change anything, just talk. (CWF 29)

Another student shared how her passion had been squelched on two occasions as a member of the student racial leadership group at Midwest.

> I was really excited to make a difference and try to eliminate racism at Midwest. I couldn't stop thinking about it. I spent time at home writing curriculum. I told an administrator and one of the advisors about it. They said they would ask me to share it at a future meeting. They never did. When I was invited to be a part of a group that would go to summit and it was all paid for, they said they couldn't send students. It was really discouraging. It felt like they were scared to do anything that might actually make a change in the school! (CWF 30)

Numerous participants, particularly those with positional power in the building or those who were involved in multiple strands of the racial-equity initiative, saw a progression in the work that was more positive. Administrators and a few other equity leaders shared their perceptions that the staff and students at Midwest had become more reflective of their interracial interactions and more conscious of the presence and role of race in teaching and learning. There was a wide range of responses regarding the central importance of conversation and processing to close the achievement gaps at Midwest High School. Most participants recognized the need to engage in focused inquiry, but others wanted more of a move to action. The perception among many staff members and students was that there was a lack of balance between reflection and action.

Reflection Over Action

Many participants shared their perceptions that the leaders in charge valued time to process and reflect on the personal learning that was being forged with the staff and students at Midwest. Some even suggested that the racial-equity initiative took on characteristics of these leaders. For staff and students who shared this learning style, the racial-equity work seemed to be going in the right direction. In fact, a few participants were happy to be problem-solving in a very "gray" area. For those who wanted things more black and white—wanting answers and specific strategies—there needed to be a concerted effort on their part to stay engaged and positive.

At Midwest High School, there seemed to be a balance of action and reflection, but some leaders at the school shared their perceptions that substantive actions were not happening fast enough. Many of the trainings conducted by PEG provided guidelines for action but focused primarily on self-reflection and institutional awareness. This focus was deemed necessary by one of the consultants, who shared his perception that Midwest could not "safely or effectively address racial-equity work until they [dealt] with the dysfunction with their staff" (personal correspondence, 2005).

The work seemed to slow down most often when staff members became concerned about how White staff would react to the racial-equity work. Through the field study, I recall numerous times when we spent the majority of a meeting talking about how to present something without facing the re-percussions of angry White staff members. Staff with positional power was often considered in the process. Staff would reflect on interactions with col-leagues and even those they had overheard in passing. One teacher shared concern about a person with considerable clout in the district trying to slow down the work because of her discomfort.

> I can't help but picture you and the professional-development leader talking over your desks. She's sitting across from you talking about, "Well, how will this be perceived by staff if we bring people of color in and they say things that are un-comfortable? Will it be piling up like when we did that fishbowl kind of thing?" You were constantly trying to defend the pace and vision of the work to those who felt it was too much, too soon. (TWM 24)

Indeed, throughout the first couple of years of intense racial-equity work at Midwest High School, there were a number of people who shared with new administrators that the equity work was being "shoved down their throat" or that they were being "being hit over the head" with it. Although participants in the study were fairly consistent in their belief that the pace and rigor of the racial-equity work had been appropriate, they suggested that various stake-holders at Midwest High School were divided on this issue. While some felt a need to slow down the pace and "do it right," others felt there was no time to slow down while "kids were being hurt" by the perpetual cycle of racism.

PERMANENCE OF RACISM

Implied in the work of antiracism is the belief that racism permeates American life and should not be regarded as an aberration (Delgado & Stefanic, 2001; Singleton & Linton, 2006). Socially constructed racial categories are currently and have historically been a fundamental organizing principle of the U.S. public school system. Individual, cultural, and institutional examples of racism re-flect the racial stratification that has become the fabric of the United States. In a CRT analysis, racism is understood as an ordinary practice and part of the dominant cultural ideology that manifests itself in multiple contexts—in schools, much like other institutions. Race and racism are central and defining factors to consider when attempting to understand individual and group expe-riences for students and staff. Racism affects the course and quality of educa-tion for all students, as it impacts the way people of color and White people experience opportunities, curriculum, enrichment, and social stratification. The permanence of racism suggests that we have all been impacted, consciously or not, by the historical and current practices of racism. Those who do not understand the permanence of racism may find sustained engagement in racial-equity work to be not only redundant but at times invasive of their professional autonomy—which in either case maintains the cycle of oppression.

Throughout my fieldwork and in the response of numerous participants, perceptions regarding the permanence of racism at Midwest High School manifested itself through four main themes: "checking it off the list," looking at data, systemic roadblocks, and addressing the pain of racism. Those themes are discussed in the following sections.

"Checking It Off the List"

Most participants in the study seemed to understand the notion of the permanence of racism within the system. Participants who had been on the site equity team particularly talked of a need to strike a balance with the dichotomy of daily diligence and the need for celebration of accomplishments. There were many who pointed to the substantive changes happening within the system and the challenges they had in keeping colleagues engaged who believed that we had achieved our goals. However, many of these changes actually perpetuated a belief that racism was exiting the system. In truth, it was just as present in the system as it was before the equity team was developed.

One White school leader said during a small meeting that consisted only of White teachers that she believed that "after the work we have done the past two years, we will never have to worry about racism at Midwest High School again." This naivete also translated into complacency among staff after seeing individual accomplishments by people of color within the system. This complacency sometimes turned to anger in response to the push by district administration and particularly some antiracism consultants who were challenging the organization to sustain its momentum in changing the system to help address the needs of Black and Brown students. During my fieldwork, I had a conversation with a staff member with considerable positional power at Midwest. She shared openly,

> I believe that the only reason some people do this [antiracism] work is to keep themselves employed. Haven't you noticed how nothing is ever good enough for them? They are constantly telling us what we need to do next and how things are not good enough. I think Pacific Educational Group actually wants racism to continue so they can keep getting money. We will keep wasting our money on them as long as we believe them when they tell us that racism still exists here. (personal correspondence, 2007)

This belief was not unique to this individual. During one of the focus groups conducted for this study, participants talked about the anger one colleague felt about the "unrelenting nature" of the equity work. Another shared a concern that many teachers had learned to say what the equity leaders wanted to hear so they could "go back to their classrooms and continue the same practices in peace" while perpetuating the cycle of racism at Midwest High School. One staff member remarked that now that the school had a Black principal, it felt like "we [could] relax because we [had] accomplished what we never thought was possible." Although important to celebrate individual accomplishments, this common feeling among many racial-equity leaders created a mentality among many leaders that they needed to move on to the next item to, as one participant put it, "check off their list." A number of participants shared their own perceptions or those of their colleagues that the individual accomplishments of a person of color signaled the end of racism. Upon the hiring of a Black principal, some equity leaders expected more outspoken leadership from the administration. On the contrary, in many ways, things became more subtle. Most participants, when asked to share how antiracism had been defined and implemented at Midwest High School, gave examples from the first year of the equity work at the site. Numerous participants shared that there was a feeling among their colleagues that they had addressed the biggest "racial issues" in the school and would soon be able to move on the "next" initiative. Staff of color were particularly cognizant of this perception. In fact, most of them shared their reluctance to be in front of the staff while directly addressing racial equity. As one colleague shared during a conversation while I was on site,

> I don't need to go out and make any grand statements in front of the staff about my beliefs in equity. You all [Whites] need to engage your colleagues in this so they can actually be comfortable with our [Black] presence. I can sense how uncomfortable it makes a lot of people whenever I open my mouth. (personal correspondence, 2006)

Numerous White equity leaders articulated a feeling of accomplishment when individual events went well and individual students or staff of color had shared something positive. What was not articulated, however, was any vision for how to create a system that would support racial equity and sustainable antiracist leadership. Nearly all White participants pointed to the hiring of Black leaders as an important step in achieving racial equity, yet none of these same participants shared any knowledge of progress for students of color within the system. This was most likely the case because, as one participant put it, "We have done a lot to make students and staff feel good about being at our school, but nothing to make sure that they will have the same chance of success in each classroom." This may be attributed to the few people who had internalized the protocol of Courageous Conversations and a lack of courageous analysis and vision when examining data.

Looking at the Data

The permanence of racism can often be traced to individual counter-stories and examples of the presence and role of Whiteness within a system. At Midwest High School, this permanence could have been measured through various aspects of qualitative and quantitative data. Throughout this period of time, even the most dedicated antiracist leaders and leadership groups rarely spent any time examining the data or asking to see if there were any substantive or negligible changes in achievement or access for students of color. With a few notable exceptions, including discipline data being disaggregated by one administrator and the enrollment of students of color in Advanced Placement classes getting tracked and addressed (something that numerous participants recognized as an area of progress), there was very little data used in decision-making. One participant lamented the lack of data involved in his own leadership experience.

> The attitudes around here have probably changed. I've heard several staff members say, "It's a more comfortable place, I don't feel as threatened, I think the African American students have noticed that, and they're happier, and they say hi to me in the hall and stuff," so people have noticed that the attitude and the atmosphere's changed. I don't have numbers, but I'm not so sure that the gap is closing that quickly. The kids I work with who are failing are still, the vast majority are African American students who aren't making it. Some are [Latinx]. These are the kids that aren't gonna graduate, who are working under their potential, so I still see things like that. There are only five African American students ranked in the top 20 percent of the 10th grade class, I mean, that's the kind of things I see. There's only one African American in this AP class or in that honors section. (SWM 15)

This was a common experience for participants from Midwest. Most staff and students wondered aloud during interviews whether or not there had been any change in student achievement data. After 3 years, all participants did not know for certain whether or not there had been any change, and three discussed that they did not even know who to ask for data on their own students. With the exception of members of the CARE team, staff did not reference their own classroom or caseload data when talking about students. Discussion remained largely anecdotal. As one participant put it,

> I don't see our staff taking any measures to look at data to address student achievement. Rather, there is an anti-data-driven sentiment among many of my peers. They think that looking at student achievement through standardized test scores is racist and I think that is short-sighted and perpetuating the problem. When we don't take responsibility for the "snapshots" of data that are part of testing we throw away a data point on the way to achieving racial equity. Of course, there is a bias toward collecting quantitative data, but we aren't even doing a good job of collecting qualitative data from our students. What if we took time to engage our students regularly in ethnographic study to measure the rigor, criticality, intellectualism, and joy in our curriculum? Wouldn't that be a story that over time could help move our school in the right direction? (TMMM 23)

Systemic Roadblocks

At Midwest High School there were numerous situations that maintained a system of racism despite the presence of random acts of antiracism. Among these roadblocks were scheduling, transportation, hiring practices, and systemic accountability.

A common theme among school personnel was the relative lack of time provided outside of other professional duties to address improved instruction and systemic change. Leaders in the racial-equity work felt a sense of urgency to collaborate with colleagues on changing their practices but shared frustration because of the subsequent resource allocation that was not in alignment with that urgency. All teacher participants mentioned time—either an allusion to their frustration with a lack of time they could devote to the work or approval that administrative leaders had sporadically devoted substantial time for staff to address issues of racial equity in depth. This was a common theme among study participants at Midwest, and one teacher shared his thoughts about the need for focused time:

> What needs to continue is for there to be a range of resources and materials, you know, available to people. What needs to change is for there to be a concerted effort and opportunity created for teachers to collaborate, teachers to be able to integrate these resources into their classrooms, and—I guess that's the part that's missing as well, because sometimes I think we kind of do these in-services, or these trainings sort of on the fly, and expect teachers to pick something and "Oh! I'm gonna try it out in my class right away." But I think it takes more time and reflection for these kinds of things to be integrated in a manner that, that is a sound way of teaching. And particularly with at-risk kids, it's not just, you know, putting on a show in front of them for 1 day because you happened to pick up on an idea that's brilliant and it works great today. But what about tomorrow? It's got to follow up and follow that constant connection with a student. (TWM 5)

Numerous staff members at Midwest believed that the "system" was impeding their progress on closing racial achievement gaps. The isolating nature of education (Dewey, 1988) seemed to be magnified for those who were engaged in racial-equity work. More than half of staff participants wished that administrators would change administrative structures to allow for more substantive talk with their colleagues. Rarely did they share ideas for these changes. A common response focused on a strong perception of what was lacking but little understanding of what would help provide those resources for staff.

> We don't have time for collaboration. We talk and care about having an opportunity for teachers of targeted students to really communicate and try, try to apply consistent practices that you're working on with a given student. Time is important. I don't know to what extent the administrative model or role needs to change. I don't know how it can change; there is a culture in the district. I don't know how—but that needs to be changed. I think there needs to be a more clear expectation and more explicitly stated expectations as to what it is we're trying to achieve and how we're going to achieve it. That's never been clearly stated. (TWF 12)

Throughout the course of this study, racial-equity leaders at Midwest High School shared ideas for scheduling classes and teachers differently. Many formal and informal meetings included discussion about how to cluster students of color and White students in ways that would be most conducive to learning. Often, there was frustration with the inequities of caseloads for teachers. Five participants suggested that a small number of teachers were seen as culturally competent and often had students of color scheduled into their classes while leaving others unaccountable for improving their teaching capacity because of the selective segregation inherent in the system. More than two-thirds of participants suggested that there needed to be an emphasis at Midwest High School on hiring more racially conscious staff—particularly staff of color. The belief of many participants was that a greater collective consciousness could help identify and eliminate institutional racism more efficiently and effectively.

One example of the depth of institutionalized racism in the Midwest system was alluded to by a few participants and was part of an ongoing discussion at one of the equity-team meetings. Students of color were disproportionately late for first-hour class because of a number of factors. One factor that was out of their control was the late busses from predominantly Black and Latinx neighborhoods that were arriving at school 2 to 15 minutes late each day. Some staff shared frustrations with the students and with the free breakfast program that many of these students attended when they arrived at school—often delaying their arrival in class by another 10 to 20 minutes. Upon further review, members of the equity team realized that the practice of the transportation department was to allow drivers to change routes if there was turnover among the drivers. The newest and often the least experienced drivers were often placed on these routes—seen as less desirable than the suburban routes that went through higher-income, White neighborhoods. Students of color were more often subjected to drivers who did not know the neighborhood, had little to no relationship with the students, and therefore were arriving to school later than the other students and busses. Upon realization of this phenomenon, a few participants from the equity team asked to meet with officials from the transportation department. Although the results of this practice were strongly seen as unacceptable, there was only some preliminary change made before the school decided to instead institute a "take back the school" initiative that punished students who were seen in the halls after the bell had rung.

Participants who discussed this situation were divided in their perceptions. While many felt that the accountability was equitable, there were examples of frustration with a lack of effectiveness in addressing the systemic problem that was impacting so many students of color disproportionately.

Students and staff alike were impacted negatively by the systemic roadblocks. Thirteen participants discussed how they were concerned that the progress at Midwest was too slow for them. Most of these participants questioned their ability to sustain their own leadership without some assurance that their discomfort would bring about some results. Discussion at Midwest often led to dialogue or testimony regarding the "pain" associated with racial-equity work.

Addressing the Pain of Racism

For many staff of color, the wounds of racism were something that reopened every time the staff would reengage in conversations about race. There were numerous times when staff of color would share their concerns about the fidelity of the school's antiracism work, and they would challenge the sincerity of White allies in the work. When this questioning would occur, wounds for White staff would manifest in defensiveness, guilt, and sometimes disengagement. The dysfunction among equity leaders at Midwest may have been heightened, but the same themes seemed to be common in multiple areas of the school. More than half of participants shared at least one incident that could be attributed to the pain associated with the personal impact of racism on staff.

In my own experience, I saw these dynamics play out regularly at Midwest. It was common for equity-team meetings and even some staff meetings to feature an airing of grievances—often feelings and beliefs that had not previously been discussed in interracial company. These incidents often produced discomfort among staff and left many equity leaders, particularly leaders of color, feeling more marginalized by the system. One participant of color shared her belief that it might be "better to not do this work at all than to do it this way." When pressed, she explained that "this way" gave a false sense of hope that racism would be eliminated and that White staff would collectively change.

Many staff shared their observations regarding the normalization of racial discourse at Midwest High School. One staff member remembered that when White staff would bring up a student of color in conversation they would often apologize for mentioning race or talk in whispers. By Year 2, racial discourse had become normalized. Seventeen of 30 participants recognized a difference in the way staff talked about race. Many of these same participants also shared perceptions that Whites might be talking about race differently, but their actions and mindsets had not changed as dramatically. Staff and student participants alluded to the pity, guilt, fear, and prejudice that often accompanied interracial dialogue and interactions. Few participants recognized these tendencies in themselves, nor did they share any knowledge of the variety of stages of racial identity that people go through. The following chapter highlights the stages of White identity and identity development for leaders of color and multiracial leaders in the Midwest School District during the 3 years of this critical ethnographic study.

CHAPTER 5

Racial-Identity Development at Midwest High School

Much like the period in U.S. history that bears its name, the Gilded Age of Antiracism at Midwest High School was one that was marked by substantial growth, extravagant displays of individual fortitude, and challenging circumstances that left some staff and students feeling marginalized and exploited. Participant interview responses were full of explicit and implicit references to their own racial-identity development and their perceptions on the racial identity of their colleagues, family members, students, teachers, and peers.

The following section includes a report and discussion of emergent themes pertaining to racial-identity development. It is divided into two main areas: (1) White racial identity and (2) identity development for people of color. In the first section, I use the racial-identity development model of Janet Helms (1994) to address themes of White racial identity. Several clustered themes will be reported and discussed in the context of five of Helms's stages of White racial-identity development. The second section will draw heavily on William Cross's (1978) model of Black racial-identity development. Sixteen clustered themes will be reported and discussed in the context of four of Cross's stages of Black racial identity. The section on identity development for people of color also includes a discussion and report of four clustered themes in the context of multiracial identity, drawing on the work of Renn (2004), who adapted the Cross and Helms models.

WHITE RACIAL IDENTITY

Helms's original model on White racial identity (1984) included five stages of White people's "racial consciousness": contact, disintegration, reintegration, pseudoindependence, and autonomy. Helms (1990) later included a sixth stage between pseudoindependence and autonomy called immersion/emersion, to reflect "the contention that it is possible for Whites to seek out accurate information about their historical, political, and cultural contributions to the world, and that the process of self-examination within this context is an important component of the process of developing a positive White identity" (p. 70).

If one is a White person in the United States, it is possible to exist without ever having to acknowledge the reality that you are White. It is likely that only when Whites come into contact with people of color could Whiteness potentially become an issue. Helms conceptualizes the six stages of White identity into a two-phase process of identity development that includes Phase 1, the abandonment of racism, and Phase 2, defining a positive White identity (Helms, 1990). The first three stages of White identity development fall under Phase 1. The first stage, contact, begins at the first encounter a White person has with a person of color. A White person in the contact stage may or may not engage in individual racism while automatically benefitting from institutional and cultural racism "without necessarily being aware that he or she is doing so" (Helms, 1990, p. 55). One's longevity in the contact stage depends on the quality and quantity of interracial experiences, particularly with respect to racial issues. The second stage of Phase 1 is disintegration, characterized by conflicted and conscious acknowledgment of one's Whiteness.

As a White person's beliefs about race become more conscious, he or she enters the reintegration stage. In this stage, a person who consciously acknowledges his or her Whiteness has to grapple with feelings of guilt or denial that may be transformed into anger directed toward people of color. White people at this stage may be frustrated by the notion of being a part of a racial group rather than just individuals (Tatum, 2008). Many White people never move past the reintegration stage, while others find themselves in a pseudoindependent stage (Lawrence & Tatum, 1997). Here, an individual gains an intellectual understanding of racism as a system of advantage but may not quite know what to do about it.

Stage five (Helms, 1990), known as immersion/emersion, is marked by a recognized need to find more positive self-definition. Whites need to seek new ways of thinking about Whiteness so they are able to move beyond their self-identity in the role of victimizer. It would make sense that White individuals who are presented with examples of other White antiracists might be able to navigate to and through this stage with more ease. The last stage in Helm's model represents the ability of White people to have flexible analysis and response to racial material, data, or experiences. This stage, autonomy, is marked by an increased effectiveness in multiracial settings.

While other models of White identity have been produced in the past 30 years, the work of Helms will be used in this study to provide a model for understanding the data that were collected at Midwest High School. Emergent themes showed strong correlations to five of Helms's identity-development stages. These stages emerged often in the data and were manifested in multiple ways. White participants in this study shared various perceptions that indicated they were moving through a cycle of White identity, not necessarily a linear progression. Participants often showed signs of moving in and out of stages with fluidity. This movement seemed to most often be impacted by encounters with people of color that perpetuated or changed previous notions of their experience or moments of White racial bonding (Sleeter, 2017) that most often resulted in unconscious or intentional disregard toward perspectives outside of their own racial group.

The Contact Stage

The contact stage, often associated with obliviousness to racism and satisfaction with the status quo, was clearly the stage that many individuals associated with Midwest High School were in. Although some White participants shared examples of their movement through the contact stage during the course of my interaction with them, there was no evidence that any of them were in that stage. It is highly likely that the criteria for participant selection impacted the lack of evidence of a contact stage among them. Participants were all leaders in the racial-equity work and volunteered their time in response to my call for participants among the various leaders that could have met the criteria. My exclusion of discussion of the contact stage does not suggest that its relative lack of presence among participants in this study is of no significance. My observations of individuals and groups in the contact stage are discussed in this chapter and my thoughts on this phenomenon will be discussed more in depth in Chapter 6. The following sections focus on discussion and findings of examples of the remaining five stages of White identity development that emerged in the data. These five stages are disintegration, reintegration, pseudoindependence, immersion/emersion, and autonomy.

Disintegration

Once White people realize that they are White, Helms (1994) suggests, the second stage of White racial-identity development is disintegration. This stage is characterized by conflicted and conscious acknowledgment of one's Whiteness. Numerous participants shared examples that seemed to place them into this stage of development.

Examples of the disintegration stage of White identity were present in 27 of the 30 participants. Eighteen of the White participants showed signs of disintegration in their own experiences as a racial leader at Midwest High School. Nine participants shared stories of their interactions and perceptions of others that may have indicated this stage. Many of the 18 White participants who showed signs of a disintegration racial identity also shared perceptions of others who seemed to be in that stage.

In my examination of the data, I looked for instances in which there seemed to be some internal conflict or anxiety provoked by unresolvable or complex racial moral dilemmas. Sometimes these dilemmas manifested themselves in the self-reflection Whites would have regarding internal conflicts between loyalty to a White racial affiliation and a decision to engage in an antiracist action. Other manifestations included a shift from colorblindness to racial consciousness, moments of self-realization that as antiracist leaders they had an obligation to address overt acts of racism and moments of ambivalence toward those who were in other racial groups. Themes of disintegration emerged most frequently in what I have categorized in the following three sections as self-reflection, color-consciousness, and "aha" moments.

Self-Reflection

For the purpose of this study, I have defined self-reflection as the process of examining the impact of personal values, communication styles, belief systems, and personal experiences on one's perceptions of race. This process falls under the status of disintegration in that it can help an individual develop a deeper understanding of racial identity, racial biases, the intersectionality of race with other aspects of one's identity, and internalized racism (Singleton, 2012.

Self-reflection about the impact of race on one's life was one of the most prolific of the emergent themes in this study. Twenty participants, including all but two of the 19 who were White, demonstrated some manifestation of self-reflection about the impact of race on their life. Numerous participants reported that they had become more "aware" about race and the disparities between Whites and students of color during their discussions with the school equity team. Five participants concluded that they had gone through a profound shift in their thinking about race in the 3 years they had been engaged in the racial-equity work. Some participants also reported that their intentional engagement in self-reflection had provided some avenues for improving their antiracist practice. One White teacher shared that self-reflection had led to a very personal experience in his classroom.

> The NSDC [National Staff Development] Conference in Philadelphia and the Beyond Diversity Seminar were experiences that got me realizing that a lot of the things I was putting in the way of progress of this journey fell away once I was able to reflect on the impact of race in my life with other people who were engaging in that reflection with me. And one of the most important things was that I needed to no longer worry about being uncomfortable. And you know, being comfortable is, I kind of realized a real ludicrous standard for life. And you know, I think after coming off a year abroad that was not comfortable, I would have been more situated to be uncomfortable with antiracism. It took the intensity of a seminar like that, engaged with a multiracial group of people to realize that I was the one in my classroom who was uncomfortable with getting my students uncomfortable . . . When I engaged my students in a discussion [about the book we were reading] that is very much about race I realized that kids got very uncomfortable once it was said. It was clear in 2005 that I was, barely ready for this kind of conversation, the kids were not ready for this kind of conversation. There was only one kid in the class who was, and he was a Black kid who had grown

up in the projects in Chicago and had moved to Midwest with his mom. He was in a place to talk about this. (TWM 6)

The discomfort with race felt by White staff and students alike was rarely discussed at Midwest High School before engaging in antiracist leadership development. Engagement in self-reflection by staff led some teachers, like the participant above, to guide students through reflective activities that asked them to explore their own will, skill, knowledge, and capacity to address racism in their school and community. Indeed, many participants discussed positively how they had come to better understand their personal beliefs, styles of communication, life experiences, and the impact those experiences had on their relationships with others, particularly students of color.

The emergence of self-reflection among so many participants at Midwest High School is not particularly surprising because of the emphasis placed on this practice by school administration and by consultants who spell out multiple examples of self-reflection in their protocol for Courageous Conversations. This protocol values self-reflection, particularly an understanding of individual and systemic belief systems about school practice. A handful of participants provided one criticism of the antiracism work at Midwest High School by asserting that there may have been too much emphasis placed on self-reflection by those leading the work. The understanding of racial-identity development by the critical participants is unclear.

Color-Consciousness

If we are living in an age of colorblindness, as some scholars have asserted, (Alexander, 2010; Bonilla-Silva, 2006), then color-consciousness is the antithesis. I define color-consciousness as a racial self-awareness that keeps Whites from using arguments, phrases, and stories that, although often subtle, ultimately justify racial inequities. Within the context of disintegration, color-consciousness is an example of White awareness of race and racism often accompanied by a positive orientation toward engaging in antiracism. Color-consciousness, however, does not necessarily lead to antiracism. It is something that can also lead to more racial alienation, guilt, and fear.

Color-consciousness emerged in the data in a number of ways. Thirteen participants shared examples of themselves moving from colorblindness to color-consciousness while working as racial-equity leaders at Midwest. Twenty-three participants shared a belief or anecdote demonstrating that it was important for individuals and the Midwest "organization" to become more color-conscious. Five participants, all White males, shared their perception that they had personally become more color-conscious but also found themselves to be colorblind in certain contexts—particularly when it came to recognizing institutional racism. Many staff and students shared that they had become increasingly aware of the "Other" in their classrooms. Although most of the participants made reference to their professional life, about half of those who shared their experiences with color-consciousness also shared a personal example. One veteran teacher shared this:

> I'm talking primarily African American and White now. I think the disparity when I travel now—I am aware there aren't many Blacks where I happen to go, which is in Colorado, or on airplanes and I wonder why, and I think 6 or 7 years ago, certainly before we did this work, I wouldn't have paid any attention to that. I think it's my sense now with the presidential election that I can see how people see the candidates differently because of my experiences with antiracism work at school. So, the significance of having a Black man run for president, I think is more significant than having a woman run for president, and more profound in many ways and, I think, could have a great impact on attitudes toward race as years progress. Personally, engaging in this work has had a deep, deep influence on me. I feel, however, that I have not done enough personally to address the issue and don't always know how. (TWM 8)

As staff engaged in the racial-equity work, many shared that they became increasingly more color-conscious. As the quote above suggests, some of them did not know what to do with the new racial awareness—a common sign of the disintegration racial-development stage. All student participants noticed an increase in their own color-consciousness and the color-consciousness of "Midwest High School," as evidenced by some cursory changes to curriculum and a small increase in the quantity of racially conscious curricular examples shared by teachers in the class.

"Aha" Moments

Color-consciousness and self-reflection were often shared to be processes that developed an internal sense of antiracism in participants in the study. While these examples took place over time, many participants also shared what I refer to as "aha" moments. Psychologist John Kounios is credited with the definition: "An *'aha' moment* is any sudden comprehension that allows you to see something in a different light. It could be a solution to a problem; it could be getting a joke or suddenly recognizing a face. It could be realizing that a friend of yours is not really a friend" (*Safire*, 2009). These are the sudden incidents, encounters, or interactions that caused people to change their comprehension of a situation or phenomenon. Within the context of disintegration, "aha" moments brought some staff members from a place of racial obliviousness—the contact stage—to one that was no longer colorblind.

In this study, 12 participants shared examples of "aha" moments. Seven of those individuals shared that those moments were a turning point in their racial-identity development. Three of five students and nine of 19 White participants expressed thankfulness for their "aha" moment, often citing a person or group that helped them understand or experience something about race they had been ignorant about before. One staff member shared the impact that these moments had on him.

> When you have that "aha" moment, whether it's—you know—maybe it's just talking with you about that thing that happened in class, or maybe it was a staff-development thing like a story shared by "my Black colleague" at a CARE meeting. All of a sudden, I look back at what I've done to welcome students at the beginning of the year and realize that I may have been responsible for a bad start for my kids of color. I'm thinking specifically about some of the small group sessions where our CARE team just sat and worked and someone who I don't spend a lot of time with at school says they would do something in a completely different way than I would. It helped me understand a bit more what the student couldn't articulate but was thinking. (TWM 1)

Some staff felt the "aha" moments were important, and one shared that he often wanted to replicate those moments for others on the staff. Some changed their instruction to bring these moments into the classroom. Some students shared examples of interactions with adults or guided by adults in classrooms that led to an "aha" moment but also led to greater self-reflection and color-consciousness. These encounters surely led many into the next stage of White racial identity: reintegration.

Reintegration

Helms (1994) believes that the third stage of White racial-identity development is reintegration. This stage often includes an idealization of one's racial or ethnic group and intolerance of other groups and their practices. After one develops more racial consciousness, some Whites may start to develop perceptions or racial differences that keep them from engaging in antiracism. These perceptions can manifest in words, thoughts, or actions.

Examples of the reintegration stage of White identity development were present in 18 of the 30 participants in this study. Fourteen of the White participants showed signs of disintegration in their own experiences as a racial leader at Midwest High School. Three participants shared stories of interactions and their perceptions of others who may have been in this stage. Seven of the 14 White participants who showed signs of a reintegration racial identity demonstrated a lack of awareness that they had entered that stage or that they were feeling things that could be characterized as reintegration.

In my examination of the data, I looked for instances when there seemed to be denigration or intolerance of groups of color. Sometimes these instances included selective perception of interactions that showed a pattern of negative distortion toward one racial group, including their own. Themes of reintegration emerged most frequently in what I have categorized in the following four sections as (1) White guilt, (2) staff anger, (3) thinking you know, but you don't, and (4) discomfort with staff of color.

White Guilt

One of the hallmarks of White racial-identity development is some time spent in a place of White guilt (Steele, 2003; Katz, 1997). White guilt is a concept that refers to the collective guilt felt by some White people, particularly once they realize they are a part of a racial group that has historically been responsible for racism toward people of color. Within the context of reintegration, White guilt often follows a time when Whites have gone through some sort of color-consciousness development or self-reflection.

White guilt emerged in the data in a number of capacities. Three White teachers shared feelings of guilt during the course of their interviews for this study. They shared that those feelings of racial guilt had developed during the course of their leadership training and still existed at the time of the interview. Two White students shared feelings of guilt that developed during the course of their antiracist leadership experience. All five participants felt that there was something keeping them from being effective as antiracist leaders. This "roadblock" to antiracism was reported to either be time, skills, or courage. One White teacher felt as though there was a standard for culturally proficient teaching that he did not meet.

> I guess I just look at a lot of things I do, and I'm constantly shuffling it, and I think guilt is more the word when I'm looking at this antiracist initiative more than just, "Oh, I really taught that lesson [in social studies] in a really bad way." You know—there's something—I guess it's because I feel this is really important—I feel like it didn't meet the bar. I think the guilt just comes from looking back at different choices I could have made, and how maybe if I would've taken a stand, or corrected a student who had said something [racist] that would have meant something to a student in the class who had been hurt by it, or felt marginalized by it, or didn't feel like I was representing them in my curriculum fairly. (TWM 1)

This "bar" was not set by anyone, but was alluded to by all three White teacher participants—a sense that they were expected to already be proficient in teaching students of color. Some staff felt that this bar was set by people of color who were engaged with them in the work. One teacher commented that a Black colleague would "not back down and accept that I was trying" (TWF 18). Despite feeling that way, she followed a protocol to stay engaged and follow up the next day but still felt like she put her foot in her mouth:

> I remember walking back up to him and he was talking about White privilege and all of the things that Whites get to do that Blacks don't get to do. And I can't believe I said this now, but I said something like, "Well, Black people, they can

always feel like they can dance, and no one's going to laugh at them because they don't look cool [but Whites have to deal with that]." He just blasted me. And, I said, "What? What? That's true!" I've experienced that several times. But, when he expressed and defined racism and privilege, it was helpful to process that you can't be racist if you don't obtain power through your situation. So even though Black people could be racist, negative, or hateful toward White people, they're not racist because they're not obtaining any power for it. (TWF 18)

White participants who shared experiences of White guilt often weaved in and out of stages of White identity. Those who stayed engaged with the people or situations that brought about the guilt shared that they were able to move through it. Those who did not stay engaged were more likely to get negative or angry.

Staff Anger

Staff anger was something that many participants discussed throughout their interviews and group discussions. Equity-team meetings and informal communication between staff members often included concerns or strategies for dealing with staff anger. One equity-team member who did not participate in the study shared with me during the break of our first equity training together that he was so mad "at this asshole, Glenn [Singleton]" that he was either going to tell him to "fuck off" or storm out of the room. What was he so angry about? He had asked the teachers and principals in the room to isolate race during the discussions at their table after the break. Isolating race became a very divisive issue for White leaders at Midwest. At leadership meetings and equity-team meetings, this notion was questioned and sporadically, from 2004 to 2008, led to arguments and visible disengagement by White staff.

Five White staff participants explicitly shared incidents in their interviews in which they had either been very angry at someone or had encountered an angry colleague when discussing racial equity. One White student shared a similar situation in which her questioning of a teacher had led to a perception that the teacher was being made to feel guilty and that it had escalated to anger. She was now uncertain about how to engage other teachers in a discussion about her perceptions of racist practices in their classrooms. One Black participant shared her frustrations with her White colleagues who were complaining about the emphasis on racial equity at Midwest High School. When I said I hadn't heard these particular staff members complain, she replied,

Of course not! You were one of the main leaders out there in front of the work. When would they come to you and say that? They found safe White colleagues to complain to—unfortunately people told me about it and then I would have to sit next to the people who complained. They would say we have too many Black kids in this school now that we started this [racial-equity] work—blaming the work for the change—they would interpret equity to mean that we're not supposed to hold kids accountable who were Black. Now that I'm at a new school, [White] people definitely let the director know how they feel about his actions. And I mean you have some of those attitudes with the White staff everywhere. Yes, I heard it. I'm sure it's not a lot of people, but just to have that come out is like, I don't even want one person to say it—the work was trying to help people get the tools, but they would get so unreasonable and angry! (TBF 24)

Participants suggested that one of the biggest detours that White staff used to derail racial equity at Midwest High School was their anger with decisions that were made to allocate resources in support of students of color. White staff referenced work to desegregate the entrances as something that infuriated a handful of their colleagues. One White teacher suggested that "it really comes out where people stand on equity—to some it was the biggest boondoggle waste of money . . . I see staff divided in our building, completely" (TWM 1). The data suggests that staff anger directed at resource allocation or a perceived favoring of students of color manifested itself covertly and overtly. In addition, it happened when some Whites were confronted with information that challenged their perceived expertise with racial equity.

Thinking You Know, but Don't

At Midwest High School for 4 years, staff of color worked closely with White staff in various racial-equity groups. During this time, interracial conflict arose, often because of strong differing opinions regarding next steps on developing programming for students and staff. Personally, some of my best learning took place when I was challenged by staff of color to reexamine a choice or course of direction I thought we should go in.

Nine participants shared examples of times that their colleagues or their peers felt like they knew what to do to address racial equity but were neither color-conscious nor considering the complexities of a situation. Most of these nine participants shared that this often came out in one of two ways—White staff blaming deficiencies of people of color for inequities in school data and a lack of understanding that their Whiteness plays a role in daily interactions with people of color, particularly students of color. Six of the nine participants who discussed these examples were people of color. For participants of color, "one of the hardest parts of the work is watching well intentioned White people go in and out of paralysis because they keep blaming people of color and often other White people for not getting it." (TMMM 23). Another teacher went on to talk about the potential impact it has on other staff who are moving through the first few stages of White racial identity.

The worst people to work with is the one—is the group that thinks they're doing something positive, but underneath it all, they're not. They're actually doing harmful stuff. They're hard to sway. They don't think they need any growth. They're very confident in how they're working with kids and families in their classes, and they can be hurtful, very hurtful. More hurtful than just the blanket idiot that says something like, you know, just blatantly outrageous, and everybody knows it's bad and we can agree it's horrible . . . they can influence people because this [equity work] is really complicated, totally grounded in a ton of history, culture, and values. [What they are doing] is not good—it makes it really like a tug-of-war with staff that is just learning this stuff and is easily influenced. I'm not a knee-jerk anti-racist. I believe I attempt to get the complexities of equity without saying let's just not kick any of them [students of color] out of class, that kind of thing So, I think sometimes that when I speak to that, that means I'm saying we don't need to work on it. And that group that thinks they get it tends to be the one that mixes that message the most. They say things like, "If they would just, if they would just"—in reference to parents and students of color. They're the hardest to work with because they think they're moving forward. They think they're an active, positive part of the initiative—and that makes them dangerous. Strong word, but true. (TMF 7)

This participant was not the only one to be concerned about the danger of White people who think they know how to help with racial equity but actually do not. Some of them realized that their White colleagues were well-intentioned and felt a need to help them work through their issues. Another believed that some had developed intolerance for people of color by taking an isolated negative incident with a person of color and transferring it to a negative view of that person's entire racial group.

Discomfort With Staff of Color

Student members of the leadership group Dare 2 Be Real at Midwest High School had a mantra, "You've got to get uncomfortable, so you can get comfortable." In conversations about race, that comfort rarely happened with adults outside of their racial affinity groups. Interracial dialogue and interactions increasing led to discomfort for many of the staff. For many Whites, discomfort with people of color became increasingly frequent when they worked closely with them as equity leaders.

None of the participants in the study admitted to having any discomfort with staff of color, but six participants shared stories that expressed discomfort when staff of color had expressed anger or frustration during their interactions. On these occasions, White staff members often couched their stories in a need to get more staff of color in the building. Rarely there was recognition among White staff that the climate for staff of color may be hostile. One participant expressed some feelings of White guilt, as well as a lack of connection between an incident on the equity team and the difficulty with adding more staff of color to the environment at Midwest.

We would get shot down primarily by the women of color who were in the group. And you know, I think that what they didn't accept was that there were some White men on that committee that were racist, not intentionally so, but unintentionally.

And when those men spoke their truth, they were chastised for it. In one instance, one of the Black female members walked out, she was so angry. Now, that didn't help anything or get to the core of the issue when you can't speak your truth. I was bothered by that. Also, professionally, I had this sense when I brought in litera-ture written by African Americans into my classroom, I had this sense that I just couldn't teach it well because I was not Black. And I know that's wrong, because I can teach Shakespeare, and I didn't live in the 16th century. But, you know, think-ing about it professionally, this goes beyond just me, but getting teachers of color in the building, I think, would be significant, really important. I know it's been tried here and the success has been limited, I guess. I'm not really sure why. (TWM 8)

For many White staff, there was recognition that there was a lack of trust in interracial circles at Midwest High School. Some White staff talked about the value that diverse perspectives brought to the leadership groups at Midwest; however, four of six participants who discussed the discomfort had very little patience for working through that tension. One White male believed that this tension contributed to a lack of results for students of color.

We stopped talking about the gap. We stopped talking about kids. It became about why certain people were angry about who said what at what meeting and how it was perceived and whether the principal had addressed it correctly. I thought this out loud, "Let's take 30 people, and instead of investing 15 hours of your life dur-ing the school year in meetings arguing about who said what, invest 15 hours into a Black kid. If all 30 of us did that, maybe 30 more kids would be successful" because I don't know if any of us got success by being angry at those meetings. (SWM 15)

Empathy for the experience of staff of color fell along a wide spectrum at Midwest High School. Although some staff did express that it was not a good climate for staff of color, there were no participants who expressed any desire to find out more about the specifics of those difficulties. The discomfort with staff of color often came when there was tension and kept many Whites from moving beyond the reintegration stage of racial identity.

Pseudoindependence

Pseudoindependence is a stage characterized by an intellectualization of racial issues. Whites in this stage may understand that racism exists and, at least at an intellectual level, that Whites benefit from racism and from unearned privi-leges based on their race. Whites who are pseudoindependent often maintain an intellectualized commitment to their own racial group and show deceptive tolerance of other groups (Helms, 1992). This tolerance may be benevolent, making life decisions to "help" other racial groups because of the pity they feel for them. In my research at Midwest High School, it appeared that Whites in this stage may struggle to see a person of color as their equal instead of someone to be helped because of their historical marginalization in society.

At Midwest High School 24 of 30 participants had responses that I categorized within the pseudoindependent stage of White racial identity. Fourteen White staff members expressed perceptions or made statements that suggested that they were either currently in or had spent time in the pseudoindependent stage of White identity. A number of participants of color shared perceptions of Whites who seemed to be operating from a pseudoindependent status.

In the following sections, I discuss the presence of pseudoindependence within the data from Midwest High School. I looked for phrases or perspectives in the interviews that indicated that participants may have been in the pseudoindependent stage. Pseudoindependence also emerged in the data as participants talked about their experiences with staff, students, and family members. I have organized my discussion of this stage of White racial identity according to three categories: awareness of multiple strands, wanting strategies, and needing inspiration.

Awareness of Multiple Strands

Whites at this stage of racial identity started to intellectualize the racial-equity work at Midwest High School. Although one may be further developed in their racial-identity development and understand the complexity of the racial-equity work, White people at this stage demonstrated at least a basic understanding of the need for systemic change if there were any hope of meeting achievement and engagement goals for all students. At times, this awareness emerged as Whites tried to find easy answers for eliminating racism. Other examples included a belief that this work was the "right thing to do," but rarely went beyond theoretical solutions or a lamenting of abstract problems.

Eighteen participants demonstrated some aspect of the pseudoindependent stage of racial identity regarding an understanding of the multiple levels and strands of racial equity to be addressed at Midwest High School. Twelve of these 18 shared their frustration with colleagues or peers who were going through pseudoindependence. Many of these same participants also demonstrated examples of their own presence in that stage of racial identity. Many White people shared a frustration with their own lack of knowledge or skill to be an effective leader. They rarely discussed how they could be a White ally to people of color or to their White peers. Six White teachers and two White students shared their frustration with people who had either explicitly or implicitly expressed their practice of colorblindness. One teacher shared her reaction to a colleague.

> I would hear people say things, how they're colorblind and we have our own Midwest culture and if the [Black] kids can't adhere to it, then they shouldn't be at our school. And I would just want to blow, and I didn't, but I didn't say much of anything [in response] either. Just hearing that and letting it play out and having those same people interacting with me on a daily basis. I realized just how

many perspectives there are and how there's very many intelligent people in our school. And I thought, "Okay, I don't have to do this all. This isn't all on me. There's other people that are saying some great things, really deep things that are bringing all of us along no matter what stage we're in." The reading that I've done has been just huge. I've read so many books. I mean I've got two whole bookshelves full of books on racism and antiracism and teaching all that. (TWF 18)

Despite the "two whole bookshelves" of racism books, the teacher struggled with the practice of Courageous Conversations About Race with her peer. There is clearly a moral outrage at the racism of the colleague, as well as an understanding that this person may be in a different stage of racial identity. As characterized by many Whites in this stage, there is also a bit of a disconnection between the theory, awareness, and practice. This awareness and frustration often emerged when staff talked of their peers in different stages and when talking about their need for culturally responsive or antiracist strategies.

Wanting Strategies

The majority of the White antiracist leaders at Midwest High School expressed a desire to learn culturally responsive strategies. This desire was often couched within a deep yearning to close achievement gaps or increase one's effectiveness in interracial situations. Despite the good intentions, desire for strategies often dismissed the permanence of racism and the need for deep systemic change. The desire for strategies also suggests a hallmark of pseudoindependence—the belief that there must be a checklist for countering racism. Many White staff members and students often asked the question, "What do we do now?" when faced with a growing awareness of systemic racial inequities. One participant shared a conversation he had with a friend and colleague at Midwest in reference to the seemingly unsuccessful closing of racial achievement gaps at Midwest. He shared that his friend told him that "people are tired of theory. We want to go beyond something that is just motivational. Tell us what to do" (TWM 8).

Nine participants—six staff members and three students—talked about their own desire for specific antiracist strategies during their time as antiracist leaders at Midwest High School. Two of the participants—staff of color—shared their frustration with Whites who were "constantly" asking for strategies. They wanted Whites to realize that it would take constant struggle and personal commitment to combat racism, not a list of "prepackaged strategies" (TBF 24). Many of the White antiracist leaders described their personal struggle to stay engaged in racial-equity work. Six of the participants shared that they were a bit disillusioned by the lack of specific strategies. Through informal conversations throughout my 3 years in the field at Midwest High

School, numerous equity-team participants who did not respond to an invitation to be a part of this study also shared their desire for strategies, while acknowledging the belief that there is no "silver bullet" for achieving equity. Many of them shared a desire to stay engaged in the work but struggled to do so because of a lack of specific strategies. Often, this seemed to be a code used to describe one's lack of will in researching or implementing theory into practice. White "will" often came out stronger directly after time with inspirational speakers or group experiences.

Needing Inspiration

As noted in the previous sections, an individual experiencing pseudoindependence gains an intellectual understanding of racism as a system of advantage but does not quite know what to do about it. The lack of knowledge about what to do with this new awareness can become paralyzing for Whites who do not want to experience the fear, pity, or guilt associated with the journey to the pseudoindependent stage. They may want to find others who will either tell them what to do or help them feel good about their commitment to antiracist leadership.

Seven participants in this study shared their need for inspiration. One White participant, referencing a conversation with a colleague of color, said that he felt like the group needed to "go to church"—to get a spiritual revival of will to do racial-equity work. Indeed, for many Whites, the need for inspiration was strong. All seven of the White participants who mentioned this need discussed it on multiple occasions. They mentioned the desire for more-frequent meetings, motivational speakers, training sessions and workshops, and knowledgeable experts who were going to help them feel better about their work as antiracist educators. One participant linked his mutual need for strategies and inspiration:

> I want two things. I want to be motivated by somebody who's really with it, but I also want tools in my toolbox. I want both. And it doesn't necessarily have to be the same person, but I want both and I want it to be all staff. I want somebody to come tell me, "I found something that works. It may not be the silver bullet, but I found something that helps." That would get me excited. (TWM 6)

Many of the White people at Midwest High School longed for inspiration from experts, particularly people of color, from outside the organization. Despite much training from experts who strongly suggested that staff, students, and parents in the organization needed to collaborate to make the most substantive change, White leaders often wanted to hear more motivational speakers. Some White leaders at Midwest suggested that their work with consultants from Pacific Educational Group and district or regional meetings were essential to their continued engagement as leaders in the work. Many of them hinted that this exposure would not only provide an "aha" moment that might help them become more interracially effective but hopefully lead to a more positive self-definition of their own Whiteness.

Immersion/Emersion

White people who are in the immersion/emersion phase of White racial identity often seek new ways of thinking about Whiteness. Whites often want to find ways of thinking about their race that take them beyond the role of victimizer. This seeking can be active or passive but is often fueled by a desire to find more positive self-definition.

Numerous Whites at Midwest High School demonstrated their being in the stage of immersion by actively seeking out alliances and partnerships with White people who were visibly engaged in antiracist leadership. Throughout my study, 23 of 30 participants shared expressions of White racial immersion. Sixteen of these 23 participants shared examples of being in this stage of development. Seven participants shared stories and recounted discussions with others who appeared to be in this stage of racial-identity development.

Through my analysis of participant responses and documentation of work in the field, I looked for examples of Whites who had not necessarily demonstrated consistent effectiveness in interracial settings but expressed a desire to have a positive influence on racial equity from their place as a White person. I also looked for themes that emerged from responses. Themes of immersion emerged in two main areas discussed in the following sections: critical White allies and dichotomy of individual/institutional.

Critical White Allies

Students and staff leaders at Midwest High School started to develop a critical eye toward White staff members whom they perceived to be operating with inequitable practices. This critical view often manifested in a disdain for White staff who were not holding students of color to the same standards as their White peers. One staff member discussed her perception of other staff members relative to her own actions and comfort with equity.

> You know, we've got a lot of paraprofessionals who just stand around and don't tell kids [of color] what they need to do. And I don't know if their perception is that they don't have the support in the office that they need, or what. But I think we definitely need to look at that. I mean, if the paras need to be getting a consistent message then we need to do some training so they get a consistent message of support . . . and that's just a frustration of mine because between third and fourth block, I get my blood pressure going up because some folks are standing, doing nothing, and the rest of us are working hard. I think there are a lot of good minor tweaks that really could be done around here that would make the tardiness

issues, the attendance issue—you know, there are a lot of people who are afraid
to walk up to a group of kids [of color] and tell them to get moving to class, and
I don't really have a problem with that. (TWF 9)

This statement suggests an awareness of the different stages of White identity development and the necessity for consistently high standards for all
students regardless of their racial background. This place of judgment also
demonstrates a not yet fully realized understanding of how to effectively be a
White ally to these colleagues. Sixteen participants "judged" a White peer or
group of peers at some point during their interview. Rarely did any of these
participants share constructive examples for how to develop rapport with
these White peers. Five of the 16 participants acknowledged moving through
a stage of judgment toward colleagues that had dissipated with a more positive
image of their own Whiteness. For all five of those participants, this shift was
accompanied by a growing awareness of their own racial-identity development. One participant summed up her experience in the immersion stage:

> The impact on me personally and professionally is intertwined. Personally, I feel
> like it has given me . . . it has helped me to move forward in my identity as a per-
> son of race. It has been really interesting to learn so much about racism and the
> stages of being a racist or being an antiracist or a White ally and all of that. When
> I think back to where I was 3 years ago or even more when we started with PEG,
> how I was feeling about being a White person and how I feel about it now. It's
> different. And then as we went into it, how I felt with my colleagues, who I didn't
> think were as far along the road as I was and the anger I felt toward them—and
> how I feel toward them now—I feel like I've moved—and yet, I know I'm always
> going to be a White person. And there's nothing I can do about that. I used to
> feel like, "Oh, I wish I wasn't White because . . ." I had this guilt associated with
> it. "Don't blame me for this and that because I didn't do it." I feel like I under-
> stand all that now. And I don't anymore feel like I wish I wasn't White or wish
> I was Black or wish I was something else. I don't feel that way anymore because
> I realized that I have a job to do. Being a White person and having power, there
> are things I can do to help our racist society, particularly to help in our school.
> (TWF 18)

This passage illustrates some characteristics of White autonomy (Helms,
1990) and also an awareness of this participant's "journey" in relation to others
in her racial group. She realizes that she has a job to do but does not necessarily understand how to forge substantive relationships with Whites who may be
operating from stages with which she no longer wants to personally associate.
As with many of the participants who demonstrated characteristics of the im-
mersion/emersion stage, she understands what she wants to be but struggles
to forge positive relationships across stages without judgment, something she
also acknowledges. The sophistication associated with this awareness was present in all 16 of the participants as they shared their own critical reflections on

interactions with their White peers and on the presence and role of Whiteness in their own professional and personal life.

Dichotomy of Individual and Institutional

The racial consciousness of participants in the immersion stage of identity development reaches a level of sophistication that helps them see the complexity of racism. This complexity includes an understanding of different levels and models of racism that include the presence of both institutional and individual racism. As Whites in this study tried to find ways to move beyond the role of victimizer, many of them shared their thinking about how to address both of these issues, both personally and professionally.

The dichotomy of individual and institutional racism emerged in interviews with 22 of 30 participants. Seventeen participants shared a specific understanding of the existence of both of these strands of racism. All 17 of these participants shared an understanding that individual and institutional racism needed to be addressed. Fourteen participants shared examples of how both of these issues had been addressed in training at Midwest. Five of these participants demonstrated an understanding of the intersecting practices of individual and institutional racism at Midwest High School. A few participants connected individual complacency with individual acts of racism to the permanence of institutional racism at Midwest. One participant summed up his thinking like this:

> I think we have been seeking out practices within the building that are inherently racist and not only put out individual acts or people, you know, that are racist. I think we're trying to battle whole systems here—policies, rules, and ways of doing things that we've traditionally done. So, I think that's one way in which we've tried to be antiracist. I think it has put out to people that maintaining the status quo is inherently racist, in and of itself. I've picked up on that, and if others have not, I think that has been put out there. We're definitely trying to get people to understand the achievement gap, getting them to understand some of the reasons behind it, getting them to understand White privilege. (SWM 2)

As suggested by this participant, Midwest's antiracist training had included at its core a focus on helping people understand the importance of systemic and individual acts of antiracism. This awareness often asked a predominantly White staff to recognize their privilege and understand the systemic roots of racially predictable achievement. Very few adult participants shared specific examples of antiracism that were used to address systemic racism. All student participants found that their leadership work had allowed for antiracist action and learning; however, White student participant responses mirrored their adult counterparts as they demonstrated a consciousness regarding the need for individual change and systemic reform, without much ownership of either. One student participant believed that her antiracist leadership experiences at Midwest had been positive, but she wanted more.

> I think all of the equity initiatives at Midwest High School to promote antiracism, the ones that exist, are very confined to Midwest High School. As someone who just graduated and is going to college, I would like more resources to bring what I've learned to my next community that I'll be in. So, whatever incarnation of Dare 2 Be Real that we have should be giving those students who are graduating tools to use while they are in college and ways to start discussions and groups or clubs or whatever. (CWF 30)

As demonstrated by this quote, an intellectual understanding for some Whites was present in the reflections on their antiracist work at Midwest. However, there was often a lack of autonomy when it came to one's own responsibility in antiracism. This blending of theory and practice is something that will be discussed in the culminating section on White racial-identity development at Midwest High School.

Autonomy

Helms (1992) refers to autonomy as the stage of White racial identity that represents a culmination of the White racial-identity development process. A person incorporates the newly defined view of Whiteness as a part of personal identity and an informed positive socioracial group commitment that may also be coupled with increased effectiveness in multiracial settings. Whites in this stage of identity development may intentionally avoid life options that require participation in racial oppression—an indication of an increased capacity to relinquish the privileges of racism. There is often a strong correlation between one's awareness and one's actions in interracial and intraracial settings.

At Midwest High School there were multiple examples of White racial autonomy that emerged in the data. Twenty-five of 30 participants alluded to their own experiences or the experiences of others that could be characterized as autonomy. As Lipsitz (1995) asserts Richard Dyer's suggestion that "White power secures its dominance by seeming not to be anything in particular" and later quotes Richard Benjamin by parlaying that ". . . to identify, analyze. and oppose the destructive consequences of White racism, we need 'presence of mind.'" My identification of White racial autonomy in the data was based on examples of participants exhibiting this "presence of mind" and an awareness of the impact of racism on themselves and their surroundings. Within the responses of the 25 participants who explicitly or implicitly addressed autonomy were more than a hundred individualized examples that included heightened racial consciousness, awareness of self and group racial identity, and other factors that could be characterized as the autonomy identity stage. I separated these examples into three categories, which encompassed the emergent themes. These themes, addressed in the following sections, are sharing power, believing in the work, and personal and professional connections.

Sharing Power

Conscious and deliberate action is necessary to break a cycle of oppression. As stated in a previous section, the permanence of racism maintains a cycle of marginalization and the dominance of White perspectives and power. This power can be shared only when Whites are aware of their own privilege and are willing to make space for perspectives from people of color. This does not suggest that people of color cannot gain power without the help of Whites, but in the context of White identity development, the sharing of power is a crucial part of being a White ally—a component of White racial autonomy alluded to in the literature.

Fifteen participants in this study shared examples of their own experiences with the sharing of power across racial groups. For some, this sharing of power may have included intentional practices to partner with parents of color or to incorporate the voices of students of color into their classroom curriculum. For others, it may have included a willingness to defer one's own perspective on addressing a systemic inequity for one from a Black colleague that may have, at first, seemed strange or counterintuitive. Thirteen participants shared examples of collaboration with students that involved empowerment of Black and Latinx students. For many, like in the example below, training about racial identity and culturally responsive teaching led to a growth in participant capacity to work interracially:

> It has helped me feel more empowered and, in turn, I have shared that power with others because the feeling you sometimes get when you're working with students of color is that you are not connected with them. You love them. You like them, but they are still depressed and frustrated [about school]. And so, I went through this stage where I felt that with certain students, just sort of like I had no control and no power to do anything to help. But, after working with the equity team, I realized that you just sometimes have to look at things from a different perspective and try different approaches—giving up is not an option. I mean, you can always try something different. I think that being authentic and real with our students is important . . . being aware and allowing space for students of color to express what is really going on is something that this team has helped me grow in my classroom. I have learned that antiracism is about sharing my privilege. (TWF 19)

White participants often talked about what they had learned in their collaboration with others on the equity team. This often translated into a renewal of their commitment to empower students, particularly students of color, in their classrooms. Rare were examples of power-sharing between colleagues or for that matter, adults, in general. Only two White participants explicitly stated that they had gained perspective from other staff of color, while two others shared examples of the positive impact of working with parents of color. For those who positively acknowledged these relationships, there was always a quick connection back to the impact of interracial adult collaboration on students, such as in this selection:

> So much of this work becomes about semantics. A certain realm of semantics might be the White world. Rather that striving to eliminate the achievement gap, I would rather have us say, "We are going to make sure that our students of color are highly successful," because that is proactive in our work with students of color. I think we could be bolder, and I wonder sometimes about why more of us don't go to students and say, do you feel that this school is antiracist?—rather than us just say we feel it is. My conversations with Black colleagues have helped me consider ways I could be more antiracist and change some of my own behaviors to respond to the needs of more Black and Brown students. (SWM 15)

Participant responses suggested an awakening of racial consciousness among some White participants who felt as though their collaboration with people of color had helped them become more interracially proficient. This consciousness was often accompanied by a reflection on one's beliefs about race and the systems that are maintaining a racial hierarchy at Midwest High School. In the case of one participant, this awakening was very specific and created a profound shift in personal choices, professional practice, and belief systems.

> I have been at Midwest High School for nearly 3 full years now. Prior to my work at Midwest High School, I had had no antiracism training. I read nothing on antiracism. Everything that had been brought to light through Glenn Singleton and his work and the equity team's work internally was fresh to me and enlightening in a lot of ways and difficult for me to face initially in light of a whole new position. Personally, it was jarring and has led me to shift my perspective on—my perception of race, my role in my community, the decisions I make on the most infinitesimal level, to the large decisions I make as far as my career and the purchases I make. I mean, these are very large decisions I make rooted in that. And professionally, within the classroom I push myself and challenge myself to view the classroom from the perspective of all students. As difficult as that is—it can be in a classroom of 38—my basic challenge is to see the classroom, and the environment, and the work from the perspective of each individual student. Which I think at its most basic level is equity and antiracism. (TWM 4)

White participant beliefs about the need for antiracism were either reinforced or developed due to their collaboration with people of color and the sharing of this power in various settings. Six White participants shared explicitly that their beliefs in racial-equity work were affirmed and deepened by their collaborative work with people of color. These beliefs and other deeply personal connections to racial equity are addressed in the following sections.

Believing in the Work

All participants spoke of their commitment to racial-equity work at some point during the course of the study, and all but one of the White participants shared examples of their belief in the urgency and importance of antiracism at Midwest High School. This belief system often went beyond a professional commitment to a set of core values that set them apart from others at Midwest High School. Participants talked about the moral imperative of antiracist practice; the spiritual awakening that accompanied their collaboration with staff, parents, and students of color; and their faith in the process of Courageous Conversations about race that were introduced by the Pacific Educational Group.

Teachers spoke highly of their beliefs in the racial-equity work. Recurring themes included time spent outside of the school day and a personal commitment to developing the will, skill, knowledge, and capacity to be an effective antiracist leader and White ally. Throughout my time at Midwest High School, a growing number of White teachers, support staff, administrators, and students expressed their desire to engage more deeply in racial-equity work because of their belief that it was the right thing to do. While no one explicitly shared a contrary belief system, many White staff and White students at Midwest showed apathy and indifference toward antiracism. Believing in the racial-equity work was something uniquely explicit in many participant responses. This belief system came out in participant responses about the effort necessary to engage in antiracism.

> So I would love it if hands were getting more dirty and if people were going above and beyond and saying, "I know I'm not getting paid for this, I know I'm not going to get paid to stay after school once a week for an hour to work with African American students who are underachieving, but I'm gonna do it. I'm gonna do it for no pay, because it needs to be done." We need to close the gap. We have got to get them through no matter what it takes. And doing it—it's hand-dirty kind of stuff I feel like doing. (SWM 2)

This person suggests that "dirty hands" and selflessness are an essential part of getting racial-equity work done effectively. This is indicative of participants who believed that racial-equity work required making sacrifices and putting in extra time outside of their required duties. This focused devotion to racial equity in the workplace was something that one participant said helped complete his personal development.

> Antiracism issues have always been so important to me and have been something that is a big part of my life. Our work at Midwest High School has made it—as

far as my career—something now that completes me. As far as antiracist curriculum in my professional life, it has always been something very important to me because it has always been something that is kind of at the forefront of what I try to do, that I'm made aware as I'm teaching. This equity-team work has actually made it kind of my focus in a sense. It has helped push me to the next level of equity for all of my students. (TWF 12)

Involvement on equity-related leadership teams was seen by many White participants as something that linked their professional practice to something personal. This was a profound connection for many participants and is discussed in the next section.

Personal/Professional Connections

For a few White participants at Midwest a commitment to antiracism came long before their work as an equity leader at the school. A merging of personal and professional practices regarding racial equity was commonplace among participants of color but more of a revelation for White participants in this study. Many of them saw antiracism as a conscious choice they were making—one that impacted their life choices and began to redefine who they were.

Twelve White participants gave specific examples of the connections that had been made between their personal and professional lives as racial-equity leaders. All White student participants, all White administrators, and more than half of White support staff and teachers shared stories that indicated that a family conversation, personal relationship, or encounter outside of work had influenced their decision to engage in antiracism at Midwest High School. These connections often happened before their tenure as a leader. In some cases, personal experiences had constructed mental models of race, racism, and antiracism that were present in the professional work of White leaders at Midwest.

> I lived in the city, and I now work with very highly concentrated populations of students of color, but most of what I have learned about people of color before I became a teacher came from movies, music, and literature. I understand that the media shaped many of the stereotypes that play like tapes in my head. I believe that my relationships with other people of color, coupled with an intellectual curiosity and passion for social justice that was nurtured by my family, has helped me make more than a superficial effort to reach out to kids who are marginalized. I see this racial-equity work not just as work that we must do, but a commitment I must make to how I live my life. As a White male, I must use my privilege to work side by side with people of color to eradicate the racial predictability of achievement in my school. I realize that this will not be as effective unless I consciously make choices to grow my own will, skill, knowledge, and capacity as an antiracist leader. (TWM 20)

A heightened racial consciousness was a common hallmark of participants who expressed strong racial connections between their personal and professional lives. Another aspect of White racial autonomy, this racial consciousness, coupled with a commitment to antiracism, was often linked to one's understanding of the intersectionality of race within other aspects of identity. For some, a strong sense of ethnic identity helped one get a clearer sense of one's race. For others, gender discrimination helped them feel a kinship to people of color and understand the varied levels of privilege in various aspects of their identity. For some, it was an acknowledgment that they were happy to be a part of a system that was working toward antiracism because they recognized that not only their heightened consciousness but also systemic support were necessary for their continued development and success as an antiracist leader.

> I'm a huge fan of the district's attempt and the school's attempt to do this—to be forward-thinking about antiracism and just be forward-thinking about where this school is going. Personally, for me, I feel like antiracism at Midwest is really positive on two levels. Level one, because it's something that I personally feel is important outside of school, antiracism outside—you know, just in communities, or whatever, so I'm a big fan of that integration—and it requires me to think more about being White on my own level. I'm also gay, so on the second level I understand the notion of discrimination, and the notion of groups that are [in the minority]. Not that it has anything to do with race, but understanding that feeling—I understand inequities around it, and I'm about pushing a group out of inequitable practices. Just as with anyone who is White, I can be just as racist, or have racial inequities in mind, so it's good to have a collaborative way to address them—to learn patience, to learn techniques, new ways about thinking about things—if I'm personally developed, that only helps me professionally. (TWM 16)

Although not fully named, this chapter focused on the nadir of "White paralysis" throughout the leaders' experiences at Midwest High School and the inability to act or function for antiracism, a devastating condition that led to the dismantling of racial-equity work at Midwest High School. It is characterized by one or more of four conditions: (1) guilt stemming from leaders' real or perceived lack of effectiveness to increase performance for students of color, (2) fear that their failures might be perceived as racist by parents of color or as an exposure of cultural incompetence by their colleagues, (3) pity toward students of color because of the growing awareness of institutional and cultural racism that seemed out of the leaders' control, or (4) blaming particularly directed toward other White people who were considered more unconscious than the leader going through paralysis. All of these conditions that sparked "White paralysis" pushed many staff to disengage from any culturally responsive or antiracist strategies and, instead, return to familiar racially unconscious behaviors. This return to unconsciousness was a common response among White leaders who were engaging in antiracism for the first time. Leaders of color operated alongside "White paralysis," as they worked in desegregated environments. Working with White peers who were experiencing paralysis led to isolation within the system for leaders of color as well.

All White participants I interviewed and nearly all with whom I had contact during the course of this 3-year study shared stories or reflections that suggested they had, in word and deed, moved into or had wanted to be perceived as falling within the second stage of White racial-identity development (pseudoindependence, immersion/emersion, autonomy), but nearly all White participants, regardless of age, gender, or position, shared reflections that suggested they had moved into Phase 1 at times during their work in racial equity. Whites in this study often moved fluidly through a cycle of White identity, suggesting that racial encounters and increased or decreased consciousness may move them forward or backward in a short period of time. I will discuss that cycle more in the final chapter. The following sections address emergent themes relating to racial-identity development for people of color.

IDENTITY DEVELOPMENT FOR PEOPLE OF COLOR

Cross (1991) has worked to critique his own work on identity development by suggesting that his research as well as that on Black racial identity would benefit from longitudinal studies, the examination of the existence of overarching racial-identity constructs and an acknowledgment of multiple nationalistic identities (Worrell, Cross, & Vandiver, 2001). This section of the chapter delves into that.

It is important to note that in the Cross model for racial-identity development, the process is ongoing, often occurring in cycles. After someone "reaches" a stage, he or she will return to a former stage as a result of encounters with racism. Such encounters perpetuate the marginalization of people of color and have a profound impact on their identity. Updates of the Cross model have addressed the discovery of a multiculturalist racial identity (Worrell, Cross, & Vandiver, 2001). In the original model (Hall, Freedle, & Cross, 1972), the "internalized" individual was described as focusing on things other than himself and his own ethnic group. The revised model (Cross, 1991) modified this stance to say that internalized individuals give "high salience to Blackness," and this salience can leave "little room for other considerations," as in the case of Black Nationalists (p. 210). The multiculturalist racial identity falls somewhere between these two notions and was not hypothesized until the early 21st century (Renn, 2001).

Although Cross describes five stages of identity in his model, only four will be discussed in this chapter. The preencounter stage (Cross, 1991) was not in evidence among participant responses. This is most likely due to the experience and age of those who took part in this study. Cross refers to the preencounter stage as one wherein the African American has absorbed many of the beliefs and values of the dominant White culture, including the notion that "White is right" and "Black is wrong." Though the internalization of negative Black stereotypes may be outside of his or her conscious awareness, the individual seeks to assimilate and be accepted by Whites and actively or passively distances him- or herself from other Blacks (Tatum, 1993).

In the following sections, I will discuss emergent themes that are associated with racial-identity development for people of color. Discussion of the encounter, immersion/emersion, internalization, and internalization-commitment stages (Cross, 1991) will be occur through the report of clustered themes that demonstrate aspects of these four stages of identity. The section concludes with emergent themes regarding multiracial identity development (Renn, 2008).

Encounter

This phase of racial-identity development is typically precipitated by an event or series of events that forces the individual to acknowledge the impact of racism in one's life (Tatum, 1993). For example, instances of social rejection by White friends or colleagues (or reading new personally relevant information about racism) may lead the individual to the conclusion that many Whites will not view him or her as an equal. Faced with the reality that he or she cannot truly be White, the individual is forced to focus on his or her identity as a member of a group targeted by racism (Cross, 1991).

Ten participants in this study identified themselves as people of color. Among these participants were six who identified as Black; two, as Asian; and two, as multiracial. All 10 participants shared examples of their own experiences in the encounter stage. White participants and participants of color discussed examples of students, family members, or peers who had been going through or were going through the encounter stage of racial identity. I characterized 31 individual responses, a few of which were multiple examples from the same participant, in the encounter stage. I included any examples in which people of color acknowledged the impact of racism on their own life and in which Whites or people of color shared their perceptions on how racism had impacted someone they knew. Participant responses to encounters fell into three main themes: (1) pain of racism, (2) acts of racism, (3) acknowledging assimilation. These three themes are discussed in the following sections.

Pain of Racism

Being the target of racism can be painful. As evidenced by the responses of many participants in this study, that pain can have immediate and long-lasting effects. Student participants talked about encounters with their peers and with teachers who had engaged in various forms of racism. Whether intentional or unintentional, the impact of racism is very real for people of color at Midwest High School. Four of six Black participants talked about the emotional impact of racism on their life. They shared examples of racism they had encountered at Midwest High School.

For most participants of color, the pain of racism had influenced their subsequent interactions with White people. Two-thirds of Black participants felt a need to understand the motivation behind White actions at the school before fully engaging in partnership with those White peers or colleagues in racial-equity work. The two Black student participants did not share that same need. They both were more inclined to trust White peers and colleagues as long as their actions were authentic. All six Black participants and many of the other participants of color who had experienced racism described an inner strength that helped them get through their pain. Often, this inner strength seemed to help participants stay engaged in antiracist leadership.

> Let's start with our equity work. Equity's been fine all along. There have been points where I did not think I could handle it because [pain of racism] is in me. It hurts. You know, I get emotional about it. At one point, the principal wondered if I should step back for a while. Nope, nope, nope, nope. I cannot do that. I just can't give up. I can't give up. If I give up, who is going to stay engaged? (TBF 14)

Participants of color discussed their pain in the context of their engagement in antiracism. Many of them saw the pain of racism as something that was undeniable when engaging in racial-equity work. Participants often acknowledged the permanence of racism in our society and that subsequent acts of racism would happen whether or not they engaged in the school's equity work.

Acts of Racism

Participants of color at Midwest High School had a rather sophisticated view of racism. They described the intentional and unintentional behaviors, as well as the individual, cultural, or institutional practices that intersected in the school environment. Some of these acts were described as being overt; others were covert acts of racism. Some were intentional and some, unintentional. All of these manifestations of racism perpetuated systemic inequities.

Nine of 10 participants shared specific examples of racism that had impacted them during their time as antiracist leaders at Midwest High School. All 10 expressed concern over acts of racism directed toward students by other students or adults in the building. Ever-present in my discussions with participants of color was an acknowledgment that racial tension was a problem at Midwest High School. Some participants even shared that racism had become normalized in the culture to the point that they had come to accept it.

> I say it affected me physically and mentally, because when you first walk in the doors, you can always sense that there was a little tension going on in the building. As I got older, I kind of got used to it, going with the flow. You become desensitized to racism. When you become desensitized to something that's wrong,

that's a problem. A lot of kids at the school are desensitized that there's racism going on at the school. Being the person that I always was, I would never just sit there and go for it. I kind of felt that something needed to be done. I have got friends of all ethnicities and when the day ends, we keep on talking to who we talk to—our own race. I've always felt that there needed to be a stand, too, to help prevent this stuff. And that was how I felt personally. Before I realized that there were different groups and organizations at the school, I thought I was the only one that saw it. I felt like people were walking so colorblinded and that it was so crazy all of this stuff was going on in the classroom—teachers being certain ways to students—and nobody was taking a stand and saying what's right and what's wrong. I feel like if somebody stood up to stop the racism at our school, all eyes would be on them. And when all eyes are on them, they don't want that. They may want the spotlight, but not the spotlight on some racial tension being brought to the surface. (CBM27)

This student talked about his experience and how his engagement as an antiracist leader in the Dare 2 Be Real antiracist leadership group had helped heal some of the pain and given him an opportunity to be himself in a system that often made him feel like he did not belong. A similar sentiment was shared by all student participants of color.

Acknowledging Assimilation

The culture at Midwest High School supported a practice of assimilation in its students. At a staff meeting in 2006, one teacher described the attrition of students of color in classes in his department to their inability to "act the Midwest way." He went so far as to exclaim that if students of color did not learn how to act the "Midwest way" we should kick them out. Typical of Midwest culture, no one challenged him on this notion at the time, but many talked about their concerns with the comment afterward. Students and staff of color acknowledged this culture of assimilation. Unlike most of the White counterparts, adults of color shared skepticism that programming would help students of color achieve with little discussion about changing teacher behavior. On the contrary, student participants of color from all racial backgrounds shared insight into the culture of assimilation at Midwest. Participants shared examples of how this culture manifested itself in confrontations over student behavior, attendance, and curriculum. One student participant shared her concern with an intensified effort to address student tardiness that appeared to perpetuate some racial inequities.

I think there has been a lot of discussion about the kids who are not in class, that population and how that correlates with students of color. So, I think this definitely has to do with race and having students feel welcome in the classroom regardless of skin color. I can tell you, there are definitely a lot of White kids who skip class all the time and get away with it because it is not noticed. (CWF 30)

The notion that White students were not noticed when engaging in behaviors that students of color were disciplined for was repeated by many participants. While ineffective colorblind efforts to address the racial predictability of achievement and behavior outcomes at Midwest were not new, the burgeoning racial consciousness of the staff and students was prompting discussion that challenged leaders to examine the casual and systemic inequities that were perpetuated by their practices. With more racially conscious and culturally proficient practice being promoted around the school, students of color were able to compare normalized practices of hypervisibility that also implied a need for assimilation by all students regardless of their cultural or racial backgrounds to a discrete set of school norms based in Whiteness.

> I'm a strong believer that if you're going to give a message, give a message that reaches everyone's ears, not just one audience. That was a problem at Midwest High School, [teachers] often only reach one audience and they expect everyone to adjust to them. I understand that the audience that happens to be at Midwest High School is majority White. I understand that. But, that doesn't mean that the other 5, 10, 25 percent should be left out. Just like everybody else has to, we have to graduate, too. And we have to feel a part . . . I say we would never have this racial tension if people really felt that they belonged at this school. If people honestly felt that they belonged at the school, you would never have these problems because students of color would realize that we're all getting taught and treated equitably. It comes when you understand your audience and that we're all not coming in the same, but all need to be taught. (CBM 28)

Although some participants of color felt that Midwest High School had made progress in its efforts to help all students and staff feel like they belong, there was still a sense that Midwest was predominately a school for Whites.

Immersion

This stage of racial identity is characterized by the simultaneous desire to surround oneself with visible symbols of one's racial identity and to actively avoid of symbols of Whiteness (Cross, 1978). Thomas Parham wrote that "at this stage, everything of value in life must be Black or relevant to Blackness. This stage is also characterized by a tendency to denigrate White people, simultaneously glorifying Black people" (1989, p. 190). As individuals enter the immersion stage, they actively seek out opportunities to explore aspects of their own history and culture with the support of peers from their own racial background. Typically, White-focused anger dissipates during this phase because so much of the person's energy is directed toward his or her own group and self-exploration. The result of this exploration is an emerging security in a newly defined and affirmed sense of self.

I did not hear many specific examples of immersion during my time at Midwest. This is not surprising, since this stage is characterized by people of color actively seeking out peers from their own racial background for support. Despite specific conversations around this topic, I observed examples of immersion in the field and did have some participants of color share reflections about their experiences with immersion. Evidence of immersion in the data is discussed in the following sections: (1) identifying with other staff of color, (2) questioning White authenticity, and (3) tiredness/fatigue regarding the process.

Identifying With Other Staff of Color

As suggested in the literature on racial identity, it is normal for people of color to seek out one another's company in a lunchroom, hallways, or social settings (Cross, 1991; Tatum, 1993). This normalcy was present at Midwest High School. It was common to see self-segregated tables in the cafeteria, racially segregated areas throughout the school during passing times, and staff seeking out those of their own racial group for support. Although an everyday occurrence for Whites, this practice was often seen as more common among people of color. The hypervisibility of the racial minority at Midwest High School increased the need for people of color to seek each other out for support—as evidenced by participant responses during the interview process and my own observations in the field.

Although self-segregation was present throughout the building, its presence was discussed in settings where racial equity was the agenda. District administration supported, as per the recommendation of equity consultants, the formation of a staff of color (STOC) support group. STOC met on a quarterly basis to offer staff of color a safe space to connect. One person of color, who did not attend regularly, felt that this group was not for her because, as she put it, she was "past the need for healing" stage of her professional career. Six of the eight staff of color who had attended the group considered this to be an essential component of the racial-equity work for them. One described it as a "safe space to decompress and just be myself." She said that she rarely could be herself while walking the halls or engaging with White staff at Midwest High School. For her, finding allies of color was a gift that allowed her to be "free to be me."

Questioning White Authenticity

As a White leader in this work, I had to remain aware of the presence and role of Whiteness in my interactions with people of color. One participant of color shared her guardedness regarding collaboration with me as a White colleague.

> For a while I questioned why you would be so involved in this work. It takes me a while to trust White people because I have not always found their motives to be in my interest, but in their own. (TBF)

This exchange reminded me of the trust that had been placed in me as a White antiracist leader. Half of the participants of color discussed their reluctance to trust Whites who were engaged in antiracism until they saw actions that backed up their words. They were much more likely to collaborate with someone who would listen to them and try things that might have a positive impact on students of color than with those who said the right things but had no actions that matched their words. Four of six Black staff members shared times that they collaborated with another person of color rather than working with a White peer. They shared that they knew that the other person would understand their perspective and there was less chance for betrayal—something that was a very familiar pattern for at least two participants. This pattern of betrayal was described by one participant as something that made her "weary."

Tiredness/Fatigue Regarding the Process

All 10 participants of color shared at least one example when they had felt tired or fatigued with the process of antiracism at Midwest High School. For many, the practice of Courageous Conversations, although essential to the individual and systemic growth of the organization, was something that was very difficult to sustain. Many participants described the perpetual stumbling of White peers throughout the process as understandable but, at times, difficult to navigate. Eight of 10 participants discussed these interactions as something that sent them home at night more tired than if they had not been engaged in the racial-equity work. One participant said she would rather not engage with White colleagues in this work than open herself up to the daily letdown she felt when she saw White peers engaging in the same racist behaviors they had professed they would change just days before. One Black staff member described this struggle.

> I can honestly say that the work was invigorating. At the same time, I've never been so tired that year I came back in all my years of teaching. I guess it was because there was no hiding anymore. I'll speak for myself. I had to be vocal, but I also had to watch and see as my [White] colleagues and people with whom I have worked for many years also struggle with the work and it was not always a pretty picture. I would sometimes avoid [a certain teacher's] office because I knew what was coming. But, to know that the [racial-equity] work was going on, and to see the movement, excitement, even if it was a small group of people, even that started out being a small group of people and it kind of grew, and grew, and grew, and how that would hopefully impact the students at the school was exciting. It's sad for me that I didn't get to see some of the end results [because I left], but I heard good things. (TBF 24)

The number of staff of color at Midwest High School increased in the first 2 years of this study, but then decreased as three staff of color left to pursue opportunities in either more diverse settings or districts that seemed to have more support systems in place for staff and students of color. Many participants discussed the climate at Midwest in a regional context, implying the White culture they had to navigate on a regular basis.

> Our state is just different in that people don't like conflict so there's all this nice-ness. I love our state. I've been here long enough. But, sometimes it is frustrating as a person of color. Just talk. It's okay if we don't agree. It's okay because in that, people learn. I'm not very patient, but I don't have a choice if I'm going to con-tinue to live here. (TBF 24)

Most of the people of color with whom I interacted had come to accept the cul-ture of the region but still felt a calling to help their peers and students and color navigate successfully through this climate. The personalization of this calling is described in the following sections.

Internalization

While still maintaining his or her connections with Black peers, the internal-ized individual is willing to establish meaningful relationships with Whites who acknowledge and are respectful of the internalized individual's self-definition. The individual is also ready to build coalitions with members of other oppressed groups because that person may see the other group's strug-gle linked to the person's own (Mun-Wah, 1994). At Midwest High School, all participants of color demonstrated some presence of internalization in their racial identity. The criteria for participation in the study was most likely a factor in having so many examples from participants fall into this stage of identity development.

Staff and students of color who participated in this study expressed will-ingness to not only engage in an interracial leadership group but also participate in a study with a White ally they were willing to support. These practices alone demonstrate some aspect of internalization or internalization-commitment identity. In the following sections, I discuss the presence of internalization among people of color in the following manifestations: collaborating with White staff, awareness of complexity, and confidence in process.

Collaborating With White Staff

All 10 participants of color, students and staff alike, shared a willingness to col-laborate with White staff in a quest for racial equity. Most participants talked very naturally of this union and spoke of the need to engage more White staff in racial-equity work to ensure the successful transformation at Midwest High School. Four participants of color discussed the difficulty of this engagement but talked openly about their internalization of cross-racial collaboration.

> Sometimes the best conversations I had [with White colleagues] were very hard. Very hard. Where I do not want to be, but I know for some, they felt more

comfortable asking me than they would have asking someone else not knowing what their response would be. But that can be tiring. I don't want to do your work. Do your own work. But, if you need to ask a question, if I'm a safe person for that, that's cool. But don't try to take a shortcut. Just do the work. I think a powerful conversation that you and I had was when you came back after the one summer you were in your new position and it was like, boom, boom, boom, you just saw so much stuff in one summer—your racial lens had been opened. I had a conversation recently and the only White person in our triad is saying she has not seen any racism. [*Sighs*] So, I need you to try. I'm not going to force [antiracism] on anybody, but once that lens becomes more critical, it's amazing. And then, I will be right there by your side. (TBF 24)

As with the participant quoted above, I noticed a conditional nature to the way staff of color would refer to their collaboration with White peers. If one perceived a commitment from Whites to increase their skills and knowledge and to develop their capacity to use a racial lens, then the person of color would be willing to stand by their White peers and support them in their quest. Many staff of color also demonstrated an understanding that cross-racial collaboration was essential for systemic reform (Singleton, 2022).

Awareness of Complexity

Participants of color were particularly insightful about the complexity of systemic antiracism. Their experience with integration and the navigation of White culture throughout much of their professional and personal lives were given as potential reasons for their understanding. Relative to their White counterparts, participants of color had internalized many of the tenets of critical race theory. This internalization may have been reinforced by academic study but was grounded in life experiences.

Each of the 10 participants of color shared stories that reflected their knowledge and experience with different levels of racial equity. Students and staff of color talked about the need to address systemic and individual racism with multiple strategies and from multiple angles. At times, participants of color reflected on how their work in a predominantly White system had contributed to a development of internalized racism. Most participants of color explained that they must be intentional in their thought process to truly bring about racial equity.

The issue is how the students, parents, and staff of color are affected, interact, are included and involved in whatever it is I'm doing. Whether it is me teaching, interacting with students in the halls, or talking with parents—even deciding whether or not I should talk with parents about issues at school or about opportunities for involvement at school. When I talk with district staff or principals about events that are coming up, things we are trying to do, it has led me to initiate new ways of thinking and sometimes—especially in my district-level position—thinking about ways to do something new in addition to what we normally do that has to happen to be more inclusive. Inclusive—I don't really like using the word *inclusive*, because, you know, it's really changing our mindset to see that these are our students. These are our families. This is our staff, and it's changing. That leads me to think not just about adjusting our systems to bring about equity, but thinking about other ways to do our work. (TAM 11)

Teachers of color, as a whole, were adamant about the need to create systems that would bring about sustainable change and about not forgetting about meeting individual needs in the moment. Many of them expressed fear that gradual change alone might lead to more kids "falling through the cracks." Along the same lines, four participants of color alluded to the difficulty associated with antiracism in a system that was built and is founded on principles that perpetuate White privilege (McIntosh, 1989).

We are dealing with a system that was not set up to serve all students, but in a time when we need to work within this system to try to meet all needs. This does not sit well with those who have had the privileges of working a system that only served them for so long. (SBM 10)

At first, I may have mistaken participant optimism for naivete, but as I looked more closely at the data I noticed that responses were often couched in knowing allusions to the cycle of oppression the participants had witnessed throughout their lives—oppression I could try to understand but had never experienced firsthand. Despite any roadblocks participants of color saw in their path to racial equity, there was a strong positive orientation about the progress of the work from all of them.

Confidence in the Process

Eight of 10 participants of color shared their belief in the antiracist process in place at Midwest High School. Many of them spoke of their trust in the leadership of the school. Although they did not make any comments that suggested otherwise, I wondered how positive their outlook on the racial-equity process would have been if the leaders at the time were to leave the system. Beyond participants' satisfaction with the direction of school leadership, there was a belief that a critical mass of staff and students were beginning to understand the need for racial equity. One staff member said he moved to Midwest High School because of the perception that Midwest was serious about racial equity but would consider leaving if the direction changed.

We're moving in the right direction. I see people putting their money where their mouth is. I took a job here because I believed in the process that district administration said they were committing to. When that starts to change, I will probably look for another place to be. I want to work with people who have a plan for [racial equity], but can only put myself out on that limb as long as I know who is going to go out there with me. (ABM 13)

For most staff and students of color, the commitment to racial equity was something they would never lose. But their commitment to Midwest High School was often tenuous. Eight of 10 participants of color said that they would seriously consider leaving Midwest High School if the focus on racial equity were to waver. When pushed to go further, participants did not suggest a lack of commitment to Midwest but rather a sense that they could not compromise their core values in a system that would not support them.

Internalization/Commitment

People of color in the fifth stage of identity development have found ways to translate their color-consciousness or "personal sense of Blackness into a plan of action or a general sense of commitment" to the concerns of Blacks as a group that is sustained over time (Cross, 1991, p. 220). Whether at the fourth or fifth stage, the process of internalization allows the individual, anchored in a positive sense of racial identity, both to perceive and transcend race proactively (Tatum, 1993). This proactive transcendence of race was present in many of the participants of color at Midwest High School. Examples of internalization-commitment can be found in two subthemes: believing in the work and personal/professional connections.

Believing in the Work

Throughout my time at Midwest High School, my own racial consciousness was raised by increased interracial dialogue. This dialogue was heightened by the unwavering racial consciousness of so many staff and students with whom I had rarely talked about race. While my racial consciousness was raised in this setting, it became clear to me that my choice to engage was something that was not as much of an option for people of color. There was a personal, local, and immediate understanding of race in their own lives that reinforced the omnipresent impact of race in the hallways, classrooms, interaction, policies, and practices of Midwest.

Eight of 10 participants of color shared a general sense of commitment to racial-equity work. Their commitment included conscious decisions to work in a diverse setting such as Midwest rather than an ethnic enclave that matched their own racial background and to help students of all backgrounds reach their full potential. Racial consciousness was clear, yet it was not seen as a choice by all. For some, their commitment to racial equity was their life work, sometimes at the expense of their own health.

I'll do what I have to do. I'll take the kid after class, work something else out. You don't want to be a part of the solution? You don't have to. So, when I'm sitting next to them, and I'm watching that the student has put that barrier up and moved on, I'm cool with it, because I know that—I'm used to it. You experience these interactions on a daily basis. If I held it in, you'd have more Black people dying of heart attacks. I mean, my girlfriend told me that the other day. She said, "Don't die like your daddy." She said, "You gotta let them go. You can't save every kid. You're gonna die." I said, "This is what I was born to do." (TBF 14)

Many people of color at Midwest saw this unwavering commitment to racial equity as something that transcended their professional commitment. Students and staff alike referred to a "calling" to engage in antiracism and a commitment to work with their White peers to make a positive difference. Two participants spoke openly about their frustrations with White peers that led them to disengage at times. Despite this discomfort, however, these two participants, as with the other people of color, discussed their desire to stay engaged through adversity.

Personal/Professional Connections

Participants shared frequently about their commitment to racial equity at work and in their personal lives. Much of the equity-focused professional development at Midwest had asked staff to engage in race on a level that is personal, local, and immediate. This work was something that could become draining on people of color if they were asked to bridge gaps of ignorance with their White peers (Katz, 2003). Indeed, this work was draining for many of our staff members, but a few of the participants talked about the fruits of their labor outweighing that drain.

> *Draining* is the first word that comes to mind. Antiracism here impacts my energy level. The impact, however, is the overall climate of this building, the impact is our educational success, the educational delivery to students here. The impact for me professionally is how we are perceived in this community. The impact of our school's work with it has been positive. It has been positive for me as an educator. I'm not going to describe myself in that educator role yet or what I may look like. The impact has been positive because of the other places I've been, the work that's been done here in this building—it matches my inner core, or my belief system. So that it has made it professionally, enjoyable to work here. The impact on our antiracism work here has made it so that when I come to work, I actually feel like I'm doing what I've been called to this earth to do. It matches me. In other districts, I had to do it covertly, at all times. Here, because it's the school's work, because of the people invested in the building, there is a liberating feeling for me personally and professionally, things are coming together at the exact same time and that feels good. (ABM 13)

Educators of color expressed contentment with the racial-equity work at Midwest High School because of the emotional connection between their personal and professional lives. Students of color engaged in antiracist leadership also articulated the emotional impact that accompanied their commitment to racial equity. They shared stories about the encounters at home and at school that had shaped their racial identity and leadership lens. Positive interracial encounters deepened their commitment to antiracism; however, they commonly referenced the mixed messages about race that accompanied their leadership development. Students of color, much like their White peers, had been taught to not mention race in interracial company. In a predominantly White community and school setting, this was seen as a way of maintaining safety and gradual success. One staff member recalled her epiphany regarding her own internalization-commitment racial identity.

> When I was parenting my boys, I kept that same framework. You don't talk about race. I would tell them that you don't come home and say somebody did something to you because he is racist. If you knew he was racist, then you should sit at another table. That's the way we were taught to think. Which really, at its heart, is that idea that you can't blame other people, you have to figure out how to exist. And then when I came here as a teacher, I ran into a lot of obstacles about people telling me what kids I could service and who not to talk to. After sitting in these meetings with the equity team, I thought about it. I figured I have got to figure out a way to make this school better. Otherwise, I'll always be a part of the problem and [maintaining] the system I want to change. So, my role is to help the system learn to change and not contribute to the problem myself. That's what has made me want to work on becoming an administrator. I don't want to be part of the problem anymore. (TBF 22)

Learning to coexist interracially was a learning process—it was not easy, but one that this participant found would be essential if she and the Black and Brown students she also considered "hers" were to survive in the Midwest system. The hope for most antiracist leaders at Midwest was that their students, their peers, and they, themselves, would not only survive, but thrive, in a multiracial society.

Multiracial Identity

Racial identity outside of the Black and White binary had been largely unexplored until the 1990s. Two models (Poston, 1990; Root, 1990) were often used to describe the experiences of biracial and multiracial youth. Not as all-age-encompassing nor as linear as the work on Black and White racial-identity development (Renn, 2004), an ecological model that helps explain the factors contributing to identity has been the hallmark of recent scholarship on multiracial identity (Renn, 2004), primarily in late adolescence and early adulthood. Using Renn's model of multiracial identity, I noticed themes in the data among multiracial participants and among other participants' perceptions of biracial and multiracial peers. One student and one staff member demonstrated multiple monoracial identities (Root, 1990), depending on the situation. Contextual factors in the participants' school and home life seemed to primarily affect which ethnic or racial group they most identified with. Two participants also held distinct multiracial identities (Root, 1990) and elected to not identify with one group or another but to be of a distinct multiracial group. One participant also held a situational identity (Root, 1990). Similar to a person who has multiple monoracial identities, situational identity describes a fluid identity pattern whereby the racial identity is stable but other identity elements are more salient in some situations (Renn, 2004).

Emergent themes support the notion that multiracial identity was implicit among participants and was influenced by factors at Midwest High School. Some participants discussed how their physical appearance may have impacted how they were perceived by others. One biracial participant shared a couple of stories about White and Black peers, suggesting that she could "pass" for White. Another participant discussed the "code-switching" that happens depending on whether or not he is with more White or more Black peers. Three multiracial themes emerged in the data coming from multiple sources. Those themes included a frustration with the Black/White racial binary, racial isolation, and the negotiation between two worlds.

Frustration With the Black/White Racial Binary

All self-described multiracial participants demonstrated cultural knowledge that often surpassed their White or Black peers. They shared examples of knowledge learned from parents, their community, their encounters, and their own personal studies. Prior knowledge regarding multiculturalism and racial dynamics led to a frustration with the Black/White binary that permeated the discussions about race at Midwest. Courageous Conversations (Singleton, 2022) often focused on the racial hierarchy in the United States of Whites over people of color, or the American racial binary of White or Black. One participant noted,

> I believe the connotation does have to be isolated to Black-White sometimes, because that is a very big and unique package of history and contemporary issues that does not reflect anything else we've got. So you have to. You have to isolate a conversation sometimes. But I think you need to recognize that you are. Then, you have to continue to add on, to continue to delve into other pieces. Because if you don't, all of a sudden you're looking around and you start wondering if we really are talking about antiracism. Or are we talking about, I don't know what you call it . . . Black America? (TMF 7)

Multiracial participants often brought up concerns about a lack of focus on antiracism while their White counterparts rarely did. There was often an approving, but critical, eye placed on discussions that were deemed to isolate race solely to discussions of Black and White. One student discussed his concern about how the term *people of color* had lumped his experience in with others who share a common link to White oppression but little else.

> It needs to become universal. When we think of racial equity, we think of a White and Black thing. We really don't put the Hispanic's opinion or the Somali person's perspective or the Laotian person's perspective out there. It always seems like a Black and White thing. It's Somali versus Black, Black versus Asian, Hispanic versus Asian, Africans versus Africans, Whites versus Blacks . . . other than a few exceptions, is always a versus whenever we discuss race in class. Why not try to put everybody together and get everybody talking about it? I've never heard of any place else in our society where we have someone speak for a whole group except for race and even there, we are asked to speak for groups where we don't even know their story. (CBM 28)

Many participants shared their concern about the dearth of stories outside of the Black-White experience. Although many acknowledged the history of oppression that linked the two groups, this became particularly troublesome for one student who realized that she had rarely, if ever, been asked to think about antiracism from a multiracial perspective.

> I think that is so interesting that you brought up [Frederick Douglass, Harriet Tubman] because when I think of people being antiracist, I automatically try to think of White people who are trying to not be a racist White person. Then, when I think of people of color, I think of many Blacks, but rarely antiracist role models of other races. Dang, I even forgot that Frederick Douglass was multiracial like Barack Obama because that never gets talked about. (CWF 30)

Isolation

For some multiracial participants, the invisibility of their experience led to feelings of isolation. For others, the discussion about race in general was liberating. For participants of all races, there was a general feeling among those with previous experience in interracial settings or prior knowledge or experiences with antiracism that the racial-equity work at Midwest was emancipatory in many ways. Many multiracial, Black, Brown, and Indigenous participants spoke of the hypervisibility, racial fatigue, and distrust that led to self-isolation over the course of their 3 years of antiracism work. Often sparked by the distrust that came from their colleagues who were experiencing White paralysis, leaders of color found it hard to stay engaged in interracial collaboration without getting burned out. There were glimmers of hope. Staying in protocol for Courageous Conversations about race on a regular basis helped leaders of color move out of isolation. For one multiracial participant who had worked with students and staff on curricular and leadership programming regarding antiracism for years, the intentionality of the racial-equity work helped her feel as though she was not doing the work alone anymore.

> It feels like we have created enough sense of focus on this issue that it has definitely led me to feel like I'm not isolated out here anymore. And I've been here for [15 years] and can think back to—regularly to times I felt pretty isolated out here. Knowing that the staff has felt this on equity has made it so that it doesn't feel so isolating. Even if this journey has not been smooth, or the community has not necessarily always been all that accepting, it doesn't feel like you're one of just a couple attempting to work on it. That's a professional issue, but also a very important personal issue, since you spend an extraordinary amount of time connected to this place, this building, and these people. That has made it significantly easier. I feel there are fewer times when I thought, "I can't do this anymore. I need to go someplace else." The people at the core of the equity initiative in our building seem to get it. As one of the very few people of color in the building—as one of the few teachers of color in the building—that's very important for me personally. (TMMF 7)

Multiple participants shared their beliefs that racial-equity work at Midwest had influenced their desire to stay and work for change within the system rather than disengage. Many participants of color shared their thoughts about leaving Midwest if the culture or direction of the school were to turn away from racial equity. Biracial and multiracial participants did not speak of this concern as explicitly. Rather, they shared hopefulness that their isolation would decrease over time and a belief that they could weather changes to the system because of their previous experience with navigating two or more racial worlds.

Navigating Two Worlds

Multiracial participants spoke freely about their navigation between two worlds—one of color and one White. At Midwest, multiracial students indicated that they were often perceived to be Black or "Mexican" by their White peers although they may have personally associated with a situational racial identity or multiple monoracial identities. Adult participants implied experiences with White peers who had devalued their multiple identities. Students, however, spoke explicitly of the navigation between racial "worlds." In a hallway discussion with a couple of biracial students in spring 2007, they spoke about how lucky they felt to know that they could understand both the Black and White cultures at their school. One of the students believed that her biracial identity would help her achieve success once she graduated because of her experience with the seamless navigation of multiple cultures. However, some students shared how difficult this navigation was for them.

Multiple student participants shared specific details about their experiences in culturally responsive classrooms and in Dare 2 Be Real, their antiracist leadership group. One student participant recalled the impact of candid discussions and activities with White peers, peers of color, and multiracial people about history, identity, and antiracism and how they related to his experience at Midwest.

> I have been labeled by people in both of my worlds. After a while, I was trying to become somebody that wasn't me. It took me a while to realize that I don't need to become somebody to make friends, because I am who I am. Once I realized that, that is when things started to get smoother for me here. Once you start realizing what your priorities are and not worry about being cool and stuff like that, success is a path that is brought to you. Midwest High School is your typical high school. You have the last-night party stories. You have the boyfriend-girlfriend drama. You've got the racial tension. We are doing a lot of work here that makes you want to believe that everything is cool. Like, I'm at the typical high school so everything is fine. Like I learned in history class, it's like the Gilded Age. All the talk makes you think everything is golden. Then, every time you start smelling something that isn't quite right, you realize that what you thought about Midwest High School was never what it really was at all. The racism is still there, stinking up the place underneath all of the glitter and gold. (CBM 28)

This student's sentiment indicates the complexity of the antiracist experience at Midwest High School, one that most likely is not unique to this school but may have been exposed by the intentionality and number of conversations about race—not always common in suburban or even urban schools. The focus on racial equity provided a vessel for profound self-exploration and growth, but the extent to which this growth brought about substantive change varied depending on with whom you spoke. For multiracial leaders, they could empathize with White colleagues and their colleagues of color who were navigating the work alongside them. One teacher commented:

> I mean, it's invigorating to be able to view the world in a new light and to do things from a different perspective, to learn to think about a racial perspective different from my own, and to approach the world in a way that I'm unaccustomed to. And it's fatiguing to interact with myself 5 years ago in so many people. (TMMM 23)

As that participant described his encounters with "himself five years ago in so many people," I was reminded again of how often people referred to the changes within themselves while engaging in antiracist leadership. The racial-equity work was not only a professional-development opportunity but a deeply personal journey for most, if not all, of those who participated. The tenets of critical race theory and cycles of racial-identity development presented obstacles and opportunities in every interracial interaction. In addition, the fatigue associated with interacting with oneself from years ago often was accompanied by concern that the people and the organization may not have been progressing as one had hoped despite the energy and resources devoted to antiracism by so many individuals.

CONCLUSION

Throughout this chapter, you have seen stages of identity development that antiracist leaders experienced throughout their work with their colleagues at Midwest High. Fatigue was particularly troublesome in one area that seemed to affect all participants: White paralysis. These disruptive cycles of work avoidance and colorblind practices may have provided a perception of self-preservation for the leaders experiencing it, but for their colleagues and students of color, it often led to isolation marked by distrust, hypervisibility, and frustration. For the White students who saw it modeled, they saw the normalization of White paralysis and the struggle to self-actualize as antiracists. Many White leaders, adults and students alike, struggled to work through this paralysis, leaving disappointment, lowered expectations, and inequities in its wake.

DiAngelo (2010) illustrates how White fragility triggers defensive moves, including the outward display of emotions such as anger, fear, and guilt. This study extends and deepens DiAngelo's work on fragility by documenting what happens to leaders in all stages of authority throughout an organization and defines the periods of inaction that come from these feelings and their isolating effect on people of color.

What is most promising about the results of this study is the roadmap it provides for leaders to reenter active antiracism and decrease the duration of their cycles of White paralysis. Frequent application of protocols for Courageous Conversations About Race (Singleton & Linton 2006), coupled with guided self-reflection that can be applied to leaders' daily work, is essential for this change. Most importantly, centering the organization around student leadership and identity development provides adult racial-equity leaders a means to connect the purpose of their profession to their antiracist practice, thus reinstating a productive zone of disequilibrium for adaptive change for both the organization and the individual (Heifetz & Linskey, 2014,).

This study represents a beginning look at ways that principals and teacher-leaders might begin to understand the inconsistency in their racial-equity movements and the need to include regular interracial discourse and student development into their strategic equity plans. It also provides a way to encourage critical self-reflection and ethnography as an important part of research and evaluation. This kind of study needs to continue in order to support new conceptions of collaboration between teachers, students, principals, and support staff to be able to create more racially equitable schools. Most importantly, our leaders need to be willing to move beyond courage and passion for racial equity to a place of strategic collaboration and empathy. As

Isabel Wilkerson, author of *The Warmth of Other Suns* and *Caste,* puts it in an op-ed piece in 2015,

> The social geography of the cities of the North, Midwest, and West are recipes for tension and mistrust, and we're dealing with that right now, at this very moment . . . what we need now, in this time is a response of radical empathy.

Indeed, the lessons that can be gleaned from the leaders at Midwest High School are lessons that can be used to heal wounds in a nation that is coming to grips with a reality that is anything but "postracial" and calls on us to be our best, collaborative selves. The need for antiracism in our schools will only increase as we begin to delve into the pain and struggle that marks the reality of our racial present.

The implications for continuing to interrupt White paralysis can be affirming to leaders who may not realize how they are getting in their own way and in the way of their colleagues of color as they work to address systemic inequities. Much like our schools were not originally designed to serve all students, nor have our reform movements been designed to foster true student integration, regular interracial and intraracial staff collaboration across positional authorities, or student development focused on the promotion of a healthy individual and collective racial identity. Ultimately, this is not work that only gifted practitioners can engage in, but rather work that can be developed strategically by fledgling antiracist educators. We need a better system than the one currently in place to address the racial predictability of achievement in our schools, and I believe that the results of the study at Midwest High School indicate the need for future replications of research of this kind at other sites. Critical ethnographic research can address the perceptions of antiracist leaders through a lens of identity development and critical race theory and may likely provide more insight into what is necessary to address a culture of White dominance that pervades most public schools. There is a good chance that further studies of this kind will help leaders and scholars recognize the likelihood of the reproduction of racism and maintenance of the status quo across school settings. The pervasive nature of White paralysis certainly requires more examination and attention and raising awareness of White paralysis should help leaders of all races understand how to effectively and consistently proceed with antiracism efforts.

CHAPTER 6

Tenets for Sustaining Antiracist School Leadership

SYSTEMIC IMPLEMENTATION

How Integrated Is Antiracist Student Leadership in Your School System?

Engaging students interracially in racial discourse requires only a small team of adults working with a small group of interracial students. However, sustaining a program requires something more systemic. The program should be fully integrated into the structures and culture of the school. One could never imagine a core class such as math not having full support to run for every student during the school day. If adults did not feel ready to teach math or suggested it just be taught after school by a paraprofessional, the community and school board would be outraged. At Midwest High School, work that was seen as siloed provided easier fodder for dismissal and alienation from other groups that had a more established voice and status within the school. As with any antiracist work, it could be easily seen as an "add-on" or fringe program. Systemic integration should include scheduling during the school day or horizontal alignment with other existing student groups in the building (see Figure 6.1). The lack of structural alignment of a student antiracism program was seen as a crucial flaw preventing the longitudinal success of the Dare 2 Be Real program at Midwest. Other iterations have included horizontal alignment within an established system for student activities and engagement that would allow it to thrive. In addition, community support and staff guidance are crucial because of the vulnerable nature of students. Therefore, structures like the one described in Figure 6.1 should have not only horizontal alignment, but vertical integration with leadership groups like a site council or building leadership team that may have multiple adult stakeholders that can learn about and legitimize the work of the students.

Many student councils continue to follow an archaic model of popularity contests and function primarily as event planners in their schools. The Dare 2 Be Real framework aligns student leadership groups with the school improvement goals in the building. Notice that the model centers the work of antiracist leadership, making it a focal point of planning. This runs counter to most systems, which make antiracist work a fringe program, if it even exists at all. Midwest High School succeeded in making Dare 2 Be Real a weekly advisory class that spent 3 weeks of the month learning, practicing, and reviewing lessons for student leaders to share with students in other advisories. On the other week of the month, students practiced their leadership actively with those in an advisory by facilitating conversations about race with other students. Where the work failed systemically was in the strategic collaboration of a team working together to support the students. Although there was support from the principal and nominal support from other teachers, the students were led by a sole White advisor whose charisma was matched by a misplaced belief that asking for help in the advisement of students would both burden overworked colleagues and slow down the momentum the student leaders had shown. The advisor of the Dare 2 Be Real group experienced a lot of success and was quite visible in the region, and was subsequently offered a job in another school district as an administrator. The group was passed on to a Black male who had been marginalized in the system from the moment he was hired. He was easily made a scapegoat when students became passionate about keeping their voice squarely at the center of conversations of school improvement and the development of antiracist school policy. Both the advisor and the student leadership group were pushed out by the administrative team within 2 years. The advisor's position was eliminated with no explanation and the Dare 2 Be Real group was disbanded, with administration saying there was no longer an advisor to facilitate. This example provides just one of many cautionary tales that calls for a framework of systemic and collaborative implementation that includes a team of adults and support from those with positional and cultural authority in order to foster sustainable student-led antiracism.

Voices From the Field: Silvy Lafayette, Director of Research, Evaluation, and Assessment, St. Louis Park Public Schools

School systems are "composed of many interdependent components working together. How well these components operate and interact determines the system's health" (https://soeonline.american.edu, 2020). In schools, systems include areas like instructional delivery models, student behavior policies, and hiring practices. More importantly, these interdependent components are socially constructed. These systems are made up of the values and beliefs that exist only when the people involved in them bring these interdependent components to life. People in school systems are constantly operationalizing their values, beliefs, and lived experiences into systems that look like curriculum choices, grading policies, hiring decisions, and teacher evaluation. When all of these interdependent components are left uninterrogated and treated as race-neutral, the health of the system gets framed only by words like *implementation, indicators,* and *scientific measurement.* Rarely is there any mention of how school leaders contribute their human experience daily to the operation of these systems.

Throughout my 20 years of working in education, I have participated in meetings wherein school systems have been described as merely technical. Goals that schools set for the year and areas where they hope to improve are often presented as being grounded in quantitative data points related to standardized testing or student discipline data—both of which are far from being without bias. As a child born to a Cambodian refugee family who selected the United States to be our next home because of its education system, I've sat in these meetings and have often wondered: What if schools measured their effectiveness by their ability to meet the aspirations of our most marginalized students and families? How much stronger would school systems be? Based on my experience, the school leaders who are able to center the voices of our most marginalized students and families and ask these questions have been those who prioritize antiracist leadership development across all levels of our school system.

From an early age, I was raised with stories of how powerful schools and an education could be. After my family escaped the civil war in Cambodia in 1982, we settled in a white working-class suburban Minnesota community. Growing up, my parents shared stories of how most of our relatives were executed by the Communist Party because they were educated in formal schooling systems. In the Khmer Rouge's attempt to create an agrarian society and eliminate all institutions and people believed to be tainted by Western influence, many of my relatives became targets and were executed. My parents were supposed to be executed on numerous occasions. Fortunately, neighbors in my parents' village lied on my parents' behalf and claimed that they were poor and illiterate. In reality, my father was a successful civil engineer and my mother had been educated to be a teacher. They were upper middle class, spoke Khmer and French, and were literate in both languages. Both of my parents came from families who valued schools and education. When my family was told that we had sponsors ready to move us from the refugee camp in Thailand to a different country, many of my extended family members chose New Zealand as their new home. My parents, on the other hand, chose the United States. I've been told many times that when they declared our new home, my father cried tears of joy because he knew that his children would have the opportunity to attend college in our new country. This was his dream. His hope was that the American educators would see the brilliance of his children.

After immigrating to the United States, my father's dream came true but only after fighting for White educators to see the brilliance of his children. In our early days of being newly settled refugees in this country, I remember being 4 years old and staying home with my younger brother while my four older siblings attended school in Minnesota. In contrast to our family's social and educational status in Cambodia, U.S. schools now identified my siblings as children with disrupted schooling, English language learners (ELLs), and students on Free and Reduced-Price Lunch (FRPL). My older siblings entered schools where the majority of their classmates were White and told them to "go back home" daily. My oldest brother physically fought White male students at Rosemount High School. After each fight, he felt like the White educators did nothing to stop his White classmates from spewing their hatred. After defending himself too many times in the halls of his first school, he was eventually expelled and sent to another high school nearby.

As my siblings attended schools in Minnesota, adult beliefs were reflected in how they approached their instruction. White staff provided remedial instruction based on the assumptions they made about my refugee family. One day, my two older sisters came home sobbing while recounting the disheartening response from their ELL teachers after sharing their dreams about attending college. Their White ELL teacher responded to their dreams by stating that my siblings should only focus on learning English so that they could get jobs. These teachers told my siblings that my parents were too poor to send any of us to college. During this time, my father worked as a church custodian and my mom worked in a local factory. Despite their jobs, my parents maintained this dream. These White educators, however, felt differently. To say that my earliest memories of my older siblings' educational journey in the United States were framed by tears, frustration, and negative hypervisibility understates the impact this experience has had on how important I believe antiracist leadership development to be.

In St. Louis Park Public Schools, I am reminded that my family's story is not unique. Our district has been enriched by the brilliance brought to it by immigrant communities and students from places like Somalia, Latin America, and now Afghanistan. The families that have chosen our school district bring their own dreams. Unlike my family's experience, I believe that the educators in our system, starting with our superintendent and school board members, prioritize the centering of these knowledgeable communities as we work to improve the interdependent components of our school system.

Our district's continuous-improvement planning process, for example, illustrates one example of how we prioritize antiracist leadership development with students. With the support of our superintendent and various stakeholders in the community, the Department of Assessment, Research, and Evaluation created the Youth Data Analyst summer internship. This summer internship hires high school and middle school students to study our system's racially disaggregated data. From their analysis, they then create recommendations for our school system (early learning to grade 12). To contextualize our district's data, students read academic texts written mostly by scholars of color in fields ranging from biological sciences to education research. Most importantly, recommendations made to sites are grounded in our students' own lived experiences as racialized beings in our school system.

As our school district strives to be more antiracist, I think about how meaningful it has been to work in a system that values antiracist leadership development. Today, I continue to ask the same questions I did 20 years ago. The difference now is that I am no longer alone. In St. Louis Park Public

Schools, educators, administrators, school board members, community leaders, and students are all asking these questions too.

Systemic-Implementation Tenet Application

District-Level Application. In St. Louis Park Public Schools, all curriculum and instructional programs are reviewed through a three-phase antiracist process that starts at Phase I with a 2-day consulting team workshop (to be explored later in Shared Experiences in Chapter 8). Design teams for each area are hired for a 3-year period to review the process through an antiracist lens by taking the first year of the process to "know thyself" by looking inward with the creation of racial-equity purpose statements (REPs) and through the examination of disaggregated data, particularly qualitative data gathered from diverse student stakeholders. Phase II asks the team to look around by "distinguishing knowledge from foolishness." This phase includes the engagement of culturally relevant scholars and collaboration with regional, national, and international exemplars that may be providing professional development in antiracist pedagogy, practice, or policy. In Phase II, new curriculum or professional development may be piloted to start getting transformation underway. Phase III is "building for eternity." This phase asks the team to engage the entire community, the school board, all staff, and students in the development of shared beliefs and recommendations for antiracist transformation of the curricular program under review. This may or may not include curriculum adoption but may be instructional, structural, or political changes that should mitigate the racial predictability of achievement and opportunity. The district cabinet leadership is responsible for the leadership development and coaching of the design teams throughout this process to ensure coherence with a racially conscious strategic plan.

School-Level Application: Horizontal Alignment of Student Leadership Through a Middle School and K-8 Model. I was hired to work as an assistant principal at South View Middle School in Edina, a suburban grades 6–9 school of 1,300 students. The year before I arrived, approximately 175 students had been suspended from school, with many of them suspended for multiple days, multiple times. During my first year at South View more than 75 percent of the referrals to the office were because of harassment, bullying, microaggressions, or fighting stemming from racial or cultural bigotry. Although only 22 percent of the students were students of color, more than 70 percent of the suspensions were students of color. Within 5 years, we reduced suspensions to 27 and had completely eliminated the racial disproportionality in the suspension rate. How did this happen? Many things were at play: a student-centered student services team, good teachers, a strong principal. However, there was also a huge cultural change that happened in the school that corresponded with the shift: the implementation of Dare 2 Be Real and the student-leadership-development model that supported it.

Figure 6.1. Sample School Antiracist Student Leadership Development Model

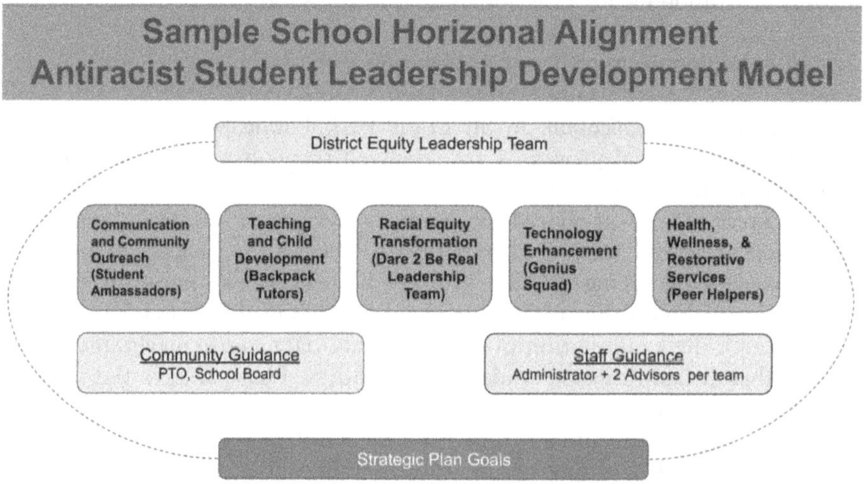

In the winter of my first year at South View, we abolished the student council. Much as in most schools, the model was archaic—a basic popularity contest consisting of tokenized roles that largely focused on the planning of one or two school dances. I decided to use my knowledge of interest convergence and Whiteness as property to develop an antiracist student leadership team model that would be sustainable far beyond my time at South View. I started by asking a colleague to partner with me at the beginning to ensure we had multiple racial perspectives to lend to the whole process.

A K–8 Model: After working at South View, I was offered a job to work as a principal in the Minneapolis Public Schools in a K–8 school, Barton Open School. I was very lucky to have been offered a great opportunity such as this. I inherited, first, a staff that was well-versed in Responsive Classroom and willing to take on new instructional strategies and leadership roles in the school and, second, a family population who wanted to be very involved in the school community. I had been recruited to be a school principal because of my commitment to racial equity, and my new staff had done some equity work but seemed to be avoiding some hard conversations. I repeatedly heard negative language around using data. The teachers did not trust standardized test scores and believed they should resist data-driven instruction. To avoid priming resistance, I started the school year with a data walk, redefining data for them by including emails from parents, student work examples, quotes from student forums, *and* the test scores. I asked staff, "What story do you see as the strengths of our school? What needs to happen? What needs to be attended to? What pieces of the story aren't told?" I summarized their responses in themes and brought them back to groups of teachers, parents, and students, asking, "Are these aspirations for the school what we stand for?"

The values were to guide everything forward, allowing us to ask whether decisions moved us toward or away from who we said we were (Kise, 2019).

I took this process to build a more-student-centered leadership development model for the school. Just as at South View, I abolished the student council program and developed a student leadership team that was horizontally aligned with Dare 2 Be Real (antiracism initiative) at the center. The difference-maker was that I also created a horizontal alignment of teacher leadership teams with equity and instructional leadership teams at the heart of the teacher work. Every adult in the school was in leadership—either on a team or advising a student leadership team. Monthly, the Dare 2 Be Real team would join our staff equity team or instructional team in equity walks and discuss what they saw, informing next steps in professional development. Older students who were partly proficient on state standardized test scores were asked to tutor K–2 students in reading and math, thus providing opportunities for not just antiracist leadership development but also the work of teaching and learning. Within 2 years we had the lowest suspension and referral rates in the city and, according to our department of research and evaluation, had narrowed our achievement gaps between Black and White students by the highest rates of any school in the previous decade.

Soon, I was asked to work with leaders in other buildings, developing their capacity to do the work. They would then develop their team's capacities. However, that vision ran into reality. Personal transformation around race frequently precedes any hope of systemic change, but people are generally in different places as to the need and the urgency. My own doctoral research focused on White paralysis—the stages of guilt, blame, pity, and fear that paralyze a person, unable to move forward. The personal work of equity was messy and the principals and teacher-leaders in my school and in other schools needed to be okay with making some mistakes. Our systems and psyches weren't set up to allow for that. Public confidence is connected to the idea of perfection. That perpetuated a culture of fear of saying the wrong thing or standing up in support of someone who may appear too radical in their approach (Kise, 2019). When I was recruited again to become a director of leadership development in St. Paul Public Schools to spread this antiracism model throughout their school district, this fear manifested itself in a difficulty of sustaining the student leadership model the way it had been sustained at South View and in other suburban schools.

This fear-driven resistance drove home yet another key reality: the power of the status quo. People were being asked to move out of the comfort zones, which provided some stability in the fishbowl of public scrutiny they were experiencing. And the equity work would eventually ask them to give up some power to allow student voice to inform best practices. I knew that the clearer my own vision—my sense of values and strengths and limitations—the easier it was to move forward the big vision of schools that work for all students. How do we help our teams recognize that by sharing power with our students, with our historically marginalized community, we aren't losing but gaining something ourselves? I believe we gain something in our own humanity (Kise, 2019).

Student Group–Level Application: In St. Louis Park we created a new antiracist talent-development program that provided gifted education for all K–5 students, providing every student in our district gifted education, 4 days a week. Below is the job description we put out and the expectations for the position of Talent Development Teacher:

DUTIES AND RESPONSIBILITIES
Primarily, the Talent Development Teacher will

- *provide culturally relevant, assets-based instruction, particularly in the areas of science, technology, education and human development, the arts, and math;*
- *identify, recognize, and cultivate the brilliance and genius of each child;*
- *assess student growth through mediative learning experiences including student observations, student interviews, focus groups, portfolios, and project-based work, both individual and collective;*
- *implement strategies that create a shared culture of confidence—a culture that recognizes and capitalizes on the assets and values of the students, their teachers, and their communities;*
- *promote a climate of rigor, relevance, and excellence;*
- *have a working knowledge of and help students understand how they can master the Minnesota State Standards; how they can better share in and understand classroom management techniques; and how they can cultivate awareness of current researched best practices and strategies for students' learning styles, the neuroscience of learning, and their needs, both academic and affective;*
- *guide students to become autonomous, culturally competent, and sociopolitically conscious learners who are both academically and socially successful;*
- *utilize specialized competencies that guide reculturation of the awareness, attitudes, beliefs, and perceptions of students about the innate potential in themselves;*
- *facilitate dialogue to garner productive classroom community investment and support;*
- *identify discrepancies between a student and a regular grade-level curriculum and provide a more optimal match between child and curriculum;*
- *engage in and facilitate Courageous Conversations About Race;*
- *guide, in collaboration with other talent development teachers and principals, the development of a system-wide vision of equity consciousness that articulates belief in and the value of the strengths and potential of each child;*

- *guide teachers in developing an ecological perspective that begins with a deep understanding and appreciation for the realities of students' lives that affect their ability to learn;*
- *participate in ongoing and regular staff, team, and individual professional development;*
- *deliver professional learning that incorporates the science of learning to arm the staff with understandings and skills that build their competence and confidence to engage student learning, foster leadership development, and motivate self-determination;*
- *employ techniques to engage the district, school staff, and school board in shared responsibility for implementing equitable practices and eradicating inequitable, marginalizing practices that perpetuate prejudice and segregation;*
- *collaborate with colleagues to implement best practices based on the needs/abilities of the students;*
- *engage in regular collaboration and teaming with the pedagogical leadership team at the school;*
- *collaborate and communicate regularly with families in making educational decisions, and use family and community resources to support learning.*

KNOWLEDGE, SKILLS, AND ABILITIES
The Talent Development Teacher will possess

- *demonstrated knowledge and application of the science of learning and the impact of culture and "Othering" on learning, performance, and self-determination;*
- *knowledge of teaching principles, practices, techniques, and developmental needs and approaches for either primary (K–2) or intermediate (3–5) student engagement;*
- *demonstrated knowledge and application of culturally responsive pedagogy;*
- *demonstrated knowledge and application of critical race theory;*
- *demonstrated knowledge and application of gifted education, interventions, and the neuroscience of learning, particularly regarding the development of elementary-aged children;*
- *knowledge and skill demonstration in the six areas of proficiency identified by the International Society for Technology in Education/National Educational Technology Standards (ISTE/NETS), including creativity and innovation, communication and collaboration, research and information fluency, critical thinking, problem-solving and decision-making; digital citizenship and global competencies;*
- *demonstrated knowledge of strategies to dynamically assess and increase students' learning growth;*

- *skill in leading culturally relevant group processes/discussions, utilizing a variety of instruction aids, strategies, and technologies;*
- *skill in facilitating authentic student engagement in culturally relevant experiences;*
- *demonstrated experience in helping students exceed expectations in science, math, reading, the arts, and education and human development;*
- *ability to write reports, lesson plans, learning objectives, and tests, and to assist in writing and reviewing curriculum using and applying professional/technical concepts, principles, and terminology;*
- *ability to work effectively and appropriately with parents, students, staff, and other educational professionals over instructional needs, concerns, or problems to gain understanding of student educational needs;*
- *demonstrated practice of collaboration on teams to support implementation of antiracism programming, culturally relevant pedagogy, and systemic transformation goals for racial equity.*

As you can see, St. Louis Park was expecting antiracist leadership from its gifted and talented teachers of all of its students.

SUPPORT FROM THE TOP

How Skilled Are We at Garnering Support From Those With Positional and Cultural Authority?

Schools are rife with leaders who carry all kinds of titles within the system. Some of the most powerful leaders in schools never leave the classroom to join the ranks of administration but rather use their cultural authority to influence positive change or subvert reform within the system. In two large urban settings in which I worked, the superintendent publicly expressed support for implementation of antiracist student leadership development, facilitating quick movement of the work throughout. In a more conservative environment, principals, teachers, and superintendents have found it necessary to garner school board support—sharing goals of the program transparently to ensure alignment with community values and mores. The greater the scrutiny of the program—and perhaps the greater fear of antiracism—the more skill needs to be employed by advisors and students in garnering support from the top.

At Midwest High School, a great level of trust existed between principal and student advisors. This trust allowed advisors to share questions with administration openly and led to strategic visioning and implementation of student leadership work. However, in many other schools, this trust was not present. Many schools are impacted by high levels of adult dysfunction that erode any sense of trust necessary to help students bring about substantive antiracist change.

Cultural Authority

Garnering support from those with cultural authority over your work— namely, the parents with competing interests, curmudgeons who subvert reform, and nonracist teammates who mean well but are obstructionists to antiracist work—requires you to build your skill and knowledge in two main areas: interest convergence and mindful inquiry.

When it comes to nonracist staff members who espouse colorblind practices and parents with competing liberal agendas who quietly (and not so quietly) devalue the prioritization of antiracism, an understanding of the critical race theory tenet of interest convergence becomes an important tool. I have worked in many liberal, urban settings, where many leaders have said they supported equity work but not antiracism work. The trap can be jumping into workshops and protocols for discussing race and improving the system before people are ready to acknowledge that they have some personal work to do around their concepts of race and racial identity. There needs to be some level of interest convergence to move the work. Sometimes this may feel like incrementalism, but to stay alive in the system I had to make it work for a little while.

I started by looking at the language that was already being used and tried to speak their language to impart my vision. In one setting, talk of race just fostered anger. So, I began by suggesting intercultural programs for students. Slowly, I peppered in the concept of race. In meetings, people would whisper, "the Black students," as if they were saying something wrong rather than acknowledging that we were talking about reality. Those conversations allowed me to introduce race in productive ways. Then I moved to another district where I was charged with beginning equity work. I assumed they were ready for race, so I started with antiracism. They definitely shared their feelings about that immediately—and I pulled back! My work is about racial equity for all students, and through that principle I want the system to outlast me. But I want to be around long enough to impact the system.

I also had to take into account the power of the status quo. Those with cultural authority don't often see themselves as leaders, but they exert incredible power over maintaining or changing the status quo. It becomes an antiracist leader's role to identify those who are gifted at subverting reform and learn how to engage in mindful inquiry with them rather than a war of words. By asking questions rather than pushing them to change, you learn more about their perspectives and therefore can understand them. The biggest mistakes I have made have come when, in anger, I have wanted to put a racist colleague on blast because he didn't want to do right by Black or Brown kids. I learned pretty quickly that those moments hurt my cause much more than they hurt the person who was the brunt of my anger. Those who have the cultural authority have people coming out of the woodwork to offer support for resistance to reform. In addition, mindful inquiry and questioning are just as important when addressing those with cultural authority who want to do antiracism work but may be working as "lone heroes." These mavericks often believe they know better than the team, believe they should be moving faster, and believe they have a better solution. It becomes important to lean into conversations with these folks without letting them sap your energy. With both types of people with cultural authority you must build your skill of questioning and the art of leaning into Courageous Conversations to garner their support. Without it, they can get in the way of systemic student leadership development for antiracism, believing they know better while actually harming kids.

Positional Authority

Garnering support from those with positional authority over your work—namely, your supervisor—boils down to three main pieces: understanding what your supervisor needs to know, seeking to understand your supervisor, and, learning how to "coach up for racial equity."

What Your Supervisor Needs to Know: It is essential that you have a keen awareness of what your supervisor needs to know about the antiracist work you are seeking to do with students. When I was supervising principals in the Anoka-Hennepin school district—the largest suburban school district in Minnesota—there was a 41-step process in place to implement any new curriculum, which included multiple viewings and approvals by the school board. This should have been enough of a wake-up call to me that approval of my passion work was going to be much different here than in other more-progressive districts. Although I had internalized the Dare 2 Be Real framework, I relied much more on the belief that if I trained principals and teachers to do the work with students in their schools, the superintendent and school board would see the value of the work and therefore approve. Unfortunately, I was neither timely in my updates nor frequent enough. I did not seek clarity early enough on what my supervisor and his supervisors needed to know about the work I was doing and, in turn, I left things open to the possibility of surprise and misunderstanding, even if I was convinced that the work we were doing with students was the right, necessary antiracist work. With an administration and board that were used to being kept in the loop on every new lesson, it became clear that doing antiracist work was going to take years, not months, to take hold, and I had to determine whether or not I was patient enough to wait it out.

Seeking to Understand: Another mistake I made in trying to garner support from positional authority in Anoka was that I did not seek to truly understand why the superintendent and the school board were so concerned about the antiracism work. It was common knowledge among school leaders that at least one board member did not want the words *White privilege* used by any staff member around students and that there was a fear of upsetting the community around this issue. We also had a referendum coming up in the months ahead of a Dare 2 Be Real retreat, and there was a fear that bringing students on a retreat that could cause any attention could harm the possibility of this passing. I believed that these excuses were fear-based and that with the proper communication, we could continue to do antiracism work with students. This all came on the heels of a number of decisions that I felt were more focused on assuaging adult comfort with our police liaisons than on looking at how they were treating our students of color. However, I failed to fully listen to those with positional authority to understand why they were unwilling to make changes with the police liaisons and what they *were* willing to accept with the Dare 2 Be Real work. Instead, I found myself concerned with what they were telling me I couldn't do. This is a common mistake I have seen many antiracist leaders do—they get angry with those in positional power telling them they can't rather than truly seeking to understand the reasons behind it. Without doing so, it becomes very difficult to coach up.

Coaching Up: I have spoken to many teachers and assistant principals over the years who have been frustrated with their principal's support. Typically, they will point out that the principal does not seem to "have their back" when it comes to racial equity or that the principal is "not present," much like the principal from Midwest High School I mentioned in Chapter 5. Most often, however, I have found that principals or superintendents just simply have not been developed themselves on how to lead for racial equity. Therefore, they are unable to develop their leaders fully. Do we have the patience to coach our supervisors the way we are willing to coach our students for antiracism? This requires more nuance, since they may not ask for your coaching.

Teachers and advisors of students need to learn the skill of garnering support from those with positional authority so they can teach it to their students. This is an important antiracist skill. For example, when I taught history at Hopkins High School, I would often play a slideshow of songs from the Civil Rights Movement with two songs in the background. The first time, I would play "We Shall Overcome," and I would ask students to write down their feelings: then I would play the same images with "Fight the Power" by Public Enemy in the background. We would discuss which song would be most effective for which audience. Students learned a valuable lesson in a very simple way about how to deliver a message about race to different people and how to evoke different feelings of sympathy, empathy, or empowerment and for whom. It sparked great discussion. It also prepared students to lead professional development when they would coach up their teachers through equity walks. If they were to speak truth to power, they needed to learn from skilled adults about how to speak to predominantly White teachers about how they needed to change the experiences they were providing for the students in their classrooms.

Voices From the Field: Astein Osei, Superintendent, St. Louis Park Public Schools

In all of my personal and professional experiences in the field of education, I have maintained a passion for changing outcomes for students. As my critical consciousness has increased, my sense of urgency has been amplified as I continue to uncover implications for students of color and Indigenous students if we stay on the same trajectory of student achievement in this country. The trajectory of public education for students of color and Indigenous students is similar to the trajectory of a speeding semi truck with no brakes headed into a crowded intersection. There is such a thing as being too late and, as a country, we are rapidly approaching a crowded intersection where our inequitable educational practices are going to collide with a democratic society that needs its citizens to be educated to survive.

As the superintendent of St. Louis Park Public Schools, I have found it important to be vulnerable, knowledgeable, and clear about the urgency of our work. In navigating the path to garner support from those with cultural and positional authority in my school district, I have learned that it requires clarity, conviction, and care. In St. Louis Park Public Schools, it is our mission to see, inspire, and empower each learner to live their brilliance in an environment that centers student voice and experience to create racially equitable learning that energizes and enhances the spirit of our community.

To actualize this mission, I must see, inspire, and empower each adult in the organization to interact with students and families in a manner that energizes and enhances their spirit. As the superintendent, my leadership is essential in creating the conditions for effective instruction and in setting the culture of the school district. One of the ways that the word support is defined is as a thing that bears the weight of something or keeps it upright. I feel this is a fitting definition of what it looks like to provide support from the top in a school district.

As the superintendent I have to "bear the weight" of keeping the strategic direction of the organization at the center of the way we utilize our human and financial resources. Making sure the strategic direction is central to every-thing we do helps to create clarity for staff members and gives them a sense of direction and security of purpose. This sense of direction and clarity in purpose is a form of support that is sometimes undervalued in school districts, but it is important in garnering support from those with cultural and positional authority.

As a superintendent, I have found it critical to consistently demonstrate an unwavering level of conviction regarding the core values and mission of the organization. A leader who does not demonstrate conviction through words and actions regarding the strategic direction of the school district that they are leading will find it difficult to garner support from those with cultural and positional authority in their organization. Additionally, a lack of conviction is a threat to an antiracist strategic direction because if the conviction, or will, is not there it will be challenging for a leader to stand in their purpose when presented with resistance. Those with cultural and positional authority in organizations appreciate leaders with strong conviction, especially when there is alignment of strongly held beliefs.

Making provisions for what is necessary for the health, welfare, and protection of students, staff, and the strategic direction of the organization is an important aspect in garnering support. Making these provisions is a demonstration of care that is central in the formation of trusting relationships. Theodore Roosevelt said, "Nobody cares how much you know, until they know how much you care." These words are helpful in thinking about the tenet known as support from the top. Successful leadership connected to this tenet requires a high level of authenticity.

Creating antiracist educational environments where students consistently achieve at high levels and have their brilliance seen and nurtured is within our reach. In order for public education systems to firmly grasp this experience for students, it will require effective support from the top.

Support-From-the-Top Tenet Application

District-Level Application: School Board Presentations on Curriculum. Around the United States the battle for the hearts and minds of the school board has become the epicenter for antiracism in schools. One of the most effective ways we have gained the support of the school board for our racial-equity work in St. Louis Park has been to maintain complete transparency and to make frequent visits to our school board meetings. Our design teams, who have gone through extensive training on critical race theory and the intersection of school leadership and have learned about the work of Heifetz and Senge on organizational change, have provided transparent presentations to our school board on an annual basis about the racial-equity transformation in which they are engaging with students, peers, and community stakeholders. This transparency is required to foster trust with the school board, a key component of sustainable antiracist work in schools. Indeed, in school districts all over the country and in our local St. Paul Public Schools, antiracist leaders were pushed out the door because of a perceived lack of transparency with the school board about efforts to transform leadership and classroom practices that would address the racial predictability of achievement. In St. Louis Park, we have our teams present to the board throughout their process, sharing their racial autobiographies and racial-equity purpose for engaging in the work sometimes a year or two before making recommendations for any structural, curricular, or instructional changes to programming. This has had the effect of enticing anticipation for change among our board members rather than trepidation about the potential for radical movements that are designed to disrupt the status quo. In addition, affirmation from the school board provides a level of confidence to our teacher-leaders and principals to move forward courageously with their antiracist work.

School-Level Application. The first school in which I worked as an administrator had the highest middle school reading and math scores in the state on our statewide standardized tests over the previous 3 years. Despite this trend, the school had one of the most persistent racial achievement gaps in the state. Black, Brown, and Indigenous students were predictably underserved and underperforming in this community. The predominantly White staff and community, however, looked at the top-ranked test scores and long-standing reputation of excellence and resisted any training or conversation about race as not only unnecessary but as finger-pointing—"Why are you blaming us for these students of color not doing well? Can't you see most of our students are doing great?"

Those with the greatest cultural authority—that is, those with the greatest influence among the staff—were among those who felt most strongly about the need to focus on colorblind initiatives rather than isolating race in our conversations. One of the strategies we decided to use, as administrators, was to engage our fledgling Dare 2 Be Real student leadership group in the development of an all-school assembly on antiracism. This particular middle school had a long tradition of excellent, culture-building assemblies built into the fabric of the calendar. One staff member was particularly gifted at coordinating these assemblies and also happened to have the ear of the entire staff. I asked the students to enlist his help in the development of the assembly, and it was game-changing. By understanding the critical-race-theory tenet of interest convergence, these students engaged this staff member with cultural authority in partnering with them to develop an excellent assembly that would reach a wide audience. By humbly asking for his help and acknowledging his expertise, but being unwavering in their outcomes, they won him over. In doing so, the students garnered his support in future conversations he had informally all over the building with staff, far outlasting the impact of the all-school assembly they cocreated, teaching the students a valuable lesson in sustaining and deepening antiracist school leadership.

Student Group-Level Application. At the same suburban middle school in which the assembly was masterfully planned by the students, the Dare 2 Be Real group never would have existed without some prior work with the support-from-the-top tenet. As you can imagine, this high-performing, predominately White school had a lot of naysayers when a new administrator suggested we center an antiracist student leadership group in school rather than have a student council. To get to that point, I had to engage in a number of conversations and iterations of FAQ sheets that spoke to why antiracist leadership would be necessary in a school such as this. The most important conversation was to ensure that the implementation of the group was directly tied to the goals of our district strategic plan and to the goals of our site council. By engaging an interracial group of students in goal-setting that would help our site and district leaders in turn meet their goals, our Dare

2 Be Real group was seen from the beginning as a potential asset to those in positional authority.

At this particular school, I enlisted the help of Anthony Galloway, the student learning coordinator for the West Metro Education Partnership, an integration district to which the school district belonged. As a Black male, Anthony was able to speak regionally with authority about the antiracist work with Dare 2 Be Real that was happening in this affluent White suburb, and I was able to speak confidently about the regional support that we had from this integration district. Not only did this have the impact of spreading the work to other school districts, but it deepened the work in my school district, building support among teachers, principals, and district administrators.

COMMON LANGUAGE AND PROTOCOL

How Have You Used Protocol and Common Language to Heighten Racial Discourse With Students and/or Staff?

Voices From the Field: Dr. Lee-Ann Stephens, Teacher and SOAR Advisor, St. Louis Park Public Schools

I often reflect on my own middle school and high school experiences. I was the only Black student in my graduating class of 350 students, which meant every year I was isolated racially. I didn't have the tools to discuss my racial experience, so I remained silent most of the time. I can't imagine how liberating it would have been for me, my White peers, and my teachers to have had the Courageous Conversations About Race protocol. I would have been able to speak my truth with the understanding that my story was just one of many stories but it was mine. Perhaps my White peers and teachers would have understood my lived experience as a Black girl, not based on their perceived bias of who I was, but through my eyes.

I remember having an 8th-grade social studies teacher who got pleasure from telling jokes about Black people. Sometimes, he would have me stand up and he would tell the jokes. I half-laughed with a mixture of embarrassment and uncertainty of how to react. Had I had the protocol, I could have told him how his jokes made me feel as the only Black student in the class. I could have told him what perception he was causing the other students to have about people who look like me. I could have asked him to examine his own racial bias that was under the guise of a joke. There is so much I could have spoken, but I simply didn't have the tools to do so; therefore, I suffered internally. My humanity suffered. Unfortunately, without the teacher's awareness, the humanity of my White classmates and that of my teacher suffered too.

Because of my experience as a middle school and high school student, I am committed to ensuring that the students I advise through Students Organized for Anti-Racism (SOAR) have the tools to have racial discourse in a manner that allows them to be seen, heard, and valued—in a manner that allows for their humanity to remain intact.

I am often dumbfounded by the fact that we have protocols for fire drills, lockdowns, hallway safety, staff meetings, and student assemblies. However, we rarely have protocols and standards for conversations about race. Yet we are having conversations about race on a daily basis, mostly impromptu, without any guidance. And when those conversations go awry, we blame the topic, instead of the lack of preparation. The Courageous Conversations About Race protocol offers such preparation and guidance.

Because our students are comfortable having these conversations, they are exemplars for teachers who aren't comfortable. I have noticed that we are very comfortable having conversations about climate change, world hunger, the women's movement, and other topics that don't necessarily center race. Perhaps those topics do not evoke feelings of helplessness or hopelessness, like maybe the topic of race and racism does. Or maybe those topics have been normalized.

Racial discourse takes intentional effort. For example, I am very methodical in how I introduce topics for racial discourse. For students who are committed to antiracism, I believe it is important for them to have knowledge of theories predicated on how our system was designed. Yes, I introduce the five tenets of critical race theory. I don't tell them what to think or how to think about any particular topic. I present the information and allow them to draw their own conclusions. Critical race theory is such a hot-button topic, so I want them to be familiar with it. The five basic tenets of CRT are permanence of racism, counter-storytelling, critique of liberalism, interest convergence, and whiteness as property. For each tenet I will give examples and then ask the students what they think. So often, their response is, "Why is this a theory, when we see it playing out in society?" My response is, "Great question!" I would rather leave them with the opportunity to answer their own questions. I don't want to give answers. That's too easy and it doesn't lend itself to getting them to think critically. Not only do I present the tenets, but I also present the argument against those tenets. It's crucial for the students to hear both sides. Students are curious beings who want to ask questions and have discussions. I wouldn't be doing my job as an educator if I didn't provide those opportunities.

We fear the unknown. We fear what's uncomfortable. What will it take for us to get on the other side of that fear? There's so much we can learn from students, because they are willing to step over that line and engage in the hard conversations that will liberate us all.

Common-Language-and-Protocol Tenet Application

District-Level Application. In St. Louis Park Public Schools, every teacher has been assigned a racial-equity instructional coach. That means that every teacher, regardless of their tenure, is observed three times a year by a coach who uses the Courageous Conversations About Race protocol and Mindful Inquiry to engage staff in understanding their own racial consciousness. In addition, the coaches align with principal observation to ensure that all teachers are engaged in high levels of culturally relevant pedagogy as defined by Gloria Ladson-Billings's work (2021a). Staff are coached and evaluated in three domains: student academic success, cultural competence, and critical (sociopolitical) consciousness. All staff in the system are reminded of this definition of culturally relevant pedagogy on a regular basis to support their planning, and Courageous Conversations protocol is modeled and normalized at all staff meetings and professional development sessions.

School-Level Application. One activity I have led on many retreats for antiracist leaders over the years has been to ask them to build a racist school. In fact, I ask them to conceptualize and present the most racist school they can possibly imagine. In short order, whether it be adults or students, groups come up with the most racist renderings one could imagine. It shows how normalized these images are in our schooling experience. However, when asked afterward to build an antiracist school, there is more of a struggle. In fact, many of the participants find themselves moving from past practices and lived experiences from the racist school activity into the theory of what an antiracist school could look like. In both of these activities, I provide numerous working definitions about race and racism and ask them to consider the work of Judith Katz in their discussion of system school racism.

Student Group-Level Application. One of the ways in which common language is taught specifically to students in St. Louis Park is through Katz's framework (1997) for understanding racism. In this framework students learn about systemic racism through the examples of covert and overt racism and of intentional and unintentional racism and descriptions of how they interact with individual, institutional, or cultural (traditions, mores) racism. This common language and understanding coupled with case studies and examples provides students with the ability to identify and discuss racism as it happens in the community.

IDENTITY DEVELOPMENT

How Are We Developing Our Individual and Collective Racial and Cultural Identity?

We only teach two things: who we are and what we know (Hartoonian, 1997). Most of our teacher and leadership preparation programs focus their efforts on developing future educators in what they know, leaving out at least half of what we teach. Knowing oneself and being conscious of how one's identity impacts others as one collaborates across various intersections present in school and society are crucial to helping students understand this truth as well.

Voices From the Field: Ezra Hudson, Black Male Student, St. Louis Park High School

Before joining Students Organized for Anti-Racism (SOAR) in St. Louis Park I had no true outlet or platform from which to catapult my fight for racial equity. Prior to joining SOAR, I had knowledge here and there about racial consciousness but mostly just anger at what I saw in the world and learned about history. I considered myself a bystander to racial-equity work, compared to being a leader now. I now refer to myself as an activist because of my growth while in SOAR.

When I first joined SOAR as a freshman in high school, I was the only male and the only underclassman among seven women of color and one white woman who were juniors and seniors. It was then that I first saw and experienced the pattern of being the one, or one of few, Black males involved in racial-equity efforts in Minnesota. As I spent my time among these amazing women, I learned so much about how the intersectionality of race and gender truly comes into play when talking about race. Over the next 2 years I would learn from this group about the compass, how to have conversations about race, how to facilitate conversations, how to challenge problems you see, and how to create systemic change. Once I reached my junior year, I felt I was able to use everything I had learned to start making big changes. I used what I had learned about the importance of collaboration in racial equity to help cofound my organization MN Teen Activists. I also was able to use the tools of facilitation I had learned to help lead my school's walkout along with debriefing and healing sessions afterward.

Putting all these things I had learned in SOAR together has had a significant impact on my identity as well. I think that I have begun to satisfy my cultural identity because I am actively fighting for it. I felt that a couple years before I was not doing enough, and now, I am on that path to enough. Personally, as a Black male I feel I have learned so much and there is so much more that I want to learn and experience. There are certain things that you just can't get out of predominantly White spaces that as a Black male you have easy access to at places like HBCUs (historically Black colleges and universities). I think on an individual level I am ready to experience the warmth and freedoms of always being around my people and fighting for change with them.

Identify-Development Tenet Application

District-Level Application. A school district that is committed to having a healthy collective racial identity is grounded in a mission and vision that supports racial consciousness and student voice explicitly. In St. Louis Park their mission, vision, and core values are stated here:

Mission Statement

St. Louis Park Public Schools sees, inspires, and empowers each learner to live their brilliance in an environment that centers student voice and experience to create racially equitable learning that energizes and enhances the spirit of our community.

Vision Statement

St. Louis Park Public Schools—Where students are seen and valued and become their best selves as racially conscious, globally minded contributors to society.
    Core Values—We believe in

- *The brilliance of ourselves and others. Everyone has the capacity and responsibility to foster the growth and brilliance of others.*
- *Authentic community engagement. Engaging and supporting our employees, families, and communities will enhance the healthy development of each learner.*
- *High expectations. Instilling and upholding high expectations empowers students and staff to higher levels of achievement.*
- *Collective responsibility. Embodying the collective and urgent responsibility of antiracist practices enriches a work and learning environment and community.*
- *Persistent effort. Through persistent effort we will create anti-racist schools and academically successful learners.*
- *Racial consciousness and cultural competence. Racial consciousness and cultural competence are essential to each person's ability to be a catalyst for change.*
- *Advocacy for equity. Everyone has equal intrinsic worth and we will advocate for the historically marginalized.*

School-Level Application. If you ask any 5th-grade student in just about any elementary school in the United States, they will be able to tell you a story about Rosa Parks. Typically, that story follows the same tired explanations. She was tired. She was old. She was a seamstress. She had had enough and decided she was not going to give up her seat on the bus. In my experience most high school students will say that they have learned this story and have heard the "I Have a Dream" speech by Martin Luther King at least five or more times in their career as a student while hearing very little else about Black history. What is missing here so often is the opportunity to teach students the antiracist lessons of the Rosa Parks story. There is a deep connection to the

Dare 2 Be Real framework and the work of Rosa—her role as the secretary of the NAACP, her training in the Highlander School (which is a great example of systemic antiracist student leadership development, if not the greatest example), and her interracial partnerships. Let's discuss the famous image of Rosa Parks sitting on a bus in Montgomery, AL (Figure 6.2). Most U.S. history textbooks show some form of this picture showing Rosa sitting on the bus looking out the window but give very little explanation of or context to this image. What most people don't know is that this picture was taken nearly a year after Ms. Parks was arrested for her act of civil disobedience. She and her antiracist counterparts were planful in their efforts to document the moment that played an integral role in the Montgomery Bus Boycott. What is also missing from the explanations in the books is anything about the White male in the background. This man is Nicholas Chriss. Mr. Chriss was a photographer for the NAACP and played the role of a White Southern racist in the photo for effect. It wasn't until decades later that this act of allyship was brought to light. There are two important lessons here about antiracist identity that can get lost quite easily. One lesson is that the work of antiracism is planful, strategic, and collaborative—not just a passive act of resistance, as is all too often the way in Rosa's courage is depicted. The second lesson involves color, race, and antiracist identity. There is little taught about the impact Rosa's light skin had on her choice of being in this picture, in being the face of the movement, and in her success in getting sympathy from Whites, where

Figure 6.2. Rosa Parks and Nicholas C. Chriss

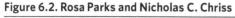

Source: Preus Museum

her darker counterparts who came before her did not. Nor do we talk to our student leaders about the impact of a White man taking on the silent role of support and ally—even willing to play the role of racist in this picture to help spread the important story of civil rights. Advisors of antiracist leadership groups and classrooms should lean upon the lessons of the Highlander School and discuss opportunities in which they can also use imagery and the documentation of stories to help spread the message of antiracism. The simplicity of an image of Rosa Parks that is known to so many, in the hands of a well-developed antiracist leader, can spark the racial consciousness and confidence of so many other student leaders, both those of color and White. The universality of the Rosa Parks story being retold through an "antiracist cultural frame" for student leaders to reference provides an entry point for the conversation about their own antiracist identity development and collective partnership with others like Rosa and Nicholas Chriss. Yvette Jackson explains how without antiracist examples, racism permeates our cultural frames:

> As educators, we must first recognize how our own cultural influences affect how we see and respond to the world. This recognition will make more comprehensible how the legacy of enslavement and residual institutional racism (which in many places have continued into the present) have been incorporated into the cultural frame of reference of our African American students. These factors affect them emotionally, and their cognition and resultant learning are in turn impacted. (Jackson, 2011, p. 47)

Student Group-Level Application. Racial autobiographies are a key way to model and share with others your racial journey. In student groups or in classes that teach antiracism I often ask each member of the class to share their first encounter with race and "chapters" of their racial autobiography that have been significant. This may also include some of the most recent encounters they have had with privilege or racism. Racial autobiographies can lead into historical conversations about community, as the focus of any student antiracist leadership development should be on individual and collective identity development. Student leaders in numerous settings have shared that their biggest "aha" moments came when learning about identity through three themes: (1) *Who we were*—our individual and collective history, (2) *Who we are*—an exploration of racial identity development as it intersects with other aspects of identity, and (3) *Who we want to be*—a particularly action-oriented movement that allows students to participate in active antiracism.

PART III

BUILDING FOR ETERNITY

The whole history of the progress of human liberty shows that all concessions yet made to her august claims have been born of earnest struggle. The conflict has been exciting, agitating, all-absorbing, and for the time being, putting all other tumults to silence. It must do this or it does nothing. If there is no struggle there is no progress. Those who profess to favor freedom and yet deprecate agitation are men who want crops without plowing up the ground; they want rain without thunder and lightning. They want the ocean without the awful roar of its many waters. This struggle may be a moral one, or it may be a physical one, and it may be both moral and physical, but it must be a struggle. Power concedes nothing without a demand. It never did and it never will. Find out just what any people will quietly submit to and you have found the exact measure of injustice and wrong which will be imposed upon them, and these will continue till they are resisted.

—Frederick Douglass

CHAPTER 7

The Story: A Gilded Age of Antiracism

In 1872, in Hartford, Connecticut, two men shared dinner and argued over the quality of modern fiction. These two men concluded that they could write a better novel than any currently popular one. Although neither had ever written a novel, together Mark Twain and Charles Dudley Warner cowrote *The Gilded Age: A Tale of Today* (1873), in which they satirized the business and politics of their day. The novel eventually gave a name to the Gilded Age—the historical period between 1860 and 1890 characterized by the sharp contrasts in society, in which America's surface gleamed with gold while camouflaging the cheap base metal underneath (Zinn, 1980).

Such symbolism was hardly lost on the ordinary people who lived through the Gilded Age and experienced tremendous hardships and losses. Whether they lived in the rapidly industrializing cities, where they had few services and even fewer opportunities for the luxuries that accompanied the wealth of a few industrial capitalists, or in small rural communities, where they endured grueling poverty, their hardships were similar. The inequities that flourished in this seemingly gilded environment fueled a new generation of struggles. Despite the keen eye for inequities in the American system, most ordinary Whites were not as sympathetic to the plight of poor people of color throughout the country. In fact, racial tolerance reached a critical nadir during the Gilded Age that resulted in deeper-seated institutionalized racism than one could have ever thought possible in a period that came on the heels of Reconstruction after the Civil War. The critical eye of historians of the 20th century helped expose the developments of the Gilded Age that included hundreds of lynch mobs, thousands of disenfranchised persons who could not vote, and millions who were denied access to equitable education. This chapter addresses the themes that emerged during what I deem to be a Gilded Age of antiracism at Midwest High School.

PROLOGUE: PHILADELPHIA

The crowd continued to approach us after our session in Philadelphia that winter. There were superintendents, principals, and teachers from across the nation asking us questions and trying to figure out how they could replicate what they had just seen presented. Midwest School District had sent seven employees from their district to Philadelphia to discuss their approach to systemic antiracism and how their leadership had permeated each aspect of their schools, structures, policies, and procedures. Most of the commentary coming from the approaching audience members highlighted the passion and high level of institutional support that was presented so clearly from this team—a team of dedicated professionals who had addressed multiple facets of their personal and professional journey as racial-equity leaders over the past 2 years of working on formal site or district equity teams. I, among them, was working as both a school leader and critical ethnographer.

Regardless of the position of the person addressing the group or the region a member of the audience came from, the discussions that ensued were founded in hope. The common theme that resonated into the evening was the potential for networking and growth that Midwest's work had awakened with the audience. One teacher from Arizona asked if this team could come speak to his staff, because of the struggle his school faced with fostering antiracism in the face of anti-immigration sentiment and covert institutionalized racism throughout the region. Principals and superintendents from Florida, Pennsylvania, and Colorado asked if they could visit Midwest High School in the next year to see the model. They discussed sending leaders from their school districts to participate in immersion or exchange programs with the district in order to learn about the "well-oiled, racial-equity machine," as one principal put it, that appeared to exist at Midwest.

As we left the room, hope was strong. We had presented a clear image of a district that from the top—the superintendent's chair—and through the ranks had prioritized antiracism that was permeating every aspect of the organization. Attendees continued to approach individuals from the conference to ask questions about the district and to find out how this work had been embedded so deeply, particularly at a high school. Fielding questions and presenting on behalf of Midwest were three district employees: the superintendent, the director of equity and integration, and the deputy superintendent; two staff members at Midwest High School; a female parent of color representative who was also a teacher at Midwest High School; a multiracial male equity coordinator and part-time teacher; an elementary teacher who worked as an instructional coach on culturally responsive teaching; and a White elementary principal. All eight of these people were key members of the Midwest racial-equity "machine." Within 3 years, due to being pushed out, moving out, or getting burned out, all seven would no longer be employed with the Midwest School District.

A year before our trip to Philadelphia, I watched the first racial-equity training at our school from a place of detachment. One thing was certain: I could not sit through another session like this. The equity team had been formed just months earlier and the direction of the program was not certain. Comprising many staff members with little to no background in antiracism or equity work, this team had been told that they needed to lead a session on racial equity for the staff at Midwest High School. The discomfort and lack of passion were both quite evident to a few staff members and to at least one school administrator. This administrator sent out a message to the staff asking if anyone would be interested in joining the existing team. Within 2 days after this session, there were four new members of the equity team, including me.

My first meeting with the equity team was actually their fourth training. The session was led by Glenn Singleton and included equity teams from sites all over the district. At first, I felt like I had to prove myself. I was the new kid on the block. However, by midday I was overtaken by a feeling that was very different from most other professional development opportunities I had experienced. It was authentic. I quickly realized that "proving myself" would not come from casually mentioning my training, the classes I taught, or even my racial or ethnic affiliation. Acceptance would come from my willingness to engage deeply and authentically in Courageous Conversations About Race, particularly from a place of reflection and vulnerability that was not common among other professional-development opportunities in which I had previously participated.

Things moved quite quickly after this preliminary meeting. I was approached by a district administrator who recognized my passion for racial equity and my knowledge of racism and the racial narrative in the United States. A few teachers had spoken candidly to district officials about their doubts regarding the administration's will, skill, knowledge, or capacity to effectively lead this work, and there was a sense of urgency to start things off well. The district administrator said she would fund a position at Midwest High School that would be similar to other teacher-leadership positions at the school. There already existed four teachers in leadership who oversaw professional development, student activities, building safety, and curriculum. A teacher coordinating equity would be the first change in that model since its inception 5 years earlier. Varying accounts accompanied the final decision to move forward with the position, but suffice it to say that staff members were sent a strong message that the equity initiative was seen as a priority of the Midwest district. Some teachers were thrilled, while many others wondered aloud about how there would be enough work to do to justify a job such as this. One said to me in passing, "I think the equity work is important and all, but what is there to do except lead the meetings?" Racial-equity work was seen as little more than an add-on in the spring of Year 1; soon it would permeate most discussions and settings at Midwest High School.

YEAR 1

The following events took place during the first year of a critical ethnographic study of antiracism in a school district. Documentation of these events was collected and created during this time period and through reflections on correspondence and journals and after experiencing these events in the field. The first year of formal racial-equity work was a significant year for antiracism at Midwest because of the resources and purposeful actions put into racial equity and the covert and overt resistance to the proposed change. The events from fall to spring of Year 1 discussed in the following section include the equity-team retreat, the decision, the conference, the work, student voices, the hire, the consultant in-house, and the student leaders.

The Equity-Team Retreat

One of the first tasks of the equity leaders was to try to build a cohesive team. I was told on numerous occasions that it would be difficult to get this group to collaborate and focus. Many members of the team were appointed, others were asked to join by administration, and others requested to join the group. There was a definite "buzz" in the building about the equity work. I was so immersed in it myself that at times it was difficult to separate it from my personal life. In retrospect, this may have been a good problem. In my study, I would find that the staff members with the most personal connections to the work were the ones who felt the most invested and positive about their contributions at the school.

I had had a lot of experience planning retreats for students, so I knew there was an essence to this sort of thing that should be replicated. I planned a retreat that would take us off-campus. I coordinated a carpool to a retreat center in a rural town about an hour away from the Midwest School District. Over the course of this 2-day retreat, participants would practice the agreements and conditions of Courageous Conversations About Race (Singleton, 2022), explore their racial identity by sharing their racial autobiographies, discuss and study film, engage in activities that would help maintain a local and immediate context, and set goals for the year.

In one particularly poignant moment, our equity team did an activity called "building a racist school" that was adapted from the work of Judith Katz (2003). This activity asked the equity team to design the most institutionally, culturally, and individually racist school they possibly could. After sharing their blueprints, policies, curriculum, schedule, and activities, the team was asked to consider how these schools were like Midwest High School. At first, there was silence. However, soon the comparisons began to flow from the mouths of team members. Leaders from multiple areas of the building commented that they had never noticed how many things were set up in our school that supported racism. This activity helped the team develop an action plan, one that included professional development, which would be implemented just a few days later, and also some new directions with policies that after 2 years had seen only minimal change.

Throughout the day, equity leaders engaged in deep and personal exploration of their own role and presence in the racial-equity work at Midwest. The equity leaders watched *The Color of Fear* (Mun Wah, 1994) and explored their own racial-identity development throughout the afternoon. At times throughout the 2-day retreat staff of color were given time to process separately and decompress from any microaggressions of unintentional or covert racism that may have occurred during the day. That evening, each leader was to share his or her racial autobiography with the rest of the group. One White staff member was particularly disengaged from the activity, sitting outside the circle even after an invitation. When asked to share, he said he did not want to focus on the past and did not see the point of the activity. Although speaking his truth, numerous team members shared that his disengagement made them feel very uncomfortable. I decided to discuss the situation with him after the session. I asked an administrator to join me because I figured this would be a difficult conversation. This administrator said he would "have my back." As I discussed the events of the evening with my colleague, things got emotional. He expressed a frustration to focus on a racist past that took time away from a future-oriented action plan. As things got heated and the discussion had gone on close to a half-hour, I turned around to find that the administrator was literally no longer behind me. This silent departure became an allegory for the year and a signal that I may not have the passionate leadership support that I would need to be a leader of systemic change.

The retreat provided a foundation for the equity work at Midwest High School that got us through many difficult times. These 2 days, in many ways, provided a glimpse into the ups and downs that the equity team would face as it went through the internal struggles to build a team and develop a culture that supported racial equity. We would draw on the lessons we learned at this retreat and never quite "retreat" from the tension and lack of trust that only made its presence known the rest of the year.

The Decision

The day we got back from our equity-team retreat, the team was excited to share their enthusiasm for racial equity with the rest of the staff. We knew we would have to build some bridges to link our passion with the competing priorities that existed throughout various leadership teams in the building. The unity of the team after the retreat resulted in a boldness and collective urgency to do this work right and do the work well. This urgency was contagious and resulted in an essential decision being made after the retreat. The equity team unanimously worked to convince the principal to devote all professional-development time for the coming year to racial equity. He said that this would have to be a decision shared by our professional development and equity teams. As liaisons to each other's teams, both the professional-development chair and I believed we could make a case for this decision with all stakeholders. A few members of the professional-development team were skeptical, but they saw that the momentum of the group was so great that the focus was inevitable.

Looking back, this was an essential decision in two ways. First, the equity team's work became the planning of multiple sessions with our staff that would lay a foundation for what antiracism would look like, sound like, and feel like at Midwest; and second, this decision was the way in which the equity team gained such visibility with staff members and how Courageous Conversations intentionally and overtly permeated the culture of the school. This decision, coupled with the intentional language placed in the Midwest High School site plan, was the result of the passion and persistence of individual leaders who had very little experience navigating the politics of change and the presence and role of Whiteness that accompany a process such as the one they had undertaken.

The Work

The equity leadership team at Midwest High School had many eventful meetings. We decided at one point that we were going to meet on a weekly basis, rotating between morning and afternoon meetings to accommodate schedules. Some team members expressed concern about the number of meetings, but the consensus among the group was that regular meeting times were important and particularly necessary if we were to lead professional-development meetings for the entire year. During these meetings, part of the time would be devoted to our own professional learning and a lot of the time would be devoted to planning and evaluating the school's antiracist professional-development plan. We decided that equity-team leaders would be paired up and would lead a series of discussions throughout the year with 25–30 staff members from the school. These sessions would focus on a discussion of Tatum's book, *Why Are All the Black Kids Sitting Together in the Cafeteria?* (1997); our own racial-identity development; and the personal, local, and immediate implications of this research on our students at Midwest High School.

Some of the greatest learning took place in the equity-team meetings themselves. It was here that many felt a heightened sense of racial consciousness that challenged both White and Black staff. On occasion, Black staff members left the room in tears, while White teachers expressed their defensiveness regarding the awareness of their association with the collective nature of "Whiteness" and the privileges that accompanied it. One memorable meeting ended when an administrator pounded his fist on the table and after an expletive, exclaimed "I'm [in charge] here, not Glenn Singleton!" This aggressive declaration silenced many of the staff of color for weeks, as White staff would discuss among themselves their own reflections on the Whiteness within the group and its implications for "the work."

"The work," as equity leaders called our racial-equity work, was becoming the centerpiece of the school year. Even the act of calling it "the work," which became more and more common throughout the fall and into the winter, centered racial equity at the core of school improvement. This personal commitment to racial equity made collaboration with other equity leaders at once exhilarating and exhausting. Equity leaders expressed great hope in the fall, but as the staff was asked to specifically explore the impact of privilege and institutional racism in the classroom, we started to feel more pushback and a developing lack of trust from within the equity team. When left to their own devices, the equity team often focused on the real and perceived dysfunction among the staff at Midwest. The pain that accompanied the work made it very difficult for some staff to stay engaged. We followed a protocol in word, but we were wildly inconsistent when the focus of the equity team turned inward. It was only when someone redirected us to our true purpose—improving the environment, instruction, and achievement for all students, especially students of color—that the focus could be regained.

Student Voices

In the December of Year 1, a consultant from the Pacific Educational Group came to Midwest High School to talk to students about their experiences in this school. A handful of the students were pulled from Diversity Seminar classes, and other African American students and Latinx students were invited to also be present for specific racial-affinity group discussions. On a Wednesday morning, from 11:30 A.M. to 2:30 P.M., 22 African American students shared their experiences at Midwest in a meeting with an African American facilitator, one White staff person, and an African American staff person from Midwest High. Earlier that morning, Latinx students were also invited to share their perspectives on student life at Midwest. The students were also asked to share their ideas about how to improve the academic success of African American students and Latinx students in their high school and in their district. This was the first time that students of color were directly engaged in a conversation about their experiences at Midwest High School. Below are a few of the questions that the facilitator asked the students and a summary of the student responses to each question. All quotes come from dialogue that took place that day.

When asked how they would describe Midwest High School one White student shared:

> I came to this school in 10th grade from Metropolis. I went to school in Metropolis. My freshman year at Washington, there was a huge difference between Washington and Lincoln, and then to come here. I can say that, at those schools, I couldn't keep myself out of the drama. But here, I haven't been in a conflict with a student in the entire 3 years that I've been here. I think that if you say, "I'm not going to be a part of this. I'm not going to talk about people behind their back. I'm going to give everyone the understanding like, if you have a problem with me, come to me," then it is fine . . . I come to school to do my schoolwork and to learn . . . I think Midwest is a really good school. I think the people, for the most part, get along—you know, the different groups. I hang out with everyone.

Others commented:

> I think a lot of people here, they are nice, but I think a lot of students here are very ignorant of other cultures, very . . . They're like afraid to say "African American"

or "Black" or they'll say "You people," and they really truly don't know what they're saying.

Some students also shared a confusion and lack of clarity regarding working definitions and language that was being used by staff and students to discuss race:

> I can't tell you how many meetings I've gone to and the [theme] of the meeting is, "What do we call students of color?" I mean, we're people. Call us by our names. [The student went on to respond to the student in the forum who stated that students get along at Midwest] I understand what you're saying about the different groups. I know that very well. I've grown up in Midwest since kindergarten. I have tons of White friends. I have people in theater, the choir, the jocks, and the skaters, whatever. I'm in every group, but I think that the one thing that is discomforting is that I like all the different people for similar reasons, but none of those groups really come together . . . If you tried to bring all of those people together, it wouldn't work . . . That's why I don't feel the school is connected because you almost have to like disassociate with people in order to get that level of respect or understanding or friendship or whatever you want to call it.

Another student disagreed that the various groups of students can't come together at Midwest:

> I have to disagree with that, from my perspective. It's probably because girls are a lot more cliquish. As a guy, I can honestly say that I hang out with the choir kids, I hang out with the band kids, I play basketball, I focus a lot on academics, so I'm hanging out with the kids who get called "dorks," and they all accept me. And when I leave one group to go to another group, they don't say, "What are you hanging out with them for?" They know who I hang out with, and I think the good part about Midwest is that it's not as cliquey as some other schools . . . People at Midwest tend to be more multifaceted.

The facilitator from the Pacific Educational Group pointed out that the context and reality of institutional, cultural, and individual racism played out at Midwest in the space and interactions between students and staff. Some students talked candidly about the self-segregation that was perpetuated by insensitivity and racial slurs:

> I think it's just that people have their places. Like the Black people on the stairs, the Somalians and Mexicans on the balcony, the Whites are in the middle.

Another student added:

> But they have names for them now. I hang out with a lot of White people, and just walking down that mall, that's a big area. You hear a lot of talkin'. Like the

stairs, I just snicker every time I hear this one—"8 Mile." I mean, come on. That is the border line to DETROIT! I can't believe people say that. Up on the balcony, that is the place where a lot of our students that are first-year immigrants stand up there, and they call that "Ellis Island." There is a section in our school in the middle where a lot of the Jewish kids stand and that's the "Jewish Community Center" . . . the thing I don't like about it is that you have the Black kids, you have the Somalians, the [Latinx], and then you just have the White kids. And the thing with the White kids is that they are able to break up into groups within that same area. You can notice the skaters, or the choir kids, or the theater kids, or the jocks. You can see all those different groups within the White people, but when people just talk about "the stairs [where many of the African American students hang out] or the Somalian or Latinx groups, people are like, "Oh, those are just the Black kids." We're not able to have our own little thing because they just look at us as the same.

Another student talked about another reason why students tend to stay in certain peer groups:

I came here in seventh grade, and everybody had their groups. It's really hard to get in their little circle of friends when they grew up together since like kindergarten. A lot of my friends, they didn't go to Midwest. We went to other schools, [so] we were like new kids. So, I think that's why all the Black people—or some of them who haven't been here in the Midwest system growing up—I think that's why a lot of them hang out together.

Several students shared their perspectives on their own racial-identity development. Many of them discussed how essential it is for students of color attending a predominately White school to figure out how to navigate and negotiate within the system. One student shared some additional thoughts:

I think with so many Black kids, it's hard to step outside the box. We were talking in sociology today about how people act how the world perceives them . . . It's hard for people to step out of the box and act in a way where someone will be like, "Whoa. I didn't expect that."'Cause, like so many people, so many White people, when I first meet them and I'm like, "Hi. How are you," I can see that like "Whoa." I think it's hard for so many Black people to say, "I'm going to decide who I am and then be okay with that." And I just think that all the Black kids altogether haven't found themselves, haven't said, "This is who I am. This is what I want to do." Because you can't say that Black people want to be stupid, or Black people don't want good grades, or they don't want to succeed in school or in life. I just think that some people are stronger than others when it comes to saying, "You know, this is who I am. It's me. Accept it or don't accept it."

The African American and Latinx students at Midwest suggested that staff should be more understanding toward African American students—as they are toward White students. According to students, staff should interact with African American students more and find out why some of them are sitting in the back of class. Students also collectively believed that staff should help students to understand and get along with people of other cultures. They spoke truthfully about their own experiences at Midwest that included a need for advocacy, consistency, and specificity from teachers that often was not there.

As this information was shared with our equity team, a couple of very interesting discussions arose. First, we wondered how we could share the voices in a way that would allow staff to "hear" them. We had already begun some Courageous Conversations with staff that had surfaced some defensiveness and a lack of trust in the counter-story of people of color. We also wondered which voices should be shared with staff and how to choose a forum that would not single out a voice that would represent an entire racial group rather than just that student's personal voice. We decided to focus on some themes that would help staff members see the impact of their actions on student performance. It became clear to many of us that there was a need to create a space for student voices to discuss race and share their multiple perspectives as students at Midwest High School. How this would happen was not clear with so much on the plates of the equity leaders at Midwest. I hoped that something would come soon. Some equity leaders were concerned about the potential danger that would accompany the use of student voice with teachers—thinking that perhaps students speaking their truth would put themselves in jeopardy of repercussions at the hands of disgruntled teachers. I thought out loud about the potential for developing a safe space for student voice that was inclusive of multiple perspectives. In the meantime, many of these student voices were able to be heard anonymously as staff and students worked to develop a forum for more-honest dialogue about race.

The Fishbowl

In February, the equity team decided to facilitate a fishbowl discussion with the entire Midwest High School staff. The fishbowl would take place in the theater and would start with a few equity leaders modeling a conversation about race. The group took great measures to ensure that the discussion would feel authentic and decided to have some open chairs in the circle so staff members could enter and exit the discussion as they saw fit. Those planning the event decided to have the discussion on the stage in the theater while staff sat in the seats.

The discussion started well, with strong engagement from the crowd. More than a dozen staff members, not affiliated with any equity leadership, volunteered to enter the discussion. At times the discussion got heated, but as the team went to close the discussion there was a roar from the crowd to keep it going. For many, this would mark the first time that staff members would engage in the discomfort of a truly honest dialogue about race. However, as some staff members began to shout their displeasure with certain comments from the seats, the dysfunction among the staff became more visible to others in the building. As one teacher talked about her fear of Black students, colleagues rushed to either judge or defend this perspective. In the planning session, administrators had been asked to monitor the rules of engagement, but as the fishbowl began, no administrators were present. For quite a few equity leaders, this furthered a perception that administration was not behind the equity work, nor were they making it a priority in their actions. The fishbowl became a turning point in the equity work at Midwest High School for two reasons. First, the equity leaders began to openly question the school administrator's commitment to racial equity, and second, the staff started to realize the importance of a protocol of conversations about race because of the judgment and vitriol that many experienced in the discussion. Many staff members longed for a shared experience, no matter how dysfunctional, that would model for them how they could contribute to progress in the school and feel a sense of belonging.

The Black/White Dichotomy

Equity leaders at Midwest could agree on one thing throughout the year: The perspectives on the equity work by our Black staff members and White staff members were quite different. In fact, the lack of clarity between staff members created substantial division, at times, among the equity leaders on the staff. Black staff often shared their perspectives along with the emotions that accompanied their viewpoints. The presence of voices of color and the emotion that accompanied it was not usual for leadership teams at Midwest. The shift was very difficult for some White staff and was particularly difficult for Black staff members who were being encouraged to follow a protocol that was not natural for these adults and certainly not comfortable for the leaders of Midwest High School.

A dichotomy between Black and White perspectives on racial equity became a running narrative throughout this intense year of work at Midwest. The division was heightened by conversations behind closed doors that perpetuated distrust and dysfunction among the staff. Although most leaders agreed that an interracial leadership group brought the multiple perspectives necessary to address the colorblindness that had been the status quo at Midwest, this work often came with judgment and little self-reflection. Numerous equity leaders shared their disdain with the lack of cohesiveness of the group, and most could pinpoint the private conversations in offices and the parking lot that had become public as the year progressed. There was a question by some about a lack of commitment from some leaders and a lack of follow-through that was often fought across racial lines. This fractious relationship was part of the disequilibrium that may have accompanied the growing individual and collective awareness of the staff of the presence and role of racism in Midwest's practices. Many wished for leadership that would bring the group together with a sense of purpose and the skill to understand this dichotomy.

The Leadership Crisis

In January of Year 1, the principal at Midwest announced his retirement. For the next few months there was less leadership presence at meetings and in the building as at least one of the principals was out of the building a minimum of 3 days a week. That February, the hiring process was initiated and it included over 20 staff members and students, many of whom had positions as equity leaders in the building. Finalists were chosen and the staff waited for a decision to be made.

During this waiting period, news about Midwest hit the papers. The district was going into statutory operating debt due to millions of dollars in financial errors. The superintendent and assistant superintendent, two of the most outspoken proponents of racial equity, resigned, and interims were moved into their places, triggering a domino effect of interim positions being filled around the district. The hiring process for Midwest High School was prolonged for weeks, and nearly 3 months after the process began, a person of color was hired. This decision was met with two distinct reactions. Some were very pleased with the hiring of a strong candidate of color for a highly influential position. Others shared their displeasure by citing the new principal's lack of qualifications and wondered aloud whether or not Midwest was ready for a principal of color. Over the coming months, some staff would wonder if we were ready for any male of color taking a leadership role in the building.

The In-House Consultant

In the spring, the Midwest equity team was still engaged in ongoing trainings that would help them to decide their course of action and to discuss how they could make the biggest gains with the staff. It was determined that conversations about race would be essential before the year ended. The equity team itself had devoted much time to the ongoing professional development of the rest of the staff. All winter, equity leaders shared their desire to have Glenn Singleton, the head consultant with Pacific Educational Group (PEG), come into our building and lead a workshop for our entire staff despite the fact that he did not typically like to do that. PEG's model centered on the role of the principal and teacher-leaders as trainers and change agents in the system. PEG's concern was that if a consultant came into a building that did not have sufficient foundation in the culture of the school or the history of the work, there would be a backlash that would look much different from that which took place when an internal leader was leading the work. It would be easy to demonize a consultant—or in some cases, put the consultant on

a pedestal—therefore keeping the work from becoming owned and lived in
the school and district as part of its mission, vision, and core values. Reliance
on external consultants like this makes it much easier for schools to move on
from the racial-equity work when it becomes uncomfortable by severing ties
with the outside organization or by claiming fiscal responsibility as a means
for not engaging in antiracist work.

The Student Leaders

Inspired by seeing staff members at Midwest High School engaged in dialogue around racial equity and by their own intellectual curiosity, a number
of students in my social studies class started reading *Why Are All the Black
Kids Sitting Together in the Cafeteria?* by Beverly Tatum in the fall of Year
1. I noticed the students outside my door during lunch and asked them how
they got the book. They had all bought copies of the book because they had
seen the book on many teachers' desks. Over the course of the next few days,
I met with this interracial group of students to discuss the book and how it
was impacting their personal views. Within a few weeks after these students
had organized their own learning community with me, two members of the
Metropolis branch of a national organization approached the school about
piloting some antiracism curriculum in four high schools in Year 1 of the
work. Their plan was to provide a one-time training in antiracism for 10–20
students at each school. I worked with two staff members of color to identify
a cross-section of students who would benefit from this training. Many of
the students involved in this initial program and in my elective class began to
develop a plan to expand the program beyond this experience. I invited students to my home and met some of them at school throughout the spring and
summer of Year 1 to develop curriculum that could be shared with more students at Midwest High School. Students had learned a lot about the history
of racism in my class. In addition, they had learned about racial identity from
the book and discussions and now wanted to work toward becoming the students they wanted to be, thus leaving a legacy at Midwest that would impart
substantive antiracist change. That August, these students who were reading
about racial identity in the hallway and who had connected with more students
through the training with the intern from the national organization planned
a half-day retreat with me that would be open to all juniors and seniors at
Midwest High School. We sent out postcards to all families and were thrilled
to have 67 students make a choice to attend on a summer day. Our new principal came to the retreat to share his support, an act that showed his commitment to students. This inspired me to develop the students' leadership and
work with them to form alliances and bring an interracial student voice to
racial equity at Midwest.

   The following year, a district administrator connected me with a professional who coordinated programming that promoted integration in various districts in the Metropolis area. Unknowingly, we had worked together

indirectly through experiential learning programs I had used with my classes in previous years. We partnered to create an ongoing leadership-development program that would incorporate themes such as confronting fear, team-building, interpersonal conflict, antiracist scholarship, and understanding racial and cultural identity as individuals and as a collective.

Students were taught to apply their skills and knowledge through conversations and presentations on race to other students and adults in their school. Over the next 5 years, numerous schools became interested in the student leadership model from Midwest. At the time of this writing, eight school districts had active groups based on the model developed at Midwest, which had begun to expand regionally and nationally to universities, colleges, and school districts in Minnesota, California, and Pennsylvania. The model has been featured on local television, and students and advisers have presented their experiences at numerous regional and national workshops and conferences, including the National Association for Multicultural Education, the Minnesota Middle School Association, the White Privilege Conference, and the Summit for Courageous Conversations in Baltimore and San Francisco. This development has been one of the longest-lasting legacies of the antiracist innovations that developed during Year 2, which are discussed in depth in Chapter 6.

YEAR 2

The following events took place during the second formal year of antiracism work at Midwest. Documentation of these events was collected and created during this time period and through reflections from correspondences and journals and from experiencing these events in the field. The second school year saw a deepening and broadening of the equity work at Midwest High School. New leadership within existing teams and new teams provided perspectives that were new to the building. The events discussed in the following section include the meeting, the instructors, the Black kids through the back door, the step back, the pattern, and the recommendations.

The Meeting

In the summer before the second year of intensive antiracism work, I set up a meeting with the new principal of our building. We decided to meet for brunch at a restaurant in the suburbs. He called me at our meeting time to say he was running a little bit late and apologized for any inconvenience this may have caused. Just a few minutes into our conversation, I recognized the gift Midwest had in this leader. He was a good listener and very authentic. His demeanor made him approachable and easy to talk to. I filled him in on my perceptions regarding the developments of the past year. He assured me that he would support me in my efforts and would appreciate the transparency from my end. I provided him with my vision for the coming year and he asked

clarifying questions while insisting that they were to help him provide support. Years later, we still reference this meeting as a time when we mutually
recognized our sincerity as allies in the equity work.

Going into a second year of the work, I felt it was important to set goals
and recommendations for our work moving forward. In September of that
year, I wrote that the focus of the previous year's professional development
had undoubtedly been on equity. The allocation of focused time to equity allowed us to build a foundation for our work in the subsequent years. For us
to continue to make strides in this work, we would need to build on the foundation we had created and monitor and adjust our practice for the changing
times. Our administration gave equity-team members an opportunity to opt
out of another year on the equity team and strategically invited three new staff
to the team who would provide new perspectives.

We engaged together in a second retreat that, much like the prior year's,
was successful in its efforts to bring the team together around focused efforts.
One of the biggest challenges from the previous year had been the division
across race by members of the equity team. This year, the team engaged in
activities that encouraged them to step into each other's racial identity and
discuss how this could impact their engagement and the perception of their
engagement as leaders. At one point in the session, an equity leader from the
previous year who had been perceived as a particularly divisive figure entered
the retreat and proceeded to sit in on discussions for over an hour. When
this person departed, the principal did what was rarely done a year before:
he stopped the meeting and named the discomfort in the room. Team members openly expressed gratitude for the authenticity of that conversation and
expressed hope for a more collaborative atmosphere in the months to come.

Unlike the previous year, equity leaders were asked to pick an area of
preference for their engagement for the coming year and then were assigned
groups that would set goals in those areas. The areas included school policies,
student development, curriculum and instruction, and professional development. Each subgroup was given the task of being an equity liaison to the
various leadership groups in the building that addressed each of these areas
of the school. This would broaden the scope of the group, but it also led to
more frustration as each team member tried to navigate the politics of other
leadership teams in the building. A lack of accountability on the part of the
equity-team liaisons and inconsistency in the other groups created tension
among many of the leaders in the school who felt like the equity team might
be trying to "police" their commitment to antiracism. It became clear that the
equity team would also benefit from having allies in the building who were
collaborating with similar goals in mind.

The Instructors

A second year of equity work also required a strong priority to be placed
on classroom instruction and curriculum. This would come from a team of

teachers charged with the task of collaborating while engaging action research in their classrooms with the specific goal of achieving racial equity. Existing equity leaders discussed potential candidates for this group and discussed criteria. The leaders determined that teachers in this group should widely represent a cross-section of curricular areas across the building. The participating teachers should also be teachers who had a combination of willingness to be intentional about their antiracism efforts in the classroom and courageous in their use of culturally responsive teaching practices. We also determined that the majority of teachers on the team should have credibility with their fellow teachers, a lesson learned from a year during which many staff members felt the judgment of peers who questioned their credibility to lead without a perceived expertise in the classroom.

I had the good fortune of sitting in on every team meeting with the leaders who were selected. I considered this group of teachers to be the second wave of equity leaders in the school, teachers who would put theory into practice and share their findings with one another and then with the entire staff. This team went through various training throughout the year with two consultants who were masters of culturally responsive pedagogy and instructional models. This group would pick strategies that they would each try between their monthly meetings and then discuss their successes and their failures—both key points in the growth of the individuals in the group. On numerous occasions, White teachers shared their guilt and frustration with their lack of success with the various strategies, but the collective passion of the group maintained a focus on the learning that could come from these failures.

After a year of monthly collaboration and classroom-based action research, this team developed a list of things they found to be successful in engaging students of color and increasing performance for all students. They also compiled a list of strategies they had tried that showed no progress for students of color and, at times, a decrease in engagement and performance. In May 2007, this team shared their findings with the staff in a large group professional-development session. While some staff were deeply moved and appreciative of the effort, others wore headphones, corrected papers, and engaged inside conversations throughout the presentation. In what I considered to be one of the defining moments of the year, a Black leader stood in front of the staff at the end of the session and said that he would take off his professional "hat" and speak from his role as a parent of two children of color. He affirmed the work of the instructional leadership team and then said that if he were sitting in this room as a parent, hearing about specific work that was being done by a portion of our staff to improve performance for students like him, and were to look around and see the brazen levels of disengagement that were quite obvious to him, he would question sending his children to this school. After the meeting, proponents of antiracism applauded this message while others shared disgust for the public nature of his comments. Despite the division, it sent a clear message about the need for more courageous dialogue among staff.

The Black Kids Through the Back Door

For close to 2 years, we had spent time talking about the de facto segregation present in our school. The equity team had discussed how the design of our bus loop and the remodeling of the school had greatly contributed to this practice. The impact affected student and staff perceptions about racial groupings in the school and resulted in more division by races than had previously been seen at Midwest. At a full staff meeting, we discussed the phenomenon and one teacher added, "How can you call this racism? I was on the committee that did that planning and not ONCE did we talk about race." The unintentional consequences of colorblindness left us considering, "Now that we know the impact of not considering race in our decisions, what does it mean for us if we do not take measures to create a more desirable outcome?"

In the spring, actions were taken to make a permanent change to the back door at Midwest. The front door at the school, where students who owned their own cars parked, was not only a welcoming door, but it also boasted gold-plated walls and a bakery that provided freshly baked goods for students each morning. The back door, where buses dropped off students, was dark, with little to no signage indicating the door was even an entrance. The students entering through the back door were disproportionately students of color. Although on the surface it appeared to only be a cosmetic change, the decision to improve the landscaping, lighting, and signage on the back door marked a commitment to following through on improvements to the culture of Midwest High School. The local paper ran an article on the changes, lauding the efforts of the equity team in championing the cause. However, some folks internally and others in editorials in the paper challenged the energy put into this effort rather than those put into improving teacher instruction. Indeed, the efforts to improve the entrances to the building may have had an impact on the physical structure of the school but the development in will, skill, knowledge, and capacity necessary to work with teachers on a change of their practice was not nearly as visible or substantive. In the weeks to come, blogs appeared on the Internet bashing the use of resources for such a frivolous act. The keepers of this blog would assert that resources such as these were being given to poor Black families at the expense of White affluent families. Local radio stations and numerous other web sites encouraged public debate that included a forum for blatant racism. These same blogs would later provide a public forum for people to anonymously bash integration and antiracist student-leadership development at Midwest and throughout the region. Although it was disheartening and frightening for some, a couple of equity leaders felt pride in the fact that their work was making enough of a difference that it would cause this sort of backlash.

The Step Back

The fear of public backlash was certainly a discussion point throughout the winter, spring, and summer following the second year of formal antiracism work at Midwest. The district was embroiled in a very divisive boundary-changing decision that became part of a public forum. District administration had decided to close the most racially diverse school in the district despite increasing enrollment in the school, while other predominantly White schools that were declining in enrollment were kept open, making students from the closed school bus to other regions of the district. This backdrop was a part of the climate when district administration decided to cut the equity-and-integration-coordinator position at the district level. This cut was seen as a manifestation of the district's retreat from a racial-equity prioritization, and too many saw it as a personal vendetta toward the most ardent supporter of the current racial-equity movement. The loss of the director was followed shortly by a severing of ties between the district and the Pacific Educational Group. Once considered by both groups to be a model partnership, the relationship between the two groups quickly dissolved, leaving questions by many site leaders about the support systems that would be in place for their work and the reasoning behind the split. For many, these decisions were inextricably linked to their move away from equity. The district strategic planning committee meeting that came on the heels of these decisions included a decision to take the words "equity" and "race" out of the strategic plan, further dismantling the intentionality of antiracism. Midwest High School leaders discussed these changes and decided to stay their course of action, even as their concerns regarding isolation became more and more a potential reality.

The Pattern

One piece of data that was addressed in the spring was the underrepresentation of students of color in Advanced Placement (AP) classes. AP U.S. History (APUSH), the only AP class offered to sophomores at Midwest, was considered a gateway course to AP because of the social groups formed and culture established among the students who took these courses. Those who did not take APUSH often found themselves not just navigating the rigorous curriculum but also navigating an exclusive culture built on shared experiences and inside jokes. The APUSH team decided to invite all students of color with a 3.0 grade point average and those identified for their leadership and academic potential to take the class. After 1 year of this practice, there were more students of color enrolled in APUSH than in the 20 previous years combined.

This effort was met with skepticism and discouragement by some staff members. In one particular case, a teacher called out one Black male in front of about 80 of his peers by telling him to leave an information session because he did not belong there, privately told an inconsistently performing Black female student that she should not take the class because she was not ready, and then told a Black male with a straight A average that the class was "not a good fit" for him. The only commonality with these students was that they were all Black. I observed this not so subtle message to students: If you are an academically successful Black student, AP is not a good fit; if you are an average Black student, you will be discouraged from taking the class; if you are a struggling Black student, you run the risk of being publicly humiliated by your teacher if you have the audacity to even find out more information about the course. This pattern demonstrated the need to go beyond token efforts to increase participation of students of color in rigorous course work and the need for courageous conversations even 2 years into the antiracism movement at Midwest.

The Recommendations

Throughout the first 2 focused years of this work at Midwest, various school leaders provided ideas for sustaining the work. The collective experience of the Midwest High School equity leaders offered a wide range of perspectives, but five areas of concern continued to resurface. The common belief among the most engaged leaders was that for Midwest to continue to make strides in this work, district administration would need to support some essential action steps. In the spring, district leaders engaged equity teams from all over the district in a fishbowl discussion, patterned after the one that had taken place at Midwest High School the year before. After spirited discussion from, as one leader put it, "the choir," some courageous leaders shared their perception that the setting was not safe for all to "speak their truth." After the fishbowl, each site was asked to discuss the state of equity in their building and share it with the larger group. The Midwest High School equity team reflected on the current state of affairs at their school and developed five statements that best reflected their concerns for the future of antiracism in their school. The list they compiled that day included very intentional wording about the passion, practice, and persistence needed to sustain progress toward racial equity at Midwest High School:

- We must continue to build strong equity leadership through our partnership with the Pacific Educational Group. Their trainings have helped the site equity team and now our instructional leadership team to increase our motivation, skills, knowledge, and capacity to work on our goals of eliminating the racial achievement gaps at Midwest High School. The sustained training and mentorship from the people in this group have empowered many staff members to be leaders in this work at a much larger scale than they ever were before.
- We must engage more of the voices of our students and families of color. The work of our [student, parent, and teacher leaders] should align with our ongoing staff development to help us reach our district and site goals for equity and excellence for all learners. These groups could utilize some of the current modes of communication we have at the high school to work in alignment with our staff.

- We must find a way to provide regular collaborative time for the staff to create professional learning communities if we are truly interested in what is best for each of our students. Research suggests strongly that sustained equity transformation is not possible without deliberate collaborative time for the staff. These professional learning communities should include a lens of racial equity that is supported by training.
- We must engage families, local universities, and other organizations as partners in our renewed focus on equity and excellence in the district. It is essential that we work specifically with our communities of color to get their perspectives as we move forward.
- We must alleviate the burden from our small and diminishing numbers of staff of color by actively recruiting talented staff of color and racially conscious White staff to work in our building. This recruitment is not enough, however. We must also find ways to maintain an environment that retains our staff of color in the building. Our staff population should reflect the population of our school, and currently it does not.

Two representatives from the racial-equity team, both White males, shared these recommendations in front of all equity teams present at the last equity-specific training in the spring. All recommendations were collected by district administration, and they were told they would consider them and get back to the team. The following year, no discussions were initiated at the district or site level to affirm, support, or discount any of the recommendations listed above.

YEAR 3

The following events took place during Year 3 of the formal racial-equity work in the Midwest School District. Documentation of these events were collected and created during this time period and through reflections on correspondence and journals and after experiencing these events in the field. The school year saw a deepening and broadening of the equity work at Midwest High School. But for many a perception that racial equity may have become less of a priority for the district as a shift in resources and support led many equity leaders to sense that they were now more isolated than ever. Antiracist professional development and integration of antiracism into various decisions was still present, and a third year of sustained efforts led many leaders to feel a sense of hope for the ongoing transformation at Midwest High School. The events from this school year discussed in the following section include the silenced dialogue, the Underground Railroad, the dumping ground, the parents, the data gap, and raising Rosa Parks.

The Silenced Dialogue

Racial-equity work in Year 3 looked and felt different from the previous 2 years. The work was ever-present but lacked the showcase of a professional-development plan like the one in Year 1 or the instructional focus it had gained in Year 2. Some staff had now begun to speak out more openly against the work and were more acutely aware of the proponents and opponents of antiracism.

In dialogue with some staff not involved in equity leadership teams, it was common to hear that "equity had been shoved down their throat," and they were ready for the next issue to come along. For proponents of the work, there was a conviction to sustain the work despite the fear that doing so might result in a similar fate to that of many of the most outspoken administrators and consultants before them. The equity leaders at Midwest often talked about doing the work "on our own" and were convinced that it would often have to be covert. This silent dialogue would be called by some an "underground railroad," one in which the intentional and institutionalized practices championed in the first 2 years would be replaced by practices shrouded in secrecy and isolation. Staff of color often spoke of this practice as a way to maintain their own safety and the safety of many students.

The Underground Railroad

As some staff began their own underground system of support for students of color, some students literally experienced the Underground Railroad themselves. The antiracist student-leadership team was now entering a second year that included their engagement in a powerful simulation of the race to freedom for many slaves. The Underground Railroad became a powerful allegory for the work of many students to bring about change at Midwest.

Student leaders were among the most courageous as they prepared bimonthly homeroom discussions and activities designed to develop the student body's collective capacity to create a more antiracist school. The passion of students was evident in their commitment to their own learning and their curriculum development. Two staff members worked closely with the students, guiding them through activities and a curriculum based on much of the known literature on antiracism. One of the staff members, upon his departure, lamented his decision to not include more staff in this important work. By not including more adults in the development of these students, the group had become somewhat dependent on one person and could not sustain the momentum without him.

The Dumping Ground

Staff members at Midwest High School were often looking for a "magic bullet." They hoped for something that would make it easier for them to eliminate racial disparities without the discomfort associated with the isolation of race and personal reflection and adjustment of classroom practice. Numerous staff members shared with me their fatigue and made various excuses—too many to list here—for disengaging from racial-equity work. One hope among many teachers was the various programs that were developed to provide interventions or the various levels of support for students who were not performing to their highest potential.

Equity leaders discussed the creation of curricular programming quite openly and shared their happiness with the opportunities that might befall some of the students engaged in such activities. However, the concern often discussed was that the programs may come to be short-sighted. Rather than addressing racial disparities through the collective change of an entire staff, a program runs the risk of becoming a dumping ground for students who just "can't make it" in the mainstream. In one piece of data shared with me in 2009, more than 70 percent of Black students at Midwest had been removed from a mainstream schedule and were involved in some form of special programming that kept them from taking music, art, or world language classes. Students of color had a wide range of experiences in Midwest programming, but the inconsistency with classroom differentiation in general education classes became even more troublesome, as some Midwest teachers now were able to deflect responsibility for the teaching of a student by claiming that the program should have gotten the student ready for the class. Now, the subculture of programming could be yet another detour for teachers who felt comfort in knowing that when they were not seeing strong performances from students of color, they were truly teaching "other people's children."

The Parents

While the teachers and students were engaged in their own strands of antiracism, a small group that consisted of two teachers, a counselor, and the equity coordinator began to develop a team that would help bring in the perspective and partnership of parents of students of color. The equity coordinator recognized the need for parent voices in the equity work and took steps to make it happen. There were numerous opinions from inside and outside the organization about how to organize such an endeavor, but after much deliberation, the group decided it would be best to invite parents of students of all students of color, not just one specific affinity group, and to be clear in our language that White parents of students of color were welcome to join the group. Before our first meeting, we sent out letters explaining the proposed meeting in the context of the racial-equity work at Midwest. We stated our goals: (1) eliminating our achievement gaps based on race while improving performance for all students, (2) providing a safe and welcoming space for our families of color to become advocates for their children, and (3) partnering with our parents of students of color so we could learn from each other how to best serve their children. Within this invitation was the assertion that we believed that the most devastating factor leading to the underperformance of students of color and their diminished capacity as learners was institutional racism. We explained that our intentionality in reaching out to parents would hopefully help us address this insidious culprit together.

We invited parents of students of color in for three meetings, the first in the winter of year 2 and the second in the spring. Each meeting included a meal and informal time for participants to connect with each other. By the third meeting, we got feedback from some parents that they wanted to get into business more quickly. Twenty-eight parents came to the first meeting. By the third meeting we had 47 parents, 13 students, and 9 staff in attendance. Our meetings had a simple format. We would begin with three discussion questions. Staff members would stay out of discussion unless called upon to clarify something being discussed.

The first meeting provided four questions:

- What do you believe are the biggest strengths of Midwest High School?
- What do you believe needs the most improvement at Midwest High School?
- In your opinion, how can Midwest High School be more successful in serving students of color?
- What do you think is necessary for us to consider in better serving students and families of color at Midwest High School?

In subsequent meetings, the staff coordinators developed slides that answered questions from the previous meeting and worked to make progress with suggestions provided by parents at these meetings. If we could not make progress, we practiced transparency in terms of the roadblocks or impediments in the way of this progress. A handful of parents of students of color became quite active partners, helping to plan future meetings, inviting more participants, and discussing future solutions. These meetings continued into the following year and led to a professional-development opportunity that included a parent panel from this group that shared their perspectives with the staff at Midwest in the spring of Year 3.

What may have been short-sighted on the part of Midwest staff was how to institutionalize the practice we had established with our parents of students of color. By Year 4, meetings for parents of students of color no longer were happening. We had not established the capacity of the community to understand the dual needs of a safe space for historically marginalized families and a strong racially integrated coalition of community leaders. Without a goal of integration, White families were not made aware of these meetings and, thus, some felt deceived when they found out after the fact. This further perpetuated a feeling of mistrust and may have contributed to the hundreds of White families who left the district by the end of the decade.

The Data Gap

One of the biggest gaps of knowledge at Midwest had to do with data. Achievement data were rarely, if ever, discussed at meetings and among staff members. For a building devoted to closing achievement gaps, data were often, surprisingly, anecdotal or not present in discussions. A lack of achievement data was magnified by the comments of some of the parents of color who partnered with Midwest staff. One prominent Black parent shared the perspective that Midwest had created over the past 2 years one of the most welcoming schools for families of color. He and many of his peers had chosen the school because of its commitment to diversity. However, it was not clear whether this transferred to high expectations, rigorous standards, and positive results for the achievement of Black and Brown children.

As the school year came to a close, many staff "felt" as though the work had made a difference, although no one knew if it had. There were no data indicating that the performance of students of color had increased or that behavioral referrals, truancy, and disengagement had decreased as a result of the equity work. One discussion about widening racial disparities the previous spring was met with the notion of an "implementation dip" that was inevitable with all of the change. However, we would never be able to see whether or not the progress would lead to positive academic results because "the work" became more and more de-institutionalized over the next year.

Raising Rosa Parks

Throughout my time at Midwest High School I felt a strong sense of pride in the progress the school was making toward racial equity. However, I was often looking for ways to continue to develop myself personally and expand my sphere of influence. I was offered a position in a neighboring school district that summer. At this time, I did not even realize how the culture at Midwest had changed so drastically over the past 3 years. In Year 1, any mention of race was done in whispers and followed by an apology. By Year 3, it was odd if someone did not bring a racial lens into any decision involving students. These changes, however, seemed to be losing some momentum. I no longer felt the same energy from my supervisors that had begun the work earlier in my tenure and I certainly could feel that resources—monetary, structural, and human resources—were dwindling.

I believed that perhaps the grass would be greener on the other side of town, so I left. In my first month there, I tried to make a token gesture to some in my new office. I had heard that some of my colleagues were hoping for new art in the school. I framed a poster of Rosa Parks and presented it to the office staff. I was surprised and saddened by the response. As they questioned why I would put that in the office, some even wondered aloud if I thought that "only Black students went to this school." It was decided that the Rosa poster would sit on the floor in the corner until the staff decided together whether or not it should go up. I walked by Rosa every day in September. In October, when asking for feedback, I learned that the poster was seen as aggressive and was told by a colleague that perhaps I should not bring my personal beliefs into school. As I passed Rosa, who still sat on the floor in November and December, my sadness often turned to frustration. By January, I felt silenced and isolated. During the next 3 months, as I walked by the framed Rosa poster that sat on the floor, I became detached but decided that the only way I was going to make a change was to take action. I forgot the poster and worked on developing authentic partnerships with parents of students of color and developed criteria based on my experiences at Midwest for the development of a group like Dare 2 Be Real. In April, I was one of many recipients of an email from the superintendent of schools, announcing that my district would be embarking on an intensive racial-equity initiative that would include site plans, equity-team development, and training with the Pacific Educational Group. When I arrived in school the next day, someone had already placed Rosa on the wall. Learning and reflecting upon the 3 years at Midwest High School while working in another setting helped me realize the truth behind the belief that with all progress there comes struggle and that racial equity cannot be achieved with courageous leadership alone but with the will, skill, knowledge, and capacity to lead as well. Sometimes, in the face of fear, those leaders may be willing only to put something on the wall but not make the necessary changes within them. When it comes to the work with children it became a metaphor for the work of helping others become antiracist leaders. It takes a village to raise a child, but it takes a village (and leaders) focused on antiracism to raise a Rosa Parks.

EPILOGUE: NEW ORLEANS

There I was, standing in the Lower Ninth Ward, where Hurricane Katrina had ravaged the city and brought national attention to the racial inequities still very much at play in the United States. I was there with "my people"—an interracial group of equity leaders from Midwest High School, who all were standing or walking in silence as they witnessed the devastation. As we observed in silence, many thoughts came to my head. I felt how important it was to be surrounded by others who cared. The community of equity leaders that supported one another at Midwest High School was unique in that, despite struggle, it had stayed heavily engaged in antiracist leadership for more than 3 years. I was very aware of my Whiteness. I had the privilege of knowing that my community would never be ravaged, purposefully, the way that this one had. I had the privilege of knowing that my own children would not have to wonder whether or not their community, their school, or their academic progress were being undervalued because of the color of their skin. I certainly wondered what role I had played in maintaining a system that I so wanted to change.

Just as Americans had witnessed publicly in the aftermath of Katrina, a lot of emotion had been poured privately into discussions and arguments about the racial inequities at Midwest High School, but what progress had been achieved? As I contemplated this question, I noticed seven beautiful new homes there amid the weeds and rubble. These were the same homes I had seen celebrities building on television months earlier. From my television at home, many miles removed, I had assumed that there was much more progress. However, the cameras had not shown, nor had the reporters shared, that these were the only houses rebuilt after all of this time. Underneath the glitter and gold, this section of New Orleans was still a wreck. I wondered what it would take to speed up this process and help restore life to this once heavily populated African American community. I wondered, much as I had while immersed in the racial-equity work at Midwest High School, what it would take to change a racist institution that could celebrate each night on Bourbon Street yet seemed to turn a blind eye to the plight of the community that was most in need. I was reminded of a quote by Frederick Douglass that had been discussed at an early equity-team meeting I had attended in 2005: "Power concedes nothing without demand. It never has, and it never will. Find out just what any people will quietly submit to and you have found the exact measure of injustice and wrong which will be imposed upon them, and these will continue till they are resisted" (Douglass, 1857). When I share the notion of moving beyond courage, I mean something other than the stance usually taken under the banner of antiracism. Like Douglass, I believe that the only way we can bring about substantive racial equity is to challenge the institutions that reproduce the same racial hierarchy we have come to predict and expect. A challenge to school systems that are so entrenched in Whiteness must be one that disrupts the normal operation and demands systemic alternatives to the status quo. To rebuild a city or even a school like Midwest, there must be leaders who have not just the courage but the will, skill, knowledge, and capacity to teach all students, to build partnerships with all parents, to seek to understand while challenging their colleagues, and to believe that each child, and nothing less, is worth fighting for.

CHAPTER 8

Deepening Antiracist Leadership

The history of racism and exclusion in U.S. education should prepare us to expect the realities of races and racism as central and permanent aspects of U.S. society and schooling. It requires both a commitment to addressing structural racism and addressing the inequities of teaching and learning if we are to overcome what has to this point been insurmountable. We must draw on ancient wisdom as well as recent scholarship to build a systemic antiracist program that can address the powerful pull of systemic racism in our schools. Antiracist school leaders must resist random acts of racial equity and have an equally systemic, long-term approach that goes beyond any individual's charisma, effort, and expertise. Sonya Douglass Horsford says in her book *Learning in a Burning House*:

> It starts with a vision—a moral vision of equal education and the moral activism that the fulfillment of such a vision demands. Although the problem of race has social, economic, political, and legal dimensions, it remains our nations' moral dilemma insofar as it perpetuates inequality, discrimination, and injustice. A vision of equal education requires a solution that targets racism and racial injustice in ways that satisfy the constitutional guarantee of equal protection under the law. As Dr. King concluded a year before his death in 1968, "We must come to see that the roots of racism are very deep in our country, and there must be something positive and massive in order to get rid of all the effects of racism and the tragedies of racial injustice." (Horsford, 2011)

Drawing from the interdisciplinary scholarship on the construction, evolution, and intersectionality of schooling, racial-identity development, critical race theory, professional development programming, and school reform, I have put forth an antiracist approach for student leadership development, heavily informed by the work of Singleton and Linton's *Courageous Conversations About Race* (2006), Horsford's *Critical Race Approach to Equal Education* (2011), Judith Katz's *White Awareness* (1977, 2003), Louise Derman-Sparks and Carol Brunson Phillips's *Developmental Approach to Teaching and Learning Anti-Racism* (1997), Yvette Jackson's *Pedagogy of Confidence* (2011), and Roland Barth's *Improving Schools From Within* (1990). I also draw heavily on the work of substantive critical race theorists, progressive educators, and antiracists who have contributed to the study of race in education (Bonilla-Silva, 2010; Brooks & Arnold, 2013; DeCuir & Dixson, 2004; Gooden & Dantley, 2012; Khalifa, 2018; Ladson-Billings, 2009, 2014, 2021a, 2021b; López, 2003, Pollock, 2008; Solórzano & Yosso, 2002; Tate, 1997, Tatum, 2017, Wood, 2014)

SHARED EXPERIENCES

How Well Are We Building a Collective Learning Identity?

Voices From the Field: Anthony Galloway, Author, Speaker, Podcaster, Faith Leader, and Consultant for St. Louis Park Public Schools

Some of the best and most memorable learning moments in my years as an educator stem from the shared experiences with young people. In helping young people develop the knowledge, skill, will, and capacity for antiracism, having experiences that take this learning beyond the intellectual and theoretical is essential. These moments can help bolster youth identity and self-confidence and build lasting relationships across racial and ethnic lines that can deepen not only their racial consciousness, but their grace and understanding for working across difference and against systemic oppression. The safe and sacred spaces that are built by these shared experiences have a lasting effect on youth participants, and it equips them with stories that bolster long-term growth in their empathy, their resolve, and their willingness to engage across perspectives.

In addition, the stories from these experiences are extremely compelling in shifting paradigms among adults who are uncomfortable with addressing systemic racial challenges. It is the essence of the adage "and a child shall lead them," a biblical reference reiterated by Dr. King. There are several moments in antiracist student leadership development work that exemplify this adage in my 15 years of work with youth antiracist student leadership groups. One example comes to mind that occurred right at the beginning of my training as a pastor in the African Methodist Episcopal Church. It was during a program called the "Civil Rights Research Experience" with students from several school districts including the St. Louis Park School District.

This experience, crafted by educators of color from across the Twin Cities area of Minnesota, centered on contributions of African Americans to civil rights in the United States. Students spent 5 weeks getting to know each other with "edutainment" sessions from local educators, artists, and community leaders from the African American community. Each district was represented by teachers of color from their schools who have backgrounds in African American history, experiential learning, and youth development. It was followed by a week of travel to civil rights sights across the South and interactions with some of the people who lived through key moments in the modern Civil Rights Era. The students then returned to their school districts and crafted art, lessons, and presentations "capstoning" their learning through teaching and storytelling.

In this particular year, spirits were extraordinarily high because we added two amazing Black female artists from a Black arts organization that I ran to support the students. Tish Jones, local poet and executive director of a poetry organization called TruArtSpeaks, helped students document their experiences through poetry. Bianca Rhodes, producer of the documentary *Rondo: Beyond the Pavement*, helped students document their experiences through film. As a storyteller and youth developer, my role was to craft experiences and help young people make connections along with leading the tour experiences. Because of this prep work, students were primed to truly experience the sites, sounds, and stories from the people who lived through this history—from Joanne Bland, who was there on Bloody Sunday, to the Mason Temple, where Dr. King gave his last speech. It was at Mason Temple that the following defining moment occurred.

We were coming to the end of our tour phase of the program, which ended with a REALLY good meal. As we have learned over the years, the dinner table makes or breaks long intensive experiences like this. This year, through one of our adult leaders, we were able to visit Mason Temple in Memphis, Tennessee. It is the headquarters of the Church of God in Christ and is the place where Dr. King gave his last speech. The students had already done their research, so their excitement could hardly be contained. We stepped off of the bus that had become our home and Dr. Lee-Ann Stephens of St. Louis Park Schools began to lead the young people into the historic church.

As Dr. Stevens did this, she demonstrated how every moment can be made a sacred learning space. She engaged the young people in reflection about all of the connections between churches and key moments in our journey and the Civil Rights Movement. Many of our youth did not share the same religious views but were able to make connections between the use of the spiritual centers to gather, uplift, and coalesce members of these movements. It was a master class in educational love to see her skilled questioning that prompted Muslim, Christian, and agnostic young people to engage across perspectives and apply their knowledge and learning to this moment. It was simultaneously a check to make sure youth understood the power of the moment. As if that wasn't enough, it also helped get the young people focused away from the other adults trying to convince the church janitor to let us have the final meal delivered to the church, as we would not make it to the restaurant before closing time if we took this opportunity.

When we got to the large sanctuary of the church, it remained very much like it was during King's speech. The seats are arranged in a near circle around the pulpit in almost a theater in the round. The red carpets accented the woodwork and individual chairs that lined two levels of the sanctuary. It was like going back in time to the era we were there to study. One of the church staff gave us a brief history of the space and mentioned that at first the church did not want to get involved in the rally that would become so famous. This caused quite a stir among the youth, who asked amazing questions after these revelations. After the presentation, he asked the young people about their journey, and this is what began to craft the sacred moment to follow.

By this time, the young people had been to Selma; Birmingham; Montgomery; Tuskegee; Jackson, Mississippi; and now Memphis. They recounted meeting civil rights leaders, standing in Medgar Evers's house, marching across the Edmund Pettis Bridge, and having lunch with 5 elders who were there on Bloody Sunday when police mercilessly attacked voting rights marchers. The youth were masterful in their storytelling and included how these experiences were shaping their learning and understanding. I could see the church staff begin to realize that a moment was developing before their eyes as they became the students and began asking questions themselves, every once in a while looking at the adults in our group as if to say, "How do I get involved?" We shrugged it off, but I felt a small sense of guilt, as we were getting credit for merely being willing to trust the experience, the youth, and do what educators are supposed to do.

By this time the janitor had joined us and was listening intently, still clearly upset about the invitation to the space we now know he had just cleaned. We as adults were still trying to figure out what to do when one of the young people asked if we could listen to Dr. King's speech. We were stunned, not only because it's a brilliant request, but because the young person was so unwavering in their request of the church staff. We had reiterated all along the journey that "closed mouths don't get fed," and we were witnessing the fruit of that mantra. The staff were taken aback, as they had never gotten this request before. They looked to us adult leaders, as now we were all involved in this education moment as a unified team.

Some of the youth grouped together to begin problem-solving as we scrambled to try to make this happen. The janitor, by this time, had softened his face and pointed out to us that the lectern mic was active. So I pulled the speech up on my phone and was going to play the first portion of the speech. As I laid the phone on the lectern and pressed play, the speech rang through the large sanctuary, and immediately we knew that this was going to be one of those moments. We were only supposed to be there for a few minutes, but neither the staff, the students, nor the adults moved as we listened to the speech and the crowd through a phone placed on the pulpit.

After the speech ended, there was almost a minute of silence broken only by another request from the youth. "Can we hold our open mic here?" As we looked back at the church staff to pass the torch back to them, it was clear that whatever we needed would be provided. Everyone could feel the sacredness of this moment and was not about to let it end. Church staff were making calls, the janitor was preparing the fellowship hall area, and we three artists and youth development leaders began prepping for our closing activity. The open mic was supposed to happen at the restaurant in the space we reserved, but now, it was going to happen here, in the place where Dr. King gave his mountaintop speech, where countless people have had spiritual awakenings, and ultimately, where a group of 30 kids and their reverence for our ancestors was about to be on full display.

The grounding work that the St. Louis Park Schools students engaged in as part of their district equity work made them perfect candidates to open the activity sharing the agreements and conditions for Courageous Conversations About Race that we used to guide our discussions and sharing. Our spoken-word artists set the context and process, and we collectively agreed that only reflections on the experience would be filmed. The poetry showed their learning and their questions and tackled issues well beyond the scope of the trip. We heard everything, including racial incidents at their school, statements of commitment to one another, affirmations of peers across racial lines, and even deep reflections from students who had not previously been aware of the experiences of youth of color in their schools. As the entire group of youth surrounded a student who spoke boldly about the sexual violence they had survived at the hands of kids in their middle school, we saw the entire group surround the young person and hold an affirmation circle, which is an activity that has now become part of the entire process. As some of the staff called the students' parents and Facetimed so they could be a part of this moment, I saw that now all of the church staff stood in awe with silent tears rolling down.

The young people then turned to the staff and began to acknowledge their role in helping to shape this moment and give affirmations to their own families and leaders in their communities. We were now all equally crafting this moment together. So when we concluded the open mic and began to transition to the meal, it was no surprise that youth had already spoken with the janitor, set rules to keep the space clean, and worked out how to help him return the space to its original state. As adults, we were aware that this was no longer our program but theirs. And we could not have been prouder.

This story illustrates the way in which sacred space and experiences undergird the powerful learning that antiracist student leadership work can bring out in young people. This multiracial, multigendered, multiethnic, and interreligious group of students showed us their empathy, learning, resolve, and willingness to not only bridge differences but turn them into a powerful learning experience for everyone involved. The recounting of this story has led to college acceptances, program changes in schools, countless presentations by the youth involved, and even systemic changes in districts after presentations from these young people. Even Mason Temple has recreated that experience with youth in their community.

Much of our educational practice avoids this level of depth and complexity when engaging youth in racial discourse and consciousness development— many times, for the sake of uncomfortable adults. I offer this story, however, to show the power that comes from resisting the urge to succumb to discomfort. When we do this, we actually make even more opportunities for sacred moments that can leave us and our systems, forever changed.

Shared-Experiences Tenet Application

District-Level Application. In St. Louis Park we start every one of our Curriculum and Instructional Review Processes with a 2-day retreat that serves as a districtwide collective learning experience for all teacher-leaders who will engage in the review process over the next 3 years. This consulting team retreat serves to provide guidance and grounding for a group of internal stakeholders who will provide input on how we adopt curriculum, change instructional practice, transform structures, develop policy, and improve collaboration for the next three years. By starting this work with an antiracist lens, they essentially start this process with a powerful shared learning experience that grounds them in the tenets of antiracist student leadership development. These tenets serve as the structure for the retreat and provide a framework for district leadership to coach teacher leaders with throughout the course of their review. Members of this team present to the school board and provide links to their work on the district website, basically centering the shared belief in student leadership development as part of our racial equity transformation plan to all stakeholders in the district.

School-Level Application. One of the most prolific shared experiences I have facilitated in staff meetings and at retreats has been the process of engaging in Courageous Conversations through a Concentric Circles activity. In *White Awareness* (Katz, 2003) and on the Facing History (2022) website, there is ample explanation of how this activity can be performed. This activity allows all staff or students to engage in 1:1 conversation with each other in a timed (and, if facilitated adeptly), safe, and sacred conversation that allows them to practice mindful inquiry and active listening.

Concentric Circles invites every student or teacher to participate as an active listener and speaker. Students sit in two concentric circles facing one another and respond to a question in a paired discussion. When prompted by the teacher, one of the circles moves to the left or right so each student now faces a new partner, with whom they discuss a new question. This kinesthetic activity works well to debrief a reading, a narrative from a racial autobiography, a check-in regarding racial consciousness, or a check-in on the Courageous Conversations compass. For example, some participants may be asked to check in with their partner on an action they are going to take based on the professional development they just experienced. Once they move to the next partner, they will be asked to share a feeling they have about being White or a person of color in this space or environment. The Concentric Circles process allows for multiple conversations and perspectives and the opportunity to share with a wide range of partners. Furthermore, because they are speaking with just one other person at a time, reticent participants might feel more comfortable sharing their ideas than they would in a group or class discussion.

Procedure (Adapted from Facing History, 2022)

1. Select racially conscious prompts, narratives, or questions.
2. Facilitate the Concentric Circles discussion.
    1. Tell the participants that you will give them a question to discuss with their partner. Explain how much time they will have for their discussions and let them know that both students need to share and listen. You might give them tips about asking follow-up questions if they finish their discussion before the allotted time is up. You may also invite them to sit in silence to allow the partner to think of other things to say in that remaining time.
    2. If you are concerned that students might not get equal time to share and listen in each round, you might provide more structure. For example, you can instruct students that for the first minute, the outside circle will share their answers to the question while the inside circle listens actively. Then for the second minute, the inside circle shares while the outside circle listens. For the third minute, the pairs discuss their ideas, commenting on places of similarity and difference while offering evidence to support their thinking. You might want to time each person and ask the partner to practice mindful listening or mindful inquiry based on your desire to build capacity in that area with your team.
    3. After the time is up, instruct students in one of the circles to move one or two spots to the right (or left) so they are now facing new partners. Then repeat the previous step with a new question.
    4. Repeat this process until the participants have answered the questions that you prepared. You might add a bonus round wherein students pose their own questions to discuss with their partners.

Student Group-Level Application. One of the key components of our retreats with student leaders over the years has been the engagement with them in an Underground Railroad simulation. In 2020, the *New Yorker* magazine ran an article on the Minnesota version of the Underground Railroad due to its longevity, gravity, and care for participants. Unlike some simulations that ask participants to act like slaves, the Kamau Kambui Circle for Cultural Learning in Minnesota simulates the antiracist acts of an interracial group of Underground Railroad conductors who worked behind the scenes to help liberate people in the antebellum South. Meeting the "spirits" of heroes like Harriet Tubman, Levi Coffin, Lucretia Mott, and Henry David Thoreau, participants learn from their narratives about how to work together to garner freedom. This simulation has become an allegory for the work of Dare 2 Be Real groups back at school sites who then, in turn, work behind the scenes to engage in liberatory antiracist practices on behalf of their peers who may or may not be conscious of the systemic racism that holds them in metaphoric bondage. The Underground Railroad has proven to be an excellent opportunity to understand history and begin healthy authentic dialogues around race and culture in a positive and safe/supportive environment. The reenactment is an exceptional and many times life-changing experiential learning program, particularly for African Americans to understand and learn about their roots.

ACTIVE ANTIRACIST LEADERSHIP

How Do We Develop the Will, Skill, Knowledge, and Capacity of Antiracist Leaders?

Voices From the Field: Patricia Magnuson, Director of Business Services, St. Louis Park Public Schools

Public school operational systems are inherently racist. It has taken me many years to be able to clearly articulate this truth. Even as I write this, it makes my chest tighten.

It is unavoidable. School operational systems have been functioning for decades—built-in systems of Whiteness that advantage Whiteness, particularly White men. It's uncanny when the work of the system, the day-to-day teaching, is the province of White women. Systems built largely by [school boards, superintendents, administrators] and operated by [custodians, bus drivers, finance and operations managers]—White men—to keep White women [teachers, cooks, bookkeepers] under control so that children can be taught to perpetuate the same cycle. It is clear and strategic what the result will be, which children will be allowed to thrive and which will be relegated to special education, remedial coursework, the hallway, suspension, detention, expulsion, and prison.

Public education has changed in many ways in the last 50 years, but much of the underlying operational systems and structures remains in place. The institutional knowledge and insider information is passed down and kept secret behind walls of acronyms; unwieldy state-required technical systems; decades-old boiler systems; industrial combi ovens; and a stack of required licenses, certifications, experiences, and knowledge that can only be accessed with the key. That key is institutional knowledge and insider information, which can only be received from the institutional holders of the knowledge and information. I have come to realize the real key has to be daylight. Clear and open operational systems are an act of antiracism.

I am getting ahead of myself. As a White woman, my journey toward antiracism is ongoing. I continue to uncover new understanding about the deep roots of my own racism and have come to accept that it will be a lifelong journey of recovery.

I came to public education in the early 1990s as a young finance professional with a few years of private industry experience. I was humbled immediately by the complexity of public education finance and worked 7 days a week for years to become an expert. Due to the retirement of my White male mentor, following a long and storied career, and his unsuccessful White male replacement, I became the operational leader at an age and level of experience that was questionable. Suddenly I had to learn about and lead school nutrition, facilities, transportation—all led by White men older than me. It was my 1980s-fed, shoulder-pad wearing, White girl Cinderella dream. I made it and I did it myself. It took years of expert racial-equity training, piles of books, and many difficult conversations to understand just what a tool I was. By tool, I mean the Urban Dictionary definition, "Someone who lacks the mental capacity to know he or she is being used."

I actually believed what I was being told. I was a rising star; I was even school business official of the year. I had received the keys. I had the respect and cooperation of the team, the community, and the school board. Until I didn't. When it became clear that I was planning to use the keys I had received to support the antiracist work of our superintendent, the ground under my feet began to crumble. I had personal home visits and office visits from school board members, well-meaning warning calls from concerned finance advisory committee members, and questions from my children about things they had heard at school, all of which eventually became an onslaught of inquiries, letters to the editor, public data requests, and questions about the intricate details of school law in search of something that had been missed. I had not earned my keys at all. I had been offered them in exchange for my cooperation with a system that had no intention of changing.

As a confused White woman, more scared than I understood at the time, I took my keys and walked away to another school district. I was a little bit wiser but I still believed that those same keys were the answer. I just had to start giving them to a more diverse population—hiring more people of color and seeking community members of color to serve as finance committee volunteers, all the while, maintaining the systems and structures that would continue to fit the keys I was passing out. Those actions placed people who trusted me into racist systems and structures that I was perpetuating. I even expected them to do the work for me: to say the difficult truths, to tell me when I was being a racist, to make the change I assumed they wanted. I was once told by a Black male colleague that my words were violent, and it was clear that he had no interest in the job of fixing me.

Through some intense training over several months about the anti-Black violence perpetrated by White women (me), I began to feel the keys I was holding in a different way. They were like the dunce cap that everyone saw but me, the note on my back that said, "Kick me." I was a tool of the system, molded and coached to perpetuate it.

Clear and open operational systems are an act of antiracism. I believe this with every fiber of my being. Systems cannot be changed if everyone is confused and scared by them; that is the strategy of Whiteness. My work has become to clarify, document, and simplify school operational systems and structures; moreover, to ensure that those who work in those systems have the will, skill, capacity, and knowledge to keep them clear and open so that they can be broken, destroyed, repaired, and transformed into antiracist systems.

I think about the work in these ways:

- Simplify and explain. It is not impressive to leave the school board meeting having wowed them all with acronyms and data but no information at all. School boards are making decisions that impact the daily lived experience of students. They should understand the decisions they are making.
- Hold high expectations. Working toward racial consciousness is not a choice. Connecting our work to unleashing the brilliance of our students is required. The operational departments are not a place where you can hide from the work. Everyone on the team must present their racial autobiography at a team meeting. Your work needs to be simple and explained well. It will be on the district website, presented for the school board, and you must be certain that the department will not come crashing down if a few holders of the keys aren't at work.
- Give high levels of support. Provide antiracism training to staff. There is a knowledge set that everyone should have access to. Often this vital training is provided only to teachers, but business office staff, cooks, custodians, and bus drivers need to have access if they are to be held to high expectations.

In order to lead in a manner that supports clear and open operational systems as an act of antiracism, I have needed to clearly articulate my purpose. Today I state the following as my Personal Racial-Equity Purpose:

> As a White female racial-equity leader, I take personal responsibility for antiracism. I am called by my faith to do justice, love kindness, and walk humbly. I will authentically engage in antiracism work in my personal and professional life. I will not become complacent and will break free from my fragile and oppressive social conditioning as a White female in the United States.
>
> I humbly seek knowledge and wisdom to recognize and interrupt oppressive systems that systemically advantage Whiteness. I will learn about and align my work with other antiracist leaders.
>
> I seek methods and practices to unleash the knowledge and creativity of the community I serve to ensure that the district budgets, finances, and overall operations reflect and support an antiracist reality for our staff, students, and community. I will have receipts.

Ultimately, the work of antiracist operational leadership requires me to understand that I work for a system of public education. That my work impacts the daily lived experience of students. That as long as I continue to take a paycheck, I am required to ensure that school operational systems become inherently antiracist, even if it makes my chest tighten.

District-Level Application. When I was at the SXSW conference a few years ago I ran into scholar Sunil Singh, who was doing a session on Punk Ideology in Math Education. Since then, I have been inspired by his words to engage our teacher-leaders in principals in the ideology of punk and hip-hop as they review curricular and instructional programs by asking the question: "What if?" By asking staff to think on the fringe, these two simple words give permission to start thinking transformatively, something that is necessary for active antiracism at a system level.

School-Level Application. Antiracist leadership needs to be visible for students to see it as sustainable. It became clear throughout the course of this study that leadership in the work needed to be visible to both others engaged in the work and those on the periphery. The transparency and courage necessary to lead for racial equity requires a visionary who can develop a clear sense of purpose among various stakeholders. Positional leadership is a key factor in bringing about any change for racial equity. The principal role at Midwest High School was pivotal in creating a sense of urgency and trust and a feeling of support among student equity leaders. The visibility of administration and key teachers as allies in antiracism work is important. Although some work always needs to be done behind the scenes, the work itself needs to be balanced between those things being done behind the scenes and those that are shared, visibly and transparently, with the whole staff and with students. Intention of purpose, language, and activities is important in sharing antiracist goals and actions. Leaders must work to develop a culture of equity that is present in all of the work they do and to help others to see the various strands (parents, students, curriculum, instruction, policies, etc.) that are being addressed throughout the school. The sustainability will come from those recognizing that racial equity is not a silo nor "another initiative," but something that has permeated the culture, structures, and classrooms in the school. This adult culture will model a culture of antiracism among students that cannot be understated.

Student Group-Level Application. A few years ago, a number of students decided to engage in an all-school assembly to discuss the growing tension between Jewish and Muslim students at the school. When they planned the event, they strategically engaged staff members who were "on the fence" about our antiracism work in the planning but who were skilled in the planning of assemblies. They also actively recruited student stakeholders from across various groups at the school to join the assembly to ensure there would be credibility in the student voice. In doing so, the students in the Students Organized for Anti-Racism (SOAR) group applied critical race theory tenets of interest convergence and counter-storytelling in the planning of their assembly, bringing strategy and sustainability to their event.

COMMUNITY/FAMILY ENGAGEMENT

How Do We Engage Families and Parents as We Develop Our Student Leaders?

Voices From the Field: Freida Bailey, Principal on Special Assignment for Racial Equity, St. Louis Park Public Schools

> It is a peculiar sensation, this double-consciousness, this sense of always looking at one's self through the eyes of others. . . . One ever feels his twoness, An American, a Negro; two souls, two thoughts, two unreconciled strivings; two warring ideals in one dark body, whose dogged strength alone keeps it from being torn asunder. W.E.B. Du Bois (1868–1963) *The Souls of Black Folk* (1903)

Hello, I'm number 11 out of 13. I say this with pride each and every day. During the first part of my racial journey, that was not always the case. But now that I understand how important those numbers are to my self-discovery, I am honored and humbled to be who I am.

When I share these numbers with people that I meet, the usual questions are: Where did you sleep? What was that like? My question to them: What comes up for you when you hear that, really? When you hear 13 in a family, what beliefs or stereotypes come to mind?

Early years. Being born in a small city, segregated schools were prevalent. All the members of my family are African American. Both of my parents grew up in Texas and both of my parents finished high school. My neighborhood was predominately African American, where most of the store owners were either Italian or Hispanic. While growing up, we watched various television shows and played with White Barbie dolls and White paper dolls.

While attending my elementary years, K–5, my teachers were of various races. Our school operated with a sense of community, belonging, enjoyment, and learning. The curriculum that was taught during those years was enriched with culture of ethnicities, science, writing, and math. We would have guest speakers come to our school and share their job experiences with us.

My first conscious racial encounter occurred when I was bussed to a junior high school in a neighborhood that felt foreign. Most of the people in the neighborhood were White. There was something that felt different but I had no words to describe those feelings. During my first year, I became withdrawn because some of my Black friends were sent to other schools. Why did they have the opportunity to stay close to our neighborhood filled with Black joy and culture? Why did I have to attend this foreign place of unease? While attending this new way of being in junior high, my parents always encouraged us to do our best academically. I was also encouraged to participate in sports and band because during my elementary years, music was integral to our family. Therefore, I joined both to become a part of the school's community. Hence the beginning of something more. Here is where I noticed most African American students were placed in lower-level classes and encouraged to play sports.

Reflecting back, I grew up with my siblings talking about race in the house and their experiences with White people, but as a child I did not truly understand. Now as a teenager, there were similarities between their conversations and mine.

In my transition to high school, the same occurred with classes and sports. My wonderings at the time were what is it about students of color? I remember being in an English class and students of color could barely write their names. They were famous on the field, winning and being great athletes. I noticed the injustices in school and decided I wanted to become a teacher so that the students in my class would not leave my room without receiving the best education possible. It was also during my time in high school that a basketball coach's daughter came up to me and asked if I could wash off my color. I did not blame her but was shocked at what she said.

As a teenager and as an adult, I have experienced the "ignore" or "follow her" status when I enter a store. Meaning, the sales rep would either ignore me as if I could not afford the items or follow me assuming that I wanted to steal something. This is something that still exists, and there are times when I just walk out of the establishment.

My work experiences in Texas were expected but when someone didn't like you or what you stood for, they would let you know to your face. As a teacher and then a principal, we constantly talked about data in dealing with Black and Brown students. Analyzing to gather meaning from data to support students but not really discussing how our social construct impacts the learning that is taking place in the system.

At one of my elementary sites, we had book studies, by Delpit, participated in Accountable Talk by Resnick but never truly discussed the impact of race—only poverty. My connections to my previous work and my wonderings started to formalize when I began to hear about Pacific Education Group and Courageous Conversations. By participating in those trainings, beginning with Glenn Singleton leading the charge, that's when I began to internalize the framework in connection to how to best support Black, Brown, and Indigenous students and families and how to vocalize my wonderings in the education system. Even as an administrator in Minnesota and participating in the workshops connected to Courageous Conversations, I knew that I had to be careful being the only Black administrator in the district. To talk about race was not an easy subject for staff, parents, and the community. Understanding the racial quagmire, and being a Black administrator, I did not want to be the one who always led conversations about race but tried to find members on my leadership team who carried the will, skill, and passion to want to see real change in connection to the work of dismantling the systemic issues that we noticed in the building and in connection to the impact on families.

By doing this, in retrospect, I noticed that there was a shift when we began to see changes in our building with students' academic and social growth. Due to the academic divide between White students and students of color being diminished, questions began swirling about me— questions such as, "Why were our discipline numbers so low?" "Are you really doing the work of protecting your own?" "Someone is telling you what to do with your staff." Being new to Minnesota and understanding that I was grappling with not only my Whiteness, which was embedded in me through my educational training as I traveled through this system, and also understanding how critical race theory now was so embedded in the work, unpacking and pulling back these layers, as a Black administrator, was painful but necessary. This journey gave me voice, vision, purpose, and understanding and I can no longer sit on the sidelines in silence and follow a system that is detrimental to not only the most marginalized students and families but to my well-being also.

Through this analysis, my connection to Courageous Conversation protocol has given me a foundation to be able to continue to do the work and lean into what is necessary for children's future, but I also noticed that there were some moral beliefs that were embedded in me because of my family foundation. It is a foundation so deeply rooted in me now that I have become immersed in truly understanding why the protocol of Courageous Conversation is so significant. It has given me a voice to address issues head-on and has helped me to internalize and question systemic racism as I see it play out now in the district office.

I'm experiencing not only function in a space as a Black female, but the conditions are providing me the opportunity to engage, sustain, and deepen conversations about race.

I now have direction and guidance on how to support the dismantling of systemic racism when I notice. Stay true to self!

One of my most recent events of dealing with race occurred when decisions were being made without my input or knowledge on people that I supervise. Instead of being notified that there was an issue, the system bypassed notifying me and went straight to the staff that I supervise. The only way that I was informed was after the "talk to" with the employee and the employee notified me. After discussing these issues with my White peers, they were notified of employees that were having difficulty or if there was an event that needed to be investigated. So, my wondering based on many conversations with my White peer—what is it about Freida, the Black female administrator, that she can't have the same opportunities as an administrator? What is it about her that is unapproachable? Why is there no conversation with her about concerns regarding staff that she is supervising? Do my White colleagues feel that I can't handle the job or feel that it is not necessary for me to be a part of the conversation, hence, the silence around me and me not being able to silence myself? I have noticed that there are times when I do self-silence and this is when I become a reflective practitioner and remember that the work is about students and family at its core. It's about building the will, skill, and capacity within myself. I must continue to stand firm in my passion and purpose, which is transforming a system that silences the most marginalized, including me.

How does this connect to family? Is family connection important to transforming a system for students?

In the area of working with parents, the suggestions revolve around one cultural theme: the educating of parents with reference to their rights, their children's rights, and their responsibilities as parents. Making this information accessible will create a positive perception of the learning community. In order to build a collaborative relationship with parents, our school must build on the parents' cultural values, foster personal contact, and create or facilitate building accessibility (Senge, 2000). Fostering communication is regarded as critical to building collaborative relationships between parents and teachers, between parents and children, and between children and teachers. Schools that incorporate effective communication strategies with parents should receive a high percentage of parental support.

I am so thankful to be 11 out of 13 because of what my parents poured into me foundationally. Love yourself, love others, and give all that you can to help others—even if they don't believe in your worth and or see you as a Black and beautiful individual. God knows your heart!

If you are silent about your pain, they'll kill you and say you enjoyed it.

—Zora Neale Hurston (1937)

Family-and-Community-Engagement Tenet Applications

District-Level Application. One of the most rewarding examples of parent and family engagement that I have ever experienced as an antiracist leader is the program Elders' Wisdom, Children's Song (EWCS). EWCS is an intergenerational multicultural curriculum created and trademarked by educator and American troubadour Larry Long. Larry Long and Anthony Galloway have been working with the talent development teachers in St. Louis Park to support the development of this program so it will honor the elders of our St. Louis Park community while fostering the brilliance, empathy, and artistry of the 4th-grade scholars. Elders' Wisdom, Children's Song (EWCS) incorporates the tools of community organizing, education, and celebration through storytelling in song and spoken word. At the heart, EWCS is an educational process called collective song-writing. It combines the collection of oral history, or oral literature, with the teaching of song-writing and poetry. Scholars are encouraged to select elders who represent the diversity of the community and then write songs and perform them in the first person—practicing empathetic storytelling, songwriting, and community celebration. Not only are the elders honored, but family members of the 4th-graders are invited to see this showcase of talent. It is a true antiracist celebration of the spirit.

School-Level Application. When I was principal at Barton Open School, I knew that my progressive community was deeply involved in their South Minneapolis School but was also very anti–standardized tests. Although I bemoan the standardizing of schooling, I also understand the importance of finding opportunities to tell the story of our learning community through data. I invited parents and elders from the community to join our staff and students in a data retreat that included not just qualitative data but also excerpts from emails I had received (redacted of course) and video footage of classrooms, student voices, and all-school assemblies. This holistic data retreat that included the entire community allowed multiple voices and counternarratives to give perspectives on our school and help provide a new strategic plan for racial-equity transformation. It also helped change the narrative about data— showing that test data, alongside voice, pictures, and video, could create a rich story about a community that could be explored through multiple angles.

Student Group-Level Application. There is literature that suggests that the role of parents is crucial for any site that wants to bring about increased racial equity (Noguera, 2008; Tatum, 2008; Ward, 2008), but most studies in this regard focus on programs focused on engaging parents of color in partnership to address racial inequities. There is a void in the current literature that illuminates the role of White parents with respect to antiracism efforts. I suggest that White parents of students engaged in antiracism efforts could be exposed to the learning of their students in much the same way we engage them in the annual ritual of parent-teacher conferences. As students learn how to apply protocols for racial dialogue, student antiracist leaders and White parents who have been exposed to antiracism training should take part in student-led interviews to gain insight into their perspectives on racial-equity initiatives in the school and community. We expect parents to show up to see their children perform in athletic events or for concerts and school plays, so must we normalize parent participation to see their children engage others in the facilitation of Courageous Conversations; assemblies for antiracism; and the sharing of poetry, spoken-word, and autobiographical presentations about their own race and ethnicity. At Midwest High School, parents were rarely, if ever, engaged in the antiracist learning of their children; this may have contributed to the lack of sustainability and deepening of antiracist work. It is essential to engage, sustain, and deepen strong parent and family engagement to become an antiracist school.

CONCLUSION

There is a good chance that further self-study and organizational study will help leaders and scholars recognize the likelihood of the reproduction of racism and maintenance of the status quo across school settings. The pervasive nature of racism certainly requires more examination and attention.

Ethnographic research inside schools is not the only way to bring about racial equity, but it certainly is important to learn more about the people and institutions impacted by racism. My growth as a leader has been greatly impacted by the people who allowed me to hear their story. I am grateful for their willingness to share and to take time to know themselves and allow me to better know them. I am reminded of poignant words of Lisa Delpit:

> Listening . . . the essential part of dialogue requires not only open eyes and ears, but open hearts and minds. We do not really see through our eyes or hear through our ears, but though our beliefs . . . It is not easy, but it is the only way to learn what it might feel like to be someone else and the only way to start the dialogue. (Delpit, 1995, pp. 46–47)

Dialogue is indeed necessary for leaders to develop more empathy for those who are different from them, but this work must go beyond dialogue, beyond love, and beyond courage to regular and purposeful action that effectively eliminates racially predictable achievement and that empowers students of all racial backgrounds to thrive in our world by developing individuals and institutions that are proficient at creating racial equity. Further collaborative and self-reflective work that engages leaders in knowing themselves racially and culturally, in distinguishing knowledge from foolishness in their practices, and in collaboratively building student-centered programs for eternity may not only provide more insight into the factors that sustain systemic cycles of racism but may help school leaders see past the gilded veneer of empty talk and promises and usher in a golden age of antiracism. That is my audacious hope.

References

Alexander, M. (2010). *The new Jim Crow: Mass incarceration in an age of colorblindness*. New Press.

Almanzan, J. (2006). *CARE team training for the West Metro education program.* (April 3, 2006) [Minnetonka, MN].

Aptheker, H. (1992) *Anti-racism in U.S. history: The first two hundred years.* Greenwood Press.

Banks, J. A. (1992). African American scholarship and the evolution of multicultural education. *Journal of Negro Education, 61*(3), 173–194.

Banks, J. A. (Ed.). (2012). *Encyclopedia of diversity in education* (4 vols.). Sage Publications.

Bell, D. (1980). Brown v. Board of Education and the interest-convergence dilemma. *Harvard Law Review, 93,* 518–533.

Bell, D. A. (1992). *Faces at the bottom of the well: The permanence of racism.* HarperCollins Publishers.

Bernier, J. D., & Rocco, T. S. (2003). Working in the margins of critical race theory and human resource development. In T. Ferro & G. Dean (Eds.), *Proceedings of the Midwest research-to-practice conference in adult, continuing, and community education* (pp. 13–18). The Ohio State University.

Bonilla-Silva, E. (2006). Racism without racists: Color-blind racism and the persistence of racial inequality in the United States. *Science and Society, 70*(3), 431–434.

Bonilla-Silva, E. (2010). *Racism without racists: Color-blind racism and racial inequality in contemporary America.* Rowman & Littlefield Publishing Group.

Bonilla-Silva, E., & Embrick, D. (2008). Recognizing the likelihood of reproducing racism. In M. Pollock (Ed.), *Every day antiracism: Getting real about race in schools.* (pp. 334–337). New Press.

Bridges, R. (1999). *Through my eyes.* Scholastic Press.

Brooks, J. S., & Arnold, N. W. (Eds.). (2013). *Antiracist school leadership: Toward equit in education for America's students.* Information Age Publishing.

Brown v. Board of Education, 347 U.S. 483 (1954).

Carney, C. G., & Kahn, K. B. (1984). Building competencies for effective cross-cultural counseling: A developmental view. *The Counseling Psychologist, 12*(1), 111–119.

Carspecken, P. F. (1996). *Critical ethnography in educational research: A theoretical and practical guide.* Routledge.

Carter, R., & Goodwin, L. (1996). Racial identity and education. In L. Darling-Hammond (Ed.), *Review of research in education* (pp. 291–336). American Educational Research Association.

Chenoweth, E. (2017). Trends in nonviolent resistance and state response: Is violence toward civilian-based movements on the rise? *Global Responsibility to Protect, 9,* 86–100.

Cherryholmes, C. (1988). *Power and criticism: Poststructural investigations in education.* Teachers College Press.

Cochran-Smith, M. (2003). The multiple meanings of multicultural teacher education: A conceptual framework. *Teacher Education Quarterly, 30*(2), 7–26.

Crenshaw, K., Gotanda,N., Peller, G., & Thomas, K. (1995). *Critical race theory: The key writings that formed the movement.* New Press.

Crenshaw, K., Lipsitz, G., & Harris, L. C. (2022). *The race track: The myth of equal opportunity defeats racial justice.* New Press.

Cross, W. E. (1978). The Thomas and Cross Models of psychological Nigrescence: A review. *Journal of Black Psychology, 5*(1), 13–31.

Cross, W. E., Jr. (1991). *Shades of Black: Diversity in African American identity.* Temple University Press

Cross, W. E., Jr. (1995). *The psychology of Nigrescence: Revising the cross model.* Sage Publications.

Cross, W. E., Jr., Parham, T. A., & Helms, J. E. (1991). The stages of Black identity development: Nigrescence models. In R. Jones (Ed.), *Black Psychology.* Cobb & Henry.

Dantley, M. E., & Tillman, L. C. (2009). Social justice and moral transformative leadership. In C. Marshall & M. Oliva (Eds.), *Leadership for social justice* (2nd ed., pp. 19–34). Allyn & Bacon.

Darling-Hammond, L. (2016). Research on teaching and teacher education and its influences on policy and practice. *Educational Researcher, 45*(2), 83–91.

DeCuir, J. T., & Dixson, A. D. (2004). "So when it comes out, they aren't that surprised that it is there": Using critical race theory as a tool of analysis of race and racism in education. *Educational Researcher* (June/July), 26–31.

Delgado, R., & Stefancic, J. (Eds.). (2001). *Critical race theory: An introduction.* New York University Press.

Delpit, L. (1988). The silenced dialogue: Power and pedagogy in educating other people's children. *Harvard Educational Review, 58,* 280–298.

Delpit, L. D. (1995). *Other people's children: Cultural conflict in the classroom.* New Press

Del Real, J., Samuels, R., & Craig, T. (2020, June 9). How the Black Lives Matter movement went mainstream. *The Washington Post.*

Denzin, J., & Lincoln, Y. (1994). *Handbook of qualitative research.* Sage Publications.

Derman-Sparks, L., & Brunson Philips, C. (1997). *Teaching/learning anti-racism: A developmental approach.* Teachers College Press.

de Tocqueville, A. (1838). *Democracy in America.* G. Dearborn & Co.

Dewey, J. (1988). *Foreign schools in Turkey in essays on politics and society 1923–1924: The middle works of John Dewey, 1899–1924.* Southern Illinois University Press. (Original work published 1924)

Diamond, J. B. (2006). Still separate and unequal: Examining race, opportunity, and school achievement in "integrated" suburbs. *Journal of Negro Education, 75,* 495–505.

DiAngelo, R. J. (2010). Why can't we all just be individuals?: Countering the discourse of individualism in anti-racist education. *InterActions: UCLA Journal of Education and Information Studies, 6*(1).

Dixson, A. D., & Rousseau, C. K. (2005). And we are still not saved: Critical race theory in education ten years later. *Race Ethnicity and Education, 8*(1), 7–27.

Douglass, F. (1857). *Narrative of the life of Frederick Douglass.* Public domain.

Du Bois, W.E.B. (1903). *The souls of black folk.* Penguin Books.

Duffy, P. (2017, November). *Dare 2 Be Real: A framework for anti-racist student leadership development* [Paper presentation]. UCEA annual meeting, Denver, CO.

Duffy, P., & Galloway, A. (2012). Developing systemic anti-racist student leadership. In G. Singleton (Ed.), *More courageous conversations about race.* Corwin Press.

Duncan, G. A. (2002). Beyond love: A critical race ethnography of the schooling of adolescent black males. *Equity and Excellence in Education, 35*(2), 131–143.

Duncan-Andrade, J. (2008). Teaching critical analysis of racial oppression. In M. Pollock (Ed.), *Everyday antiracism: Getting real about race in schools* (pp. 156–160). New Press.

Elliot, P. R., & Nieto, S. (1996). *Testifying on racism: African-American educators, racial identity and anti-racism staff development in schools.* University of Massachusetts, Amherst.

Facing History & Ourselves. (2022). Retrieved April 27, 2022, from https://www.facinghistory.org/

Firestone, W. A. (1993). Alternative arguments for generalizing from data as applied to qualitative research. *Educational Researcher, 22*(4), 16–23.

Freire, P. (1998). *Pedagogy of freedom: Ethics, democracy, and civic courage.* Rowman & Littlefield Publishers.

Gall, M. D., Gall, J. P., & Borg, W. R. (2003). *Educational research: An introduction* (7th ed.). Allyn & Bacon.

Ganter, G. (1977). The socio-conditions of the white practitioner: New perspectives. *Journal of Contemporary Psychotherapy, 9*(1), 26–32.

Garrett, J. T., & Walking Stick Garrett, M. (1994). The path of good medicine: Understanding and counseling native American Indians. *Journal of Multicultural Counseling and Development, 22,* 134–144.

Gay, G. (1995). Mirror images on common images: Parallels between multicultural education and critical pedagogy. In C. E. Sleeter & P. McLaren (Eds.), *Multicultural education, critical pedagogy, and the politics of difference* (pp. 155–189). State University of New York Press.

Gay, G. (2005). Politics of multicultural teacher education. *Journal of Teacher Education, 56*(3), 221–228.

Gay, G. (2012) "Our children need . . . education for resistance." *Journal of Educational Controversy: 6*(1), Article 8.

Gilborn, D. (2005). Education policy as an act of white supremacy: Whiteness, critical race theory and education reform. *Journal of Education Policy, 20*(4), 485–505.

Giroux, H. (1997). Racial politics and the pedagogy of whiteness. In M. Hill (Ed.), *Whiteness: A critical reader* (pp. 294–315). New York University Press.

Gooden, M., & Dantley, M. (2012). Centering race in a framework for leadership preparation. *Journal of Research on Leadership Education, 7*(2), 237–253.

Gorski, P. (2008). Good intentions are not enough: A decolonizing intercultural education. *Intercultural Education, (19)*6, 515–525.

Gregory, A., Skiba, R. J., & Noguera, P. A. (2010). The achievement gap and the discipline gap: Two sides of the same coin? *Educational Researcher, 39*(1), 59–68.

Gupta, A., & Ferguson, J. (1992). Beyond "culture": Space, identity, and the politics of difference. *Cultural Anthropology*, 7(1), 6–23.

Hacker, A. (1992). *Two nations: Black and white, separate, hostile, and unequal.* Balentine Books.

Haggis, P. (Director). (2004). *Crash* [Film]. Lions Gate Entertainment.

Hall, W. S., Freedle, R., & Cross, W. E. (1972). Stages in the development of a black identity. *ACT Research Reports, 50,* 21.

Hartoonian, H. M. (1997). Personal correspondence

Haycock, K., & Chenoweth, K. (2005). *Choosing to make a difference: How schools and districts are beating the odds and narrowing the achievement gap.*

Heifetz, R. A., Linsky, M., & Grashow, A. (2009). *The practice of adaptive leadership.* Harvard Business Review Press.

Heifetz, R. A., & Linsky, M. (2014). *Adaptive leadership: The Heifetz collection (3 items).* Harvard Business Review Press.

Helms, J. (1984). Toward a theoretical explanation of the effects of race on counseling: A black and white model. *The Counseling Psychologist, 12*(4), 153–165.

Helms, J. E. (Ed.). (1990). *Black and white racial identity: Theory, research and practice.* Greenwood Press.

Helms, J. E. (1991). *A training manual to accompany black and white racial identity.* Content Communications.

Helms, J. E. (1992). *A race is a nice thing to have: A guide to being a white person or understanding the white persons in your life.* Content Communications.

Helms, J. E. (1993). I also said White racial identity influences White researchers. *The Counseling Psychologist, 21,* 240–243.

Helms, J. E. (1994). Identity development and classroom dynamics. In J. Carey & P. Pedersen (Eds.), *Multicultural counseling in the schools.* Allyn & Bacon.

Helms, J. E. (1999). Another meta-analysis of the White Racial Identity Attitude Scale. *Measurement and Evaluation in Counseling and Guidance.*

Henze, R., Katz, A., Norte, E., Sather, S. E., & Walker, E. (2002). *Leading for diversity: How school leaders promote positive interethnic relations.* Sage Publications

Henze, R., Lucas, T., & Scott, B. (1998). Dancing with the monster: Teachers discuss racism, power, and white privilege in education. *The Urban Review,* 30(3), 187–210.

Hilliard, A. (1992). Behavioral style, culture, and teaching and learning. *Journal of Negro Education, 61*(3), 370–377.

hooks, b. (2018). *All about love: New visions.* William Morrow Books.

Horsford, S. D. (2011). *Learning in a burning house: Educational inequality, ideology, and (dis)integration.* Teachers College Press.

Howard, G. (2016). *We can't teach what we don't know: White teachers, multiracial schools.* (3rd ed.). Teachers College Press.

Huerta, D. (1984). California agriculture oral history project [interview]. Dolores Huerta Papers, Walter P. Reuther Library, Archives of Labor and Urban Affairs, Wayne State University.

Hurston, Z. N. (1937). *Their eyes were watching god.* Virago Press.

Ignatiev, N. (1995). *How the Irish became white.* Routledge.

Jacobs, H. (1861). *Incidents in the life of a slave girl.* L. Maria Child.

Jackson, Y. (2011). *The pedagogy of confidence: Inspiring high intellectual performance in urban schools.* Teachers College Press

Jensen, R. (2005) The heart of whiteness: confronting race, racism and white privilege. City Lights.

Jones, J. M., & Carter, R. T. (1996). Racism and White racial identity: Merging realities. In B. P. Bowser & R. G. Hunt (Eds.), *Impacts of racism on White Americans* (pp. 1–23). Sage Publications.

Joseph, Chief (1911). *Chief Joseph's Own Story*. Glen Adams.

Kailin, J. (1994). Anti-racist staff development. *Teaching and Teacher Education, 10*, 169–184.

Kailin, J. (1996). *Engaging teachers in anti-racist pedagogy: An historical and ethnographic study* [Doctoral dissertation, University of Wisconsin–Madison].

Kantor, H., & Lowe, R. (1995). Class, race, and the emergence of federal education policy: From the New Deal to the Great Society. *Educational Researcher, 24*(3), 4–21.

Katz, J. H. (1997). *White awareness: Handbook for anti-racism training* (2nd ed.). University of Oklahoma Press.

Katz, J. H., & Ivey, A. (1977). White awareness: The frontier of Racism Awareness Training. *Personnel and Guidance Journal, 55*(8), 485–489.

Kelly, S. (2009). The Black-White gap in mathematics course taking. *Sociology of Education, 82*(1), 47–69.

Khalifa, M. (2018). *Culturally responsive school leadership*. Harvard Education Press.

Kinchloe, L. J., & McLaren, P. (2000). *Rethinking critical theory and qualitative research*. Sage Publications.

Kise, J. (2019). *Holistic leadership, thriving schools*. Solution Tree.

Klingner, J., Artiles, A., Kozleski, E., Harry, B., Zion, S., & Tate, W. (2005). Addressing the disproportionate representation of culturally and linguistically diverse students in special education through culturally responsive educational systems. *Educational Policy Analysis Archives, 13*(38). https://doi.org/10.14507/epaa .v13n38.2005

Kluegel, J., & Smith, E. (1986). *Beliefs about inequality: Americans' views of what is and what ought to be*. de Gruyter.

Ladson-Billings, G. (1999). Preparing teachers for diverse student populations: A critical race theory perspective. *Journal of Teacher Education, 21*(1), 211–247.

Ladson-Billings, G. (2000). Fighting for our lives: Preparing teachers to teach African-American students. *Journal of Teacher Education, 51*(3), 206–214.

Ladson-Billings, G. (2001). *Crossing over to Canaan*. Jossey-Bass.

Ladson-Billings, G. (2005a). *Beyond the big house: African-American educators on teacher education*. Teachers College Press.

Ladson-Billings, G. (2005b). Reading, writing, and race: Literacy practices of teachers in diverse classrooms. In T. McCarty (Ed.), *Language, literacy, and power in schooling* (pp. 133-150). Lawrence Erlbaum.

Ladson-Billings, G. (2009). *The dreamkeepers: Successful teachers of African-American children*. Jossey-Bass.

Ladson-Billings, G. (2021a). *Culturally relevant pedagogy: Asking a different question*. Teachers College, Columbia University.

Ladson-Billings, G. (2021b). *Critical race theory in education: A scholar's journey*. Teachers College, Columbia University.

Ladson-Billings, G., & Tate, W. F., IV. (1995). Toward a critical race theory of education. *Teachers College Record, 97*(1), 47–68.

Landsman, J. (2001). *A white teacher talks about race*. Scarecrow Press

Lawrence, S. M. (1995). Beyond race awareness: White racial identity and multicultural teaching. *Journal of Teacher Education, 48*(2), 108–117.

Lawrence, S. M. (2005). Contextual matters: Teachers' perceptions of the success of antiracist classroom practices. *Journal of Educational Research, 98*(6), 350–365.

Lawrence, S. M., & Bunche, T. (1996). Feeling and dealing: Teaching white students about racial privilege. *Teaching and Teacher Education, 12*(5), 531–542.

Lawrence, S. M., & Tatum, B. D. (1997). Teachers in transition: The impact of antiracist professional development on classroom practice. *Teachers College Record, 99*(2), 162–178.

Lincoln, Y., & Guba, E. (2003). *Naturalistic inquiry.* Sage Publications.

Lindsey, R. B., Robins, K. N., & Terrell, R. D. (2009). *Cultural proficiency: A manual for school leaders.* Corwin Press.

Lipsitz, G. (1995). The possessive investment in whiteness: Racialized social democracy and the "white" problem in American studies. *American Quarterly, 47*(3), 369–387.

Lipsitz, G. (2006). *The possessive investment in whiteness* (Revised ed.). Temple University Press.

Loewen, J. (1996). *Lies my teacher told me.* New Press.

Loewen, J. (2005). *Sundown towns: A hidden dimension of American racism.* New Press.

López, G. R. (2003). The (racially neutral) politics of education: A critical race theory perspective. *Educational Administration Quarterly, 39*(1), 68–94.

Lucas, J. (February 17 & 24, 2020). *Can slavery enactments set us free?* New Yorker Magazine.

Lynn, M., & Adams, M. (2002). Introductory overview to the special issue critical race theory and education: Recent developments in the field. *Equity & Excellence in Education, 35*(2), 87–92

Lynn, M., Yosso, T. J., Solórzano, D. G., & Parker, L. (2002). Critical race theory and education: Qualitative research in the new millennium. *Qualitative Inquiry, 8*(1), 3–6.

Madison, D. S. (2005). *Critical ethnography: Method, ethics, and performance.* Sage Publications.

McIntosh, P. (1999). White privilege: Unpacking the invisible knapsack. In M. McGoldrick (Ed.), *Re-visioning family therapy: Race, culture, and gender in clinical practice* (pp. 147–152).

McIntyre, A. (1997). *Making meaning of whiteness.* State University of New York Press.

McIntyre, A. (2008). Engaging diverse groups of colleagues in conversation. In M. Pollock (Ed.), *Every day antiracism: Getting real about race in schools* (pp. 279–282). New Press.

McLaren, P. (1997). Decentering whiteness: In search of a revolutionary multiculturalism. *Multicultural Education, 5*, 4–11.

Merriam, S. B. (1998). *Qualitative research and case study applications in education.* Jossey-Bass Publishers.

Mun Wah, L. (Director). (1994). *The color of fear* [Film]. Stir Fry Productions.

Mun Wah, L. (2004). *The art of mindful inquiry.* Stir Fry.

National Council of Teachers of Mathematics. (2014). *Principles to actions: Ensuring mathematical success for all.* Author.

Nieto, S. (1995). *Affirming diversity: The sociopolitical context of multicultural education* (2nd ed.). Longman.

Nieto, S. (2000). Placing equity front and center: Some thoughts on transforming teacher education for a new century. *Journal of Teacher Education, 51*(3), 180–187.

Nieto, S. (2008). Nice is not enough: Defining caring for students of color. In M. Pollock (Ed.), *Everyday antiracism: Getting real about race in schools* (pp. 28–32). New Press.

No Child Left Behind Act of 2001, 20 U.S.C. § 6319 (2008).

Noguera, P. (2003). *City schools and the American dream: Reclaiming the promise of public education*. Teachers College Press.

Noguera, P. A. (2008) *The trouble with black boys and other reflections on race, equity and the future of public education*. John Wiley.

Noguera, P. A., & Wing, J. Y. (Eds.). (2006). *Unfinished business: Closing the achievement in our schools*. Josey Bass.

Palmer, P. (2011). *Healing the heart of democracy: The courage to create a politics worthy of the human spirit*. Jossey-Bass.

Parents Involved in Community Schools v. Seattle School Dist. No. 1, 551 U.S. 701 (2007).

Parham, T. (1989). Cycles of psychological Nigrescence. *The Counseling Psychologist, 17*(2), 187–226.

Parker, L., Deyhle, D., & Villenas, S. (Eds.). (1999). *Race is . . . race isn't: Critical race theory and qualitative studies in education*. Westview Press.

Parker, L., & Lynn, M. (2002). What's race got to do with it? Critical race theory's conflicts with and connections to qualitative research methodology and epistemology. *Qualitative Inquiry, 8*(1), 7–22

Parmar, P., & Steinberg, S. (2008). Locating yourself for your students. In M. Pollock (Ed.), *Everyday antiracism: Getting real about race in schools* (pp. 283–286). New Press.

Pollock, M. (2008). *Everyday antiracism: Getting real about race in school*. New Press: Distributed by W.W. Norton & Co.

Poston, C. W. (1990). The biracial identity development model: A needed addition. *Journal of Counseling and Development, 69,* 152–155.

Powell, J. A., (1996) The multiple self: Exploring between and beyond Modernity and Postmodernity. *Minnesota Law Review.*

Renn, K. A. (2001). Patterns of situational identity among biracial and multiracial college students. *The Review of Higher Education 23*(4), 399–420.

Renn, K. (2004). *Mixed race students in college: The ecology of race, identity, and community*. SUNY Press.

Renn, K. A. (2008). Research on biracial and multiracial identity development: Overview and synthesis. *New Directions for Student Services, 2008*(123), 13–21.

Report of the National Advisory Commission on Civil Disorders. (1968. [Washington: United States, Kerner Commission: U.S. G.P.O.

Rocco, T. S., Bernier, J. D., & Bowman, L. (2014). Critical race theory and HRD: Moving race front and center. *Advances in Developing Human Resources, 16*(4), 457–470.

Roediger, D. (1994). *Towards the abolition of whiteness: Essays on race, politics, and working class history*. Verso.

Roediger, D. (1999). *The wages of Whiteness*. Verso Press.

Roediger, D. (2002) *Colored White*. University of California Press.

Roithmayr, D. (1999). Introduction to critical race theory in educational research and praxis. In L. Parker, D. Deyhle, & S. Villenas (Eds.), *Race is . . . race isn't: Critical race theory and qualitative studies in education* (pp. 2–6). CO: Westview.

Root, M. P. (1990). Resolving "other status": Identity development of biracial individuals. *Women & Therapy Journal*, 185–205.

Safire, W. (2009, July 1). *On aha and senior moments*. New York Times.

Scheurich, J. J. (1993). Toward a white discourse on white racism. *Educational Researcher*, 22(8), 5–10.

Scheurich, J. J. (2002). *Anti-racist scholarship: An advocacy*. State University of New York Press.

Scheurich, J. J., & Skrla, L. (2003). *Leadership for equity and excellence: Creating high-achievement classrooms, schools, and districts*. Corwin Press.

Senge, P. (2000). *Schools that learn: A fifth discipline fieldbook for educators, parents, and everyone who cares about education*. Doubleday.

Shakur, T. (1996). *The rose that grew from concrete*. Simon & Schuster.

Singleton, G. (2012). *More courageous conversations about race*. Corwin Press.

Singleton, G. (2022). *Courageous conversations about race: A field guide for achieving equity in schools and beyond* (3rd ed.). Corwin.

Singelton, G. & Hayes, C. (2008). Beginning courageous conversations about race. In M. Pollock (Ed.). *Every day antiracism: Getting real about race in schools* (pp.18–23). New Press.

Singleton, G., & Linton, C. (2006). *Courageous conversations about race: A field guide for achieving equity in schools*: Corwin Press.

Singleton, J. (Director). (1991). *Boyz n the hood* [Film]. Columbia Pictures.

Sleeter, C. E. (1990). Staff development for desegregated schooling. *Phi Delta Kappan*, 72, 33–40.

Sleeter, C. E. (2017). Critical race theory and the whiteness of teacher education. *Urban Education*, 52(2), 155–169.

Sleeter, C. E., & Delgado Bernal, D. (2003). Critical pedagogy, critical race theory, and anti-racist education: Their implications for multicultural education. In J. A. Banks & C. A. Banks (Eds.), *Handbook of research on multicultural education*. Jossey-Bass.

Smith, J. (Director). (1995). *Dangerous minds* [Motion picture]. Available from Hollywood Pictures.

Smith-Maddox, R., & Solórzano, D. G. (2002). Using critical race theory, Paulo Freire's problem-posing method, and case study research to confront race and racism in education. *Qualitative Inquiry*, 8(1), 66–84.

Solórzano, D. G., & Bernal D. D. (2001). Examining transformational resistance through a critical race and LatCrit theory framework: Chicana and Chicano students in an urban context. *Urban Education*, 36, 308–342.

Solórzano, D. G., & Yosso, T. J. (2002). Critical race and LatCrit theory and method: Counter-storytelling Chicana and Chicano graduate school experiences. *International Journal of Qualitative Studies in Education*, 4(1), 471–495.

Steele, C. (2003). Race and the schooling of Black Americans. In S. Plous (Ed.), *Understanding prejudice and discrimination* (pp. 98–107). McGraw-Hill.

Takaki, R. T. (1993). *A different mirror: A history of multicultural America*. Little, Brown & Co.

Tate, W. F. (1994). From inner city to ivory tower: Does my voice matter in the academy? *Urban Education, 29*(3), 245–269.

Tate, W. F. (1997). Critical race theory and education: History, theory, and implications. *Review of Research in Education, 22,* 195–247.

Tate, W. F., Ladson-Billings, G., & Grant, C. A. (1993). The *Brown* decision revisited: mathematizing social problems. *Educational Policy, 7*(3), 255–275.

Tatum, B. D. (1993). Teaching White students about racism: The search for White allies and the restoration of hope. *Teachers College Record, 95*(4), 462–476.

Tatum, B. D. (1997). *Why are all the Black kids sitting together in the cafeteria?* Basic Books.

Tatum, B. (2008). Cultivating the trust of your black parents. In M. Pollock (Ed.), *Everyday antiracism: Getting real about race in schools* (pp. 310–313). New Press.

Tatum, B. D. (2017). *Why are all the Black kids sitting together in the cafeteria?* (Rev. Ed.). Basic Books.

Terry, R. (1970). *For Whites only* [Paper presentation]. Detroit Industrial Mission, (February 1965), Detroit, MI.

Thompson, A. (2008). Resisting the "lone hero" stance. In M. Pollock (Ed.), *Everyday antiracism: Getting real about race in schools* (pp. 327–333). New Press.

Troyna, B. (1987). Beyond multiculturalism: Towards the enactment of anti-racist education in policy, provision and pedagogy. *Oxford Review of Education, 13*(3), 307–320.

Twain, M. & Warner, C. D. (1872). *The Gilded Age: A tale of to-day.* The American Publishing Company.

U.S. Reports: *Brown v. Board of Education,* 347 U.S. 483 (1954).

Ward, J. (2008). Helping parents fight stereotypes about their children. In M. Pollock (Ed.), *Everyday antiracism: Getting real about race in schools* (pp. 314–317). New Press.

Weidman, J. C., & Stein, E. L. (2003). Socialization of doctoral students to academic norms. *Research in Higher Education, 44*(6), 641–656.

Wells-Barnett, I. B. *(1892). Southern horrors and other writings: The anti-lynching campaign of Ida B. Wells.* Bedford Books

Wesley, C. H. (1939). Organised labor and the Negro. *Faculty Reprints,* 213.

Wiedeman, C. R. (2002). Teacher preparation, social justice, equity: A review of the literature. *Equity and Excellence in Education, 35*(3), 200–213.

Wilkerson, I. (2011). *The warmth of other suns: The epic story of America's great migration.* Vintage Books.

Wilkerson, I. (2015, Jan. 11). When will the North face its racism? *New York Times.* Section SR, page 6.

Winthrop, J. (1630). *A model of Christian charity,* Massachusetts Bay Colony.

Wise, T. (2009). *Between Barack and a hard place: Racism and white denial in the age of Obama.* City Light Books

Wood, C. (2014). *Yardsticks: Child and adolescent development ages 4-14* (4th ed.). Center for Responsive Schools.

Worrell, F. C., Cross, W. E., Jr., & Vandiver, B. J. (2001). Nigrescence theory: Current status and challenges for the future. *Journal of Multicultural Counseling and Development, 29*(3), 201–213.

Yosso, T. J., Parker, L., Solórzano, D. G., & Lynn, M. (2004). From Jim Crow to af-
firmative action and back again: A critical race discussion of racialized rationales
and access to higher education. *Review of Research in Education*, 28, 1–25.

Yosso, T., Smith, W., Ceja, M., & Solórzano, D. (2009). Critical race theory, racial
microaggressions, and campus racial climate for Latina/o undergraduates. *Harvard Educational Review*, 79, 659–691.

Young, J. (1911). *Chief Joseph's own story*. Glen Adams.

Young, W. (1970). *Exceptional children*. Speech presented at Council for Exceptional
Children, Reston, VA.

Zinn, H. (1980). *A people's history of the United States*. HarperCollins.

Index

About the Author

Dr. Patrick Duffy grew up in the small Lake Superior community of Grand Marais, Minnesota and attended the University of Minnesota and the American Academy of Dramatic Arts in New York. Patrick followed his calling as a teacher and currently works as the Director of Teaching, Learning, and Leadership in the St. Louis Park Public Schools district and as an adjunct professor at the University of Minnesota, Twin Cities in Educational Policy and Human Development. Patrick was honored by the American Educational Research Association (AERA) in 2012 for his critical ethnographic dissertation and has presented nationally on student leadership development, racial equity transformation, and demystifying Arab American voices in leadership. Patrick is a 2023 graduate of the AASA National Urban Superintendents cohort through Howard University and attended the Harvard Graduate School of Education's Urban Principal Institute. Patrick previously published with the Reverend Anthony Galloway in *More Courageous Conversations about Race* (Singleton, 2012) on Systemic Student Leadership. Some of his work as a principal in Minneapolis was also featured in *Holistic Leadership, Thriving Schools* (Kise, 2019). Patrick has worked in the three largest school districts in Minnesota (Minneapolis, Saint Paul, and Anoka-Hennepin) as a principal, principal supervisor, and director of leadership development. Patrick is the proud father of Keira and William Duffy